Legendary Sessions

BOB DYLAN

HIGHWAY 61 REVISITED

Legendary Sessions

BOB DYLAN

HIGHWAY 61 REVISITED

Colin Irwin

Foreword by David Hutcheon

Billboard Books

an imprint of Watson-Guptill Publications / New York

Publisher and Creative Director: Nick Wells
Editor: Julia Rolf
Consultant Editor: David Hutcheon
Project Editor: Polly Willis
Picture Research: Gemma Walters
Art Director: Mike Spender
Digital Design and Production: Chris Herbert
Layout Design: Vanessa Green

Special thanks to: Geoffrey Meadon, Helen Tovey and Claire Walker

This edition published in 2008 by Billboard Books
an imprint of Watson-Guptill Publications, Nielsen Business Media,
a division of The Nielsen Company
770 Broadway, New York, NY 10003
www.watsonguptill.com

Created and produced by
FLAME TREE PUBLISHING
Crabtree Hall, Crabtree Lane
Fulham, London SW6 6TY
United Kingdom
www.flametreepublishing.com

09 11 10 08
1 3 5 7 9 10 8 6 4 2

Flame Tree Publishing is part of the Foundry Creative Media Co. Ltd.
© 2008 The Foundry Creative Media Co. Ltd.

ISBN-13: 978-0-8230-8398-5
ISBN-10: 0-8230-8398-5
Library of Congress Control Number: 2007935031

Every effort has been made to contact copyright holders. In the event of an oversight the
publishers would be glad to rectify any omissions in future editions of this book.

Printed in China

To Bobby and Eliza Heard,
Dylanologists of the future.

List of Illustrations

CONTENTS

FOREWORD

Highway 61 Revisited starts with an explosion, a smart crack and kick from drummer Bobby Gregg that was heard all around the world. It introduces one of the keystone texts of all rock music, and long is the list of musicians who remember where they were when they first encountered it.

But where and when did this noise begin? Was it really on *Bringing It All Back Home?* Some might have first heard it on that November day in Dallas when John F. Kennedy was assassinated and America was forced to face up to the fact that it was not Camelot; others might say the first time they heard 'Rock Around The Clock', and Billy Gussack's similar, two-beat introduction to the modern age; somebody might suggest the explosion began at a lynching in Duluth, Minnesota, in June 1920. Within a fortnight, they were selling postcards of that hanging.

Highway 61 changed everything, but what had changed Bob Dylan? He went from protest singer to wayward folkie to avatar of the rock era, during the 12 months in which he burnt brighter than any star since Elvis Presley. It didn't matter what was on the other side of the doors he was kicking down, because once he stepped through, nothing would ever be the same again. Folk imploded, rock expanded, pop art mingled, the mainstream succumbed and show business was turned on its head: for songwriting, arrangements and lengths there is a before *Highway 61* and an after.

In September 2005, *Mojo* magazine published a list of the 100 greatest Dylan songs. Among the likes of 'Idiot Wind', 'Mr Tambourine Man' and

'Sad Eyed Lady Of The Lowlands' in the Top 20 were five songs that were recorded during the session for *Highway 61*, including positions four ('Desolation Row'), two ('Positively 4th Street') and one ('Like A Rolling Stone') – songs written and recorded in the period when the finger-pointing folkies deserted Dylan for Barry McGuire.

Dylan started 1965 a hero to some and ended it a Judas in the eyes of those same fans. In the blurred eye of a hurricane, in the haze of a life being lived way too close to the sun, he set it all to music. When he began recording the songs that would comprise his second album of 1965, Dylan had only just decided he wanted to be neither the new Woody Guthrie nor the old Bob Dylan. The folk certainties – don't follow leaders, times change – were no longer challenging. He'd started out on burgundy and was about to hit the harder stuff.

This is the story of the journeys that led to the explosion that led to *Highway 61*, of the roads never travelled that run parallel to it, of the slip roads, crossroads and cul de sacs, of the freeways that sped Dylan further from the orbit he had once inhabited.

And how does it begin? 'Once upon a time ...'

David Hutcheon
London, 2007

Chapter 1

AND GOD SAID
TO ABRAHAM,
KILL ME A SON

---

*'I'm never gonna make a record better than that one, it's just
too good. There's a lot of stuff on there I would listen to...'*
Bob Dylan on the release of *Highway 61 Revisited*

Stretching 1,700 miles all the way from New Orleans to the Canadian border, Highway 61 had acquired an almost mythical identity in American folklore long before Bob Dylan ever got hold of it.

Bessie Smith, the 'Empress of the Blues', was killed in a car crash near this highway in the area of Clarksdale, Mississippi, in 1937. Her career was in freefall and her 43-year-old body was ravaged by years of hard living and strong gin, but John Hammond, her producer and mentor, was convinced she could recapture past glories and was on his way to Mississippi to collect her to make a new record. Although it is a conspiracy theory that has since been comprehensively devalued by hard facts, the way Hammond told it, Bessie's arm was all but ripped off in the crash and she died from loss of blood after a hospital refused to help her because she was black.

Blues legend Robert Johnson is also reputed to have sold his soul to the devil at the Clarksdale crossroads where Highway 61 intersects with Highway 49: 'I went down to the crossroads, fell down on my knees / Asked the Lord above, have mercy, save poor Bob if you please ...'. Despite the iron sculpture of a guitar marking the spot this, too, is more than likely to be an urban myth. And surely if Johnson and Satan did strike such a deal, one of the graveyards a mile or so away would have been a more suitable site?

In 1968 Martin Luther King Jr was shot dead in a motel along the highway; Ike Turner, Sam Cooke, John Lee Hooker and Elvis Presley spent their early years at different locations along the route; Mississippi Fred McDowell sang about it in his song '61 Highway': 'Sixty one is the longest road I know / She run from New York city to the Gulf of Mexico'. Running right through the Mississippi Delta, the road has been a spiritual symbol for blues artists through the years.

Born on the path of Highway 61 in Duluth, Minnesota, Bob Dylan was well versed with the road's mythical credentials. A succession of great singers, from Muddy Waters to Elmore James, used it as an escape route to find success with their music to Memphis and it became known as the 'Blues Highway'. The significance of its name still rings loud and clear through the very heartbeat of American folk music in all its multi-coloured guises.

Small wonder that Dylan embraced the highway's symbols of freedom and escape in 1965 so voraciously. The name Highway 61 alone conjures up such a well of diverse images – roots, rebellion, movement, growth, drama, speed, bohemianism, flight – that it perfectly captured the dizzying swirl of triumphs and travails that had consumed Dylan and led him to an almost desperate need for radical reassessment. His *Highway 61 Revisited* album was born of turbulence, confusion and frantic genius, and while Dylan himself has never wished to debate the whys and wherefores, it changed contemporary music forever.

It was a time when the world itself was in turmoil. JFK was assassinated in 1963 and the shock waves were still resonating on an international environment already unnerved by the growing tensions of the Cold War. In 1962 the Cuban missile crisis had brought the world to the brink of nuclear conflict as Kennedy and Khrushchev, respective leaders of the world's two super-powers, locked horns over the deadly weapons the Soviets were pointing at the US. After a terrifying week of nuclear poker that threatened large-scale devastation, Khrushchev finally blinked and agreed to remove his rockets from Cuba. But it was an uneasy agreement, and the distrust and enmity between East and West remained a black cloud over international politics for many years afterwards.

The West had already long been paranoid about Communism, as some of those who had inspired Dylan in the first place discovered to their cost when Senator Joe McCarthy embarked on his witch hunt to rid America of the 'red threat' in the 1950s. Anybody who had left-wing leanings – and some who did not – was scooped up in McCarthy's freewheeling cleansing campaign against Communist sympathizers.

McCarthy's obsessive pursuit of American Communists had been triggered by the death of the former US Secretary of Defense James Forrestal, who at 2 am on 22 May 1949 had seemingly jumped to his death from a 16th floor window at the Bethesda Naval Hospital. All manner of conspiracy theories arose around the death of Forrestal, who had suffered a breakdown in the wake of Harry S. Truman's surprise 1948 presidential victory over Thomas Dewey and was being treated at the hospital for 'involutional melancholia'. Forrestal, constantly at loggerheads with Air Force Secretary Stuart Symington and distrustful of Truman, became increasingly unstable, claimed he was being followed, harassed and ultimately forced out of office, accusing Zionist agents, the FBI and Communists of spying on him, with some theorists suggesting that UFOs were involved in his downfall.

Like many others at the time, Senator McCarthy believed Forrestal was murdered and pledged to avenge him. 'While I am not a sentimental man,' said McCarthy, 'I was touched deeply and left numb by the news of Forrestal's murder. But I was affected more deeply when I heard of the Communist celebration when *they* heard of Forrestal's murder. On that night I dedicated part of this fight to Jim Forrestal.'

McCarthy's avowed method of achieving this was to rid America of all Communists. He started with perceived traitors within the government and received plenty of public support for his efforts, however flaky the evidence he provided to back up his emotive accusations. By 1953, when McCarthy was appointed chairman of the Senate Committee on Government Operations, he was already out of control, pursuing a ruthless agenda, hauling in people from all walks of life suspected of having leftie leanings, and naming and shaming those who refused to co-operate with his Senate committee.

The unofficial blacklist that emerged as a result stifled the careers of many entertainers. They included some of those who had such a profound influence on Dylan's early style. Although severely afflicted by the effects of the debilitating Huntington's Disease, Woody Guthrie was under constant scrutiny, while The Weavers – the group formed by Pete Seeger, Lee Hays, Fred Hellerman and Ronnie Gilbert, who took Leadbelly's 'Goodnight Irene' and Guthrie's 'So Long, It's Been Good To Know You' into the American Top Ten — were suddenly denied airplay and television exposure. Pete Seeger himself spent a day in prison in 1961 and did not appear on network television for 17 years after refusing to testify before the House Un-American Activities Committee in 1955, even though the case against him was dismissed in 1962.

'Reds under the bed' paranoia wasn't exclusive to the United States. Soviet spies such as Kim Philby, Donald Maclean and Guy Burgess were unmasked in the British establishment, and fear of what was being hatched behind the Iron Curtain was rife throughout Europe. On the other side, Colonel Oleg Penkovsky, a colonel in the Soviet Military Intelligence agency, was sentenced to death in Moscow in 1963 for passing Soviet secrets to British and American intelligence agents. The world was very jumpy.

Racial tensions also intensified. The iniquities of apartheid had become fully apparent in South Africa, with the non-white majority forced to endure the humiliation of segregation, limited voting rights and second-class citizen status. The 1960 uprising at Sharpeville focused the world on the horror of what was happening in South Africa, but while there were gestures, the world was either powerless or felt disinclined to get involved. Internal opposition was brutally cut down; the initially nonviolent African National Congress was banned and one of its leaders, Nelson Mandela, became a marked man.

Wanted for 'incitement' after being named as one of the ringleaders in an attempted national strike in 1961, Mandela was on the run for 17 months before being captured and given a five-year prison sentence, with the CIA strongly implicated in his arrest. In 1964 that was extended to a life sentence on further charges of sabotage and conspiracy to connive in a plot to invade South Africa and Mandela went to prison on Robben Island for what turned out to be a 26-year imprisonment.

By the early 1960s, black civil rights had also become a major issue in America. Nearly a decade on from the day Rosa Parks incited a black uprising when she refused to accede to local segregation laws and give up her seat in a whites-only section of a bus in Montgomery, Alabama, black issues were at the forefront of the American psyche.

In 1963 Alabama governor George Wallace rigorously fought the federal government's attempts to enforce its desegregation laws, and when Dr Martin Luther King and Dr Ralph Abernathy were arrested leading a peaceful protest through Birmingham, Alabama, the event ignited a bloody battle with the police to a background of marchers singing 'We Shall Overcome'. Alabama was described by the Attorney General, Bobby Kennedy, as 'like a foreign country' and troops were sent in to quell the riots and violence across the state.

Dylan joined Marlon Brando, Burt Lancaster, Judy Garland, Martin Luther King and over 200,000 others at the biggest civil-rights march ever in Washington later in August 1963, an event that President Kennedy said had advanced the cause of 20 million blacks. Both Dylan and Kennedy were upstaged, though, by Dr King, who stood on the steps of the Lincoln Memorial to deliver his epochal 'I have a dream ...' speech. 'I have a dream that one day on the red hills of Georgia, the sons of former slaves and the sons of former slave owners will be able to sit down together at the table to brotherhood,' he said, calling for unity and peace. 'Let us not seek to satisfy our thirst for freedom by drinking from the cup of bitterness and hatred.'

He had a dream. Civil rights marching with Martin Luther King in 1963.

Three months later, the President was shot dead in Dallas, America's optimistic new dawn was in tatters and the world watched nervously.

But the new President, Lyndon Johnson, resolved to continue Kennedy's civil-rights reforms, outlawing racial discrimination in all aspects of society. In February 1964, the seemingly invincible Sonny Liston sat on his stool and refused to get up for the seventh round of a world heavyweight bout, giving the boxing world heavyweight title to Cassius Clay. The black community had found a noisy new icon.

Suddenly, everything was up for grabs. Now in the thrall of Beatlemania, the teenage audience was freshly empowered with its own music, voice and style and the youth-culture revolution exploded. Long hair and short skirts became loaded fashion statements and the establishment reeled.

Lyndon Johnson won the landslide 1964 presidential election victory over the millionaire right-wing Republican candidate Barry Goldwater, but the era of rebellion and protest was in full swing as international trouble areas flared.

In 1964 the National Guard moved in to quell race riots in New York State; India wept as its beloved leader Nehru died of a heart attack; Kruschev was deposed as Soviet Prime Minister by Brezhnev and former terrorist Jomo Kenyatta became president of Kenya. In 1965 Rhodesian leader Ian Smith strove to maintain white supremacy with a unilateral declaration of independence from Britain, while US troops poured in to quell the Communist threat in the Dominican Republic and Indonesian paratroopers landed in Malaysia.

Awarded the Nobel Peace Prize in October 1964, Martin Luther King found himself in prison just over three months later for parading in Selma, Alabama, without a permit. Protesters took to the streets again as Johnson sent Marines to Southeast Asia in March 1965 as the Vietnam conflict escalated into a full-scale war. America, it seemed, was no longer prepared to go blindly along with the decisions of its leaders – and the early protest albums of Bob Dylan might well have played a role in that.

This was the torrid global backdrop from which Dylan, himself emerging from a fraught few years, approached his new album. He had got through the madness of those early years, after descending on New York in search of Woody Guthrie and finding friends in some of the prime movers and shakers of the nascent Greenwich Village folk scene.

There was acoustic blues pioneer Dave Van Ronk, the 'Mayor Of MacDougal Street', who acted as an unofficial guru to so many of the aspiring young folk singers, offered streetwise comforts and musical guidance, and gave Dylan his first big break in New York by inviting Bob to join him on stage at the Gaslight.

There was also Izzy Young, who ran the Folklore Center where Dylan first met Van Ronk, and introduced Bob to countless obscure folk records in addition to losing money promoting Dylan's first New York headline concert at Carnegie Chapter Hall – a gig that attracted just 53 people. Fred Neil, already a songwriter of some repute, was one of the Village's most charismatic performers by the time Bob arrived (he later wrote the massive Harry Nilsson hit 'Everybody's Talkin'). Another rising singer was Afro-American Richie Havens, who went on to international stardom after a spectacular appearance at the Woodstock Festival in 1969.

From the grubby modesty of the Gaslight, Gerdes Folk City and other Greenwich Village folk-music haunts, it had been a long, eventful and often confusing journey for Dylan that had occasionally got completely out of hand. After being signed to CBS by John Hammond, he had dealt with the almost hysterical adulation of the folk scene and those endless unwanted 'spokesman of a generation' tags that had been hanging heavily round his neck following his second album *The Freewheelin' Bob Dylan* in 1963. The mystically barbed lyricism of 'Blowin' In The Wind', 'A Hard Rain's A-Gonna Fall', 'Talking World War III Blues' and, especially, 'Masters Of War' (his mercilessly uncompromising verbal assault on unscrupulous leaders calling the shots), had already turned him from the darling of the Village folk scene to a youth icon, vocalizing student rebellion and the dismay and anger of the anti-war movement. The irony of it all was that an acutely embarrassed Dylan wanted none of it.

His escalating reputation as a visionary, an original thinker and a brilliant poet spread internationally with his third album, 1964's *The Times They Are A-Changin'*, the title track even giving him a British hit single, as well as an anthem for the younger generations to holler at their bemused elders. It included 'The Lonesome Death Of Hattie Carroll', a bruisingly bitter condemnation of the trial of William Zantzinger (changed to Zanzinger in the song), a privileged white boy in Maryland who killed a 51-year-old black waitress and mother of 11 – apparently because she was too slow serving his drink – and was given only a six months' sentence for manslaughter. Whether he wanted it or not – and, much later, he vigorously protested that he did not – Dylan's reputation as a social commentator and a fearless fighter of causes reached explosive new heights.

Yet he was already showing signs of wanting to escape the shackles of expectation and his anointed roles as the saviour of folk music and the prince of protest. He had been acclaimed a hero at the Newport Folk

Hail the king and queen of folk: Dylan and Baez in 1965.

Festival, almost canonized by Pete Seeger and the rest of folk-music royalty, sharing a stage and a bed with the already well-established Joan Baez. But he wanted more, so much more. He was ambitious all right, but he was already exasperated by the demands of celebrity and the futility of fame, ridiculing a succession of hapless interviewers and their banal questions about the meaning of protest and the biographical minutiae of his background.

Asked by a kindly but bewildered old-school journalist from the British pop magazine *Disc & Music Echo* why he was being so hostile in the interview, he said 'Because you're hostile to me. You're *using* me. I'm an object to you. I don't want to be bothered by your paper. I don't want to be part of it…. You have the gall to ask me what influences me and why do I think I'm so accepted. I don't want to be interviewed by your paper.' And he walked out.

Other seismic developments were hitting the music world at this time. The Beatles were turning contemporary music on its head and making their own first steps towards the transition from lovable mop-tops to more bedraggled spiritual beings, as the simple, bushy tailed pop of 'She Loves You' and 'I Want To Hold Your Hand' gave way to songs of a darker nature such as 'I'm A Loser' and 'Baby's In Black'. They had opened up a new world of rock that was already light years removed from Tin Pan Alley and pop crooners and, like everyone else, Dylan was duly affected. The feeling was mutual. 'Beatles Dig Dylan' roared the front page of the British music weekly *Melody Maker* in 1964, despite his early dismissals of their 'bubblegum' music.

Dylan became an avowed Beatles fan and the two giants of the new music of the 1960s had a profound influence on one another. Dylan was also impressed by some of the other emergent young groups flying out of Britain at a furious rate to make their mark on the rest of the world. In particular, he had been impressed by The Animals' moody and emotional rock version of 'House Of The Rising Sun', the old blues classic about a New Orleans whorehouse that he had covered on his first album.

There were early clues to the impact of all this in his 1964 album *Another Side Of Bob Dylan*, with the more insular lyrical style of 'My Back Pages', 'It Ain't Me Babe' and 'Chimes Of Freedom'. Dylan was suddenly looking inward and the protest music with which he'd become synonymous was clearly getting the elbow. His manager, Albert Grossman, aggressively propelled him into the mainstream pop arena, beyond protest and the folk-music scene whence he had emerged with such venom.

Within a year, the Dylan circus was careering along with greater force than ever, at times looking scarily wayward and more and more out of control the further it went round the world. As the tours got bigger, the press conferences grew more surreal and Dylan's patience got thinner.

It was a stormy period in social history, as well as in Dylan's personal journey. He effectively abandoned Baez, his sometime partner on and off stage, and hooked up with a model, Sara Lownds (her name is often mistakenly spelt Lowndes). They moved in together, living for a while at the Chelsea Hotel, Manhattan's famous landmark for bohemian artists, where he would write most of the songs that appeared on his fifth album, *Bringing It All Back Home*.

Dylan was fuelled by a meeting with The Beatles at the Hotel Delmonico in New York's Manhattan Park Avenue one Sunday in August 1964. In a piece for *Q* magazine three decades later, the rock critic Al Aronowitz, a friend of both parties, claimed that he had not only set up the meeting but also introduced marijuana into the equation.

Aronowitz, who died in 2005, had known Dylan since hanging out with him in Greenwich Village soon after Bob's arrival in New York. Dylan occasionally stayed with Aronowitz, who knew most of New York's grooviest people and introduced him to someone else who was to have a big influence on him, Allen Ginsberg. Dylan even wrote 'Mr Tambourine Man' in Al's kitchen. Asked at a press conference in 1965 who could save the world, Dylan answered: 'Al Aronowitz'.

So when Al travelled to Liverpool to interview The Beatles and John Lennon said he'd like to meet Dylan, he resolved to make it happen. The way he told it later, there was an initial awkwardness as he introduced them as 'nobody wanted to step on anybody else's ego'. But Al was to describe it as one of the greatest moments of his life. 'I was well aware at the time that I was brokering the most fruitful union in the history of pop music.... I was engineering, participating in and chronicling a milestone moment in history.'

The Beatles' *Hard Day's Night* movie had just opened and the group were at the height of their fame, with five singles in the American charts. The previous night they had played to an hysterical audience at Forest Hills Tennis Stadium, and security was intense as hordes of excitable fans milled around the Hotel Delmonico. Dylan had driven down from Woodstock with his roadie, Victor Maimudes, picking up Aronowitz en route, and they had to battle their way through the crowds, police, press and C-list celebrities in order to reach The Beatles' suite. They were greeted by an attentive Beatles manager, Brian Epstein, who said 'I'm afraid we only have champagne', when Dylan asked for his usual tipple, a glass of cheap wine. 'Alcohol was always Bob's number one drug of choice,' said Aronowitz.

When the ice was broken, they adjourned to a more private room and Aronowitz started rolling a joint. Dylan had misheard part of the lyric of 'I Want To Hold Your Hand' as 'I get high, I get high, I get high' (it was actually 'I can't hide, I can't hide, I can't hide') and assumed marijuana was a regular part of The Beatles' lifestyle. He was shocked when Lennon told him they'd never tried it before. Before long, they were all partaking and the night disappeared in a haze of giggles and garbled philosophizing.

Yet the meeting did appear to leave an indelible imprint on both parties. Lennon started to write more reflective material such as 'You've Got To Hide Your Love Away' and 'It's Only Love' (both on 1965's *Help!* album) almost in homage to Dylan, while Bob resolved his future lay in rock, not folk music. As Aronowitz said: 'The Beatles' magic was in their sound, Bob's magic was in his words. After they met, The Beatles' words got grittier and Bob invented folk/rock.'

Exhausted and bored by the constant dissection of his lyrics and the unwanted responsibility foisted on him by an expectant, hero-worshipping folk scene, Dylan was frustrated by the limitations of playing solo. He needed a fresh challenge and felt there was only one way to go to break new ground and embrace the challenges and musical excitement that he craved: rock music.

Dylan wrote much of *Bringing It All Back Home* during a month-long stay at his manager Albert Grossman's house in Woodstock (Grossman's wife Sally is pictured on the front sleeve). Joan Baez, who was with Dylan at the time, recalls him chain-smoking and drinking endless glasses of red wine, hunched over a typewriter for hours on end, falling asleep and waking halfway through the night to start again.

By the time he met The Beatles, he already had 'Mr Tambourine Man' (originally written for but omitted from *Another Side Of Bob Dylan*), 'Gates Of Eden' and 'It's Alright, Ma (I'm Only Bleeding)', full of intense, rambling prose and obtuse imagery. The majority of the rest of the album was conceived at New York's Chelsea Hotel, when the idea of placing some of the songs in an electric setting really took root.

With the approval of Al Grossman, producer Tom Wilson, primarily noted for his work with progressive jazz acts such as Cecil Taylor, John Coltrane and Sun Ra, was again Columbia's house producer on the album, continuing his association with Dylan first initiated on the final day recording *The Freewheelin' Bob Dylan* in April 1963. Unaffected by any of the normal hang-ups of folk musicians harming the purity of their sound, and having done something similar with Simon & Garfunkel's 'The Sound of Silence', Wilson overdubbed a few of Dylan's earliest recordings with electric rhythms, just to see what they sounded like. Among the experiments was a Fats Domino-flavoured rock arrangement of Bob's 1961 recording of 'House Of The Rising Sun'.

Dylan's head was also being turned by the work of John Hammond Jr, the son of the man who'd originally signed Bob to a five-year deal with Columbia when he heard him as a 20-year-old playing harmonica on a Carolyn Hester recording session. Already making his mark as a fine blues guitarist and singer, Hammond had recruited three members of a Canadian bar band, The Hawks – guitarist Robbie Robertson, drummer Levon Helm and organist Garth Hudson – to infuse his solo acoustic sound with the power of an electric-rock setting on his third album, 1965's *So Many Roads*. Dylan heard the thrillingly savage results of Hammond's sessions with the R&B band and was both impressed and inspired.

The first day of recording *Bringing It All Back Home*, at Columbia's Studio A in New York on 13 January 1965, was dedicated to Dylan on his own, playing piano and acoustic guitar. He recorded 10 tracks, including 'Farewell Angelina', 'Subterranean Homesick Blues', 'Love Minus Zero/No Limit', 'It's All Over Now, Baby Blue', 'She Belongs To Me' and 'Bob Dylan's 115th Dream', although after these tracks were revisited over the next two days with other musicians and heavier settings, none of these recordings were to make it on to the finished album.

Tom Wilson booked the majority of the session musicians who

assembled at Studio A on 14 January. They included guitarists Kenny Rankin, Al Gorgoni and Bruce Langhorne, bassists Joseph Macho Jr and William E Lee, pianist Paul Griffin and drummer Bobby Gregg. There was no proper rehearsal, no schedule and no planning, but in the manner that was to become a common feature of Dylan recording sessions for years to come, they just intuitively played though most of the songs Dylan had attempted on his own the day before. Dylan let them hear the songs, explained briefly how he wanted them to sound and let the band loose. Three and a half hours later, 'Love Minus Zero/No Limit', 'Subterranean Homesick Blues', 'Outlaw Blues', 'She Belongs To Me' and 'Bob Dylan's 115th Dream' had been nailed, virtually all in one take.

After a break for dinner, Dylan went back into the studio, with John Hammond Jr playing guitar alongside Bruce Langhorne and, on bass, John Sebastian, soon to be a superstar in his own right as leader of the Lovin' Spoonful (whose likable mix of folk, blues, rock and jug band music would result in a huge international hit in 1966 with 'Daydream').

The next day, the same personnel assembled – with the addition of Frank Owens who sat in on piano in place of the absent Paul Griffin – and together they knocked the album into shape. They recorded 'Maggie's Farm' in one take and, barely pausing for breath, whipped through 'On The Road Again', 'It's Alright, Ma (I'm Only Bleeding)', 'Gates Of Eden', 'Mr Tambourine Man' and 'It's All Over Now, Baby Blue', none of which took more than four takes. They also recorded 'If You Gotta Go, Go Now' at that session, although it would not be included on the album.

Bringing It All Back Home turned out to be a toe in the water. It had one acoustic side, to appease the old guard, with 'Gates Of Eden', 'Mr Tambourine Man' and 'It's Alright, Ma (I'm Only Bleeding)'. The other side sent Dylan off on a brave new adventure, placing the surreal, rambling observational reflections of 'Maggie's Farm', 'Subterranean Homesick Blues' and 'Love Minus Zero/No Limit' in a rockier setting. As baffling and poetically surreal as they often were, the songs on *Bringing It All Back Home* seemed to lift Dylan to a different plane.

'You don't need a weather man to know which way the wind blows,' he barked on 'Subterranean Homesick Blues'. 'Don't follow leaders, watch the parkin' meters …'. Amid the rampaging, endless flood of words and apparently incomprehensible narrative, Dylan seemed to be offering a very potent sacrifice of his old self.

By April 1965, the excitement surrounding Dylan began to approach the scale of Beatlemania. Fans camped out in the rain at London Airport to welcome him when he flew in for a British tour, wearing their CND anti-war badges and signature Dylan caps and shades. The press thrust cameras into his face, pounding him with questions about Donovan (Britain's 'answer' to Dylan) and asked if he was going to marry Joan Baez, still dutifully at his side, but by now forlornly sidelined and oblivious to the fact that Bob had set up home with Sara Lownds.

Baez rather naively assumed that as she had given Dylan a significant leg-up by inviting him to share a stage with her when he was starting out and she was the bigger star, Bobby would return the favour now that his star was so fully in the ascendant. She was to be sadly disappointed. A chastened Baez became an increasingly alienated figure in the entourage, an unwanted symbol of the past at a time when Dylan had eyes only for the future. When he refused to join her on a street demo against the Vietnam War, she realized she'd lost him, both as a lover and a protest singer. A humiliated Baez flew out as Dylan's future wife Sara flew in.

On stage, all seemed the same as it ever was. Dylan was playing – as it turned out, for the last time in a long while – entirely solo and acoustic, snarling his way through most of the old calling cards with his customary venom. The folk fans were to have their reservations about the electric half of *Bringing It All Back Home* but British audiences only got to hear it as the UK tour neared its end in April, and they still flocked to see Dylan and devour his increasingly mystifying mantras in awe and adulation. Pioneering Illinois-born film-maker D. A. Pennebaker, on the tour shooting the *Don't Look Back* documentary, described the scene awaiting them as they arrived at gigs as 'some sort of druid council working for us'.

But the times they were indeed a-changing at a furious rate, and a lot of the rage that Dylan exuded on stage on the tour seemed borne out of frustration with the parameters of his solo-acoustic environment. On stage, Dylan was hurtling to the end of a road; off it, with a noisy entourage along for the ride, accompanying him from one party to the next, there was a sense of things spiralling out of control.

He held court in his hotel room as a long line of British musicians came to pay homage. Among them, notably, was Donovan, who had overcome the attempts at a Dylan v Donovan feud stirred by the media but part-incited at a London concert by Dylan's own disparaging reference to the British singer during the song 'Talking World War III Blues', a comment that inspired a bout of pantomime jeering from the audience.

On 8 May *Melody Maker* ran the headline 'Dylan Digs Donovan', which helped to smooth over any awkwardness. Following an introduction by Joan Baez, the 18-year-old Donovan was accepted into Bob's inner sanctum. At beat poet Allen Ginsberg's suggestion, he even helped to write out the lyrics of 'Subterranean Homesick Blues' on pieces of card for Dylan to display in front of D. A. Pennebaker's camera in an alley at the back of London's Savoy Hotel for the *Don't Look Back* movie. The sequence became synonymous with 'Subterranean Homesick Blues' with the advent of music television years later.

When he came to write his own autobiography, *The Hurdy-Gurdy Man*, Donovan described the Dylan of the time as 'a very pretty young man with bad teeth and curiously solid hands. His slim features were widened at the jawline with powerful muscles. Definitely the thinking girl's crumpet.' He also picked up on the madness surrounding Dylan at the time, which he largely attributed to drugs. One clip in Pennebaker's film shows an adoring Donovan feyly singing one of his own ditties, 'To Sing For You', to an apparently deeply underwhelmed Dylan. 'For years people thought Dylan was putting me down,' he told the *Guardian* in 2005. 'He may have been a bit edgy, but those New Yorkers were into amphetamine. Their jawlines were about 12 inches wide. I put it down to a lot of agitation, a lot of adulation and a lot of stress that Bob was under. I wasn't copying him but we were stuck together because I was going to do what he did – I was going to be the poet folk singer who invaded the charts.'

Other acolytes partying with Dylan during the tour included Eric Clapton and other members of John Mayall's Bluesbreakers, and Alan Price, about to launch his solo career after walking out of The Animals. Pennebaker barely knew where to point his camera next. 'Those guys were completely drifting on their own,' he said. 'I was just busy trying to keep up with them.'

Also on the tour was the waspish-tongued Bob Neuwirth, a stalwart of the Cambridge, Massachussetts, folk scene and himself a rising singer songwriter. Even at the best of times, Dylan didn't suffer fools gladly and Neuwirth's acidic wit and taste for excessive partying goaded Dylan to unleash his brutal humour ever more mercilessly on anyone who rubbed him up the wrong way. He savagely berated the idiocy of a succession of hapless journalists who came seeking wisdom, and as the tour partied on Dylan must have known there was no direction home. Not to the old ways at least.

In a rare coherent intercourse with a journalist at the Savoy during the tour, he hinted at his frustrations and the changes afoot. 'I don't hate pop music,' he told *Melody Maker* Ray Coleman. 'Somebody's got to be a little wacky to say, "I don't like electrified guitar." People say, "How can it be folk music if you've got electrified guitar and drums." Ha! These instruments are real. I like them.'

He also bitterly renounced his persistent image as spokesman for a generation. 'The message isn't in the words. I don't do anything with a sort of message. I'm just transferring my thoughts into music. Nobody can give you a message like that. All I can hope to do is sing what I'm thinking. Don't put me down as a man with a message. My songs are just me talking to myself. Maybe that's an egotistical thing to say but it is what it is. I have no responsibility to anybody except myself. If people like me – fine. If they don't, then maybe I'll do something else.'

He was, however, cagey about the specifics of his future direction at that point. 'I live in the present … it's hard for me to look beyond today. Every time I try to do otherwise and plan for the future, it doesn't pay off. I know I'll write a lot of stuff, but exactly what shape it'll take has yet to be decided.'

Back in the States, the Dylan bandwagon was rumbling along at an even more ferocious pace. The Byrds had recorded an irresistibly catchy jangling folk-rock cover of 'Mr Tambourine Man', which soared to the top of the charts both in Britain and the US that summer. The British pop/R&B band Manfred Mann followed it with a cover of another Dylan song, 'If You Gotta Go, Go Now', scoring another huge hit despite the singer, Paul Jones, declaring 'I loathe and detest folk music', a comment that seemed to indicate firmly where he felt Dylan was heading on the folk/rock divide. Once it was just Peter, Paul & Mary, also managed by Al Grossman, who had hits with genteel treatments of Dylan's songs, but now the range of covers stretched from Bobby Darin to Marlene Dietrich, Cher, The Animals and The Turtles.

While Dylan's attitude and his whole musical stance had changed radically during that epic UK solo tour, the world – and more specifically *his* world – had also irrevocably shifted in his absence. His songs had taken on a life of their own and been transported into the chart mainstream and a rock environment that must have seemed a million miles away when he was singing 'Blowin' In The Wind' in coffee houses in Greenwich Village. If the dissenting voices had raised any doubts in his mind about the validity of the electric side of *Bringing It All Back Home*, then the rapidly changing winds of the day surely blew them all away.

It was time to put his music where his heart lay. Time to embrace fully the potential that rock music presented. Time to turn his back on solo acoustic Bob Dylan. Time to take the great leap forward.

Time for *Highway 61 Revisited* …

Chapter 2

FAR FROM THE TWISTED REACH OF CRAZY SORROW

---

*'My weariness amazes me, I'm branded on my feet / I have no one
to meet / And the ancient empty street's too dead for dreaming'*
Bob Dylan, 'Mr Tambourine Man'

The Byrds topped the US singles charts on 26 June 1965, with their
irresistibly tuneful version of 'Mr Tambourine Man'. It only held the
top spot for one week but it had a profound impact on an American music
scene in the dual grip of the fledgling English beat scene and the might
of Motown.

The Beatles started the year at No. 1 with 'I Feel Fine', before being
dislodged by British songbird Petula Clark's 'Downtown', which was in
turn toppled two weeks later by the Phil Spector Wall of Sound classic
'You've Lost That Lovin' Feelin'' by The Righteous Brothers. Subsequent
No. 1s included 'This Diamond Ring' by Gary Lewis & The Playboys (co-
written by Al Kooper, soon to play his own pivotal role in the *Highway 61
Revisited* story), 'My Girl' by The Temptations, 'I'm Telling You Now' by
Freddie & The Dreamers, 'Game Of Love' by Wayne Fontana & The
Mindbenders, 'Mrs Brown You've Got A Lovely Daughter' by Herman's
Hermits and 'Help Me Rhonda' by The Beach Boys. There were also two
more Beatles' No. 1s ('Eight Days A Week' and 'Ticket To Ride') and three

more from Motown ('Stop! In The Name Of Love' and 'Back In My Arms Again' by The Supremes and 'I Can't Help Myself' by The Four Tops).

Interrupting The Four Tops' stay at No. 1, 'Mr Tambourine Man' was entirely different. As it boomed out of radios in 1965, its freshness resonated around the country and there was a sense of something new emerging. It had a pop sensibility but it sounded distinctively American after the barrage of British records, while its poetic, cryptic lyrics suggested the mainstream was suddenly being assaulted by some friendly alien with its own agenda. It was written by Bob Dylan, who was famously a folk singer, yet it had all the trimmings of a different kind of rock music. The press dubbed the sound 'folk rock', a term that Dylan himself hated. 'Folk rock?' he snapped to Nora Ephron and Susan Edmiston after his concert at Forest Hills on the eve of the release of *Highway 61 Revisited*. 'I've never even said that word. It has a hard gutter sound. Circussy atmosphere. It's nose-thumbing. Sounds like you're looking down on what it is … fantastic, great music.'

Rock journalist Al Aronowitz claimed that Dylan wrote 'Mr Tambourine Man' in his kitchen at Berkeley Heights, New Jersey, late in April 1964, although in fact it was already a work in progress by then, initiated a couple of months earlier on an epic road trip through the South that took in the Mardi Gras in New Orleans and wound up in California – a trip during which Dylan also wrote 'Chimes Of Freedom'.

'He asked to borrow my portable typewriter,' said Aronowitz. 'He said he had something he needed to write. Bob must have stayed up past dawn, rapping away at the keys in his cigarette fog. He had just broken up with Suze … for him it was a long step further into loneliness. I found a waste basket full of crumpled false starts. I took it out the side door to empty it into the trash can when a whispering emotion caught me. I took the crumpled sheets, smoothed them out, read the crazy, leaping lines, smiled to myself at the leaps that never landed and then put the sheets into a file folder.'

Another insight offered by Aronowitz was that Dylan repeatedly listened to Marvin Gaye's 'Can I Get A Witness' as he wrote, having to get up every few minutes to replace the needle back at the start of the disc. 'I'll bet you can find every note of 'Can I Get A Witness' in 'Mr Tambourine Man' if you looked for them,' Beatle George Harrison once said, although many Dylan fans are still searching.

Judy Collins, an enthusiastic interpreter of Dylan from his early days in Greenwich Village, covered 'Mr Tambourine Man' on *Judy Collins' Fifth-Album* and recalled visiting Joan Baez in 1964 and hearing Dylan singing it softly in another room and was immediately struck by the riddle of the lyrics. It's a riddle that has sustained Dylanologists ever since.

Some claim it's a reflection of Dylan's love of Fellini's black and white 'neo-realism' film *La Strada (The Road)* with its surreal travelling-show imagery. But with some justification, the most common assumption is that the song is all about drugs. 'Take me on a trip upon your magic swirlin' ship / My senses have been stripped / My hands can't feel to grip / My toes too numb to step / Wait only for my boot heels /To be wanderin' ...' The commonly held theory – alluded to in the 1995 movie *Dangerous Minds* starring Michelle Pfeiffer as a teacher who is trying to inspire ghetto schoolkids by studying Dylan's lyrics, and identifies the Tambourine Man as a drug dealer – is that the song relates to the journey Dylan had taken to LA via the South with fellow singer Paul Clayton (noted for his sea shanties and whaling songs) and his good friends Victor Maimudes and Pete Karman. The travellers were fuelled by marijuana Dylan had mailed in advance to post offices along the route to avoid being busted for possession. Others speculate that the trip he takes is more likely to have been on LSD.

Suggesting that it is more about a sense of freedom, Dylan himself has denied that theory: 'Drugs never played a part in that song, drugs were never a big thing with me.' In an interview accompanying the *Biograph* box set, he said it was specifically inspired by the guitarist Bruce Langhorne, a friend from the early days in Greenwich Village.

Langhorne was a highly regarded musician who recorded with the charismatic Irish folk group The Clancy Brothers and on the 1962 Carolyn Hester album on Columbia, which also featured the unsigned Dylan playing harmonica. Langhorne was a house musician at the Bitter End and Gerdes Folk City, where he accompanied the M. C. Brother John Sellers and first met Dylan. He was subsequently hired to play a prominent role on the 1963 album *The Freewheelin' Bob Dylan* and added electric guitar to Dylan's aborted rock single 'Mixed-Up Confusion'. Langhorne also played a significant role on *Bringing It All Back Home*, his guitar in the front line on 'She Belongs To Me' and 'Love Minus Zero/No Limit'.

'Mr Tambourine Man, I think, was inspired by Bruce Langhorne,' said Dylan in the *Biograph* notes. 'Bruce was playing guitar with me on a bunch of the early records. On one session, the producer, Tom Wilson, asked him to play tambourine. And he had this gigantic tambourine. It was like, really big. As big as a wagonwheel. He was playing, and this vision of him playing this tambourine just stuck in my mind. He was one of those characters.'

All of which was news to Langhorne himself. He confirms he was the proud owner of a huge Turkish frame drum that looked like a giant tambourine and that he had played with Richard Fariña, a charismatic author and dulcimer player playing in a popular duo with his second wife, Joan Baez's sister Mimi; however Langhorne did not realize that the instrument had left such an impression on Dylan until he read about it in the *Biograph* notes. 'He didn't tell me about that,' said Langhorne. 'And ... if he did tell anybody he'd probably deny it. He just would. He has a wonderful sense of humour and a wonderful ability to let people just let out enough rope to hang themselves. He'd probably do that with me.'

Dylan first recorded 'Mr Tambourine Man' with Rambling Jack Elliott on backing vocals during the *Another Side Of Bob Dylan* sessions. In the end, he decided against including it on *Another Side* – 'I felt too close to it to put it on', he told an interviewer from the Canadian Broadcasting Company cryptically in 1966. Indeed, with 'Chimes Of Freedom' and 'My Back Pages' already earmarked, the additional inclusion of 'Mr Tambourine Man' may well have made *Another Side* overly challenging for Dylan fans grappling with his new taste for involved language games.

However, it emerged in 1965 as one of the key tracks on *Bringing It All Back Home*, savage yet accessible, with Langhorne playing a subdued electric-guitar counterpoint to Dylan's own acoustic. By this time, The Byrds had already worked up their own version of the song after their manager, Jim Dickson, had acquired a Dylan demo that included the song.

The Byrds' Jim McGuinn – he changed his name to Roger as a 'spiritual exercise' in 1967 – knew all about Dylan. As a folk singer himself, he had played sessions for Judy Collins and Hoyt Axton and worked as a sideman with the Chad Mitchell Trio and Bobby Darin, for whom he played 12-string guitar and banjo. He met Gene Clark, a former member of The New Christy Minstrels also looking for a more contemporary outlet, at the LA Troubador in the summer of 1964, following which they met and teamed up with David Crosby to make some demos as The Jet Set.

The first Beatles movie hits Times Square, New York, August 1964.

The big revelation for them was seeing The Beatles' movie *A Hard Day's Night*, featuring George Harrison playing an electric 12-string. It convinced them the future was electric. They recorded a single 'Please Let Me Love You' for Elektra using the name The Beefeaters, but Elektra passed on the option to release an album when it sank without trace. That might have been the end of the story, but The Jet Set stuck together with the addition of Chris Hillman on bass and Michael Clarke on drums (he couldn't actually play drums but he had a Beatle haircut and that was the important thing), and they began work on some new demos.

Recognizing its maverick genius, Jim Dickson played them Dylan's 'Mr Tambourine Man' demo and urged them to rework it. They also included several other Dylan songs on the demos – 'Spanish Harlem Incident', 'All I Really Want To Do' and 'Chimes Of Freedom' all subsequently appeared on their debut album – but 'Mr Tambourine Man' was the one that stood out. It was good enough, at least, to convince CBS's West Coast A&R man Allen Stanton to sign them to Columbia. The band's decision to change the signature from two/four to four/four immediately turned it into a rock record, and with McGuinn's heavily compressed Rickenbacker guitar sounding like a chiming bell, their Beatle-ization of Dylan had a spectacular impact. It was, said McGuinn later, a conscious and determined effort to merge the sound of Dylan with The Beatles, with a few Everly Brothers harmonies and Beach Boys falsettos thrown in for good measure.

Not everyone thought that 'Mr Tambourine Man' was a good idea. Dylan's manager Albert Grossman disapproved and attempted to prevent Columbia releasing it, believing it would undermine and devalue Dylan's own version. But even Grossman didn't have the muscle to stop this one and Columbia deputed its youngest producer, Terry Melcher – Doris Day's son – to work it.

Controversially, Melcher decided the band were not up to the job of playing their own arrangement of 'Mr Tambourine Man'. Faced with limited studio time, Melcher recruited session musicians – guitarist Glen Campbell, drummer Hal Blaine and bassist Larry Knechtel and keyboard player Leon Russell – to record the track as fast as possible (although Russell was mixed out of the final version). McGuinn was the only member of The Byrds who played a note on 'Mr Tambourine Man', with Crosby harmonizing behind McGuinn's lead vocals. Clark also sang harmonies on the track, but he, too, was edited out.

Melcher had a troubled relationship with The Byrds – hardly surprising considering he had effectively told them that they were not good enough to play on their own record. Then again, Melcher had a somewhat troubled life; in 1969, he was linked to the Manson family murders when Roman Polanski's wife, the actress Sharon Tate, was among five people killed in a house on Cielo Drive, Los Angeles, that had previously been Melcher's home. Many people came to the conclusion that the murders were a result of the cult seeking to wreak revenge after the producer had rebuffed Manson's attempts to become a recording artist. Melcher was reunited with The Byrds in 1971 for the album *Byrdmaniax*, but with Melcher adding lush strings to the record against the band's wishes while they were away on tour, it was no happier an occasion and far less successful than their first meeting of minds.

Yet there's no disputing that Melcher crafted a classic out of 'Mr Tambourine Man', which, in an event of blissful symmetry, was detonating on the unsuspecting American public while Dylan was on his UK tour. It was entirely coincidental, but The Byrds entering the charts with their rock treatment of 'Mr Tambourine Man' effectively marked the end of Bob Dylan as a folk singer.

It was only halfway through 1965 but it had already been a frenetic year for Dylan, with the release of *Bringing It All Back Home* and the wild British tour, during which he had unceremoniously dumped Joan Baez for Sara Lownds. And then The Byrds changed everything. Their version of 'Mr Tambourine Man' was to stay in the US charts for three months and turn Dylan from cult idol and folk-singing hero into someone who delivered hits. The revelation that he held genuine commercial appeal made the establishment sit up and take notice. His back catalogue was suddenly being scrutinized for other potential rock hits. The Turtles were soon in the studio recording 'It Ain't Me Babe', while Cher covered 'All I Really Want To Do'. Suddenly, Dylan's star had shifted up several notches and he was *seriously* hot. Still only 24 and going through a year of crazy highs and lows that saw him bounce erratically between fresh creative peaks and dark threats to give it all up, Bob Dylan was verging on becoming a household name.

The road to *Highway 61 Revisited* had initially been taken a year earlier when he'd been working on the *Another Side Of Bob Dylan* album and consciously moved away from what he described as 'finger-pointing' songs. 'I don't want to write for people any more, y'know, be a *spokesman*,' he told journalist Nat Hentoff, sleevenotes writer for *The Freewheelin' Bob Dylan*. 'From now on I want to write from inside me … the way I like to write is for it to come out the way I walk or talk … the bomb is getting boring because what's wrong goes much deeper than the bomb.'

And while he still ostensibly remained the darling of the folk world, there had been a few dissenting voices when he had played the 1964 Newport Festival and introduced more obtuse material such as 'Mr Tambourine Man' and 'To Ramona'. It invoked a worried response from the folk music bible *Sing Out!*. Editor and renowned socialist Irwin Silber wrote an open letter to Dylan, questioning the new direction of his songwriting. 'You seem to be in a different kind of bag now, Bob – and I'm worried about it.' He accused Dylan of losing contact with people at Newport, fretting that 'the paraphernalia of fame' was getting in the way. 'Your new songs seem to be all inner directed now, inner probing, self-conscious – maybe even a little maudlin or a little cruel on occasion. And it's happening on stage too. You seem to be relating to a handful of cronies behind the scenes now rather than to the rest of us out front.…'

If it was intended to prick Dylan's conscience, it failed miserably. As he told Hentoff in the *New Yorker* magazine, the idea of his words being interpreted as a representation of others appalled him. 'I'm part of no movement. If I was I wouldn't be able to do anything else but be in The

Movement. I just can't make it with any organization.'

The signs of Dylan's discomfort with his iconic status as a protest singer had been there much earlier. At the Grand Ballroom of the Americana Hotel, New York, in December 1963, he was presented with the Tom Paine Award at the Emergency Civil Liberties Committee's annual Bill of Rights dinner. The Committee was honouring him for his civil-rights songs, but Dylan took one look at what he identified as champagne socialists rooted in outdated left-wing ideals and recoiled in distaste.

At first he refused to accept the award, but when prevailed to stand up and speak, he launched into an impromptu rant at the guests. 'You people should be at the beach,' he told them. 'You should be out there and you should be swimming and relaxing in the time you have to relax. It's not an old people's world. It has nothing to do with old people. Old people when their hair grows out, *they* should go out. And I look down to see the people that are governing me and making my rules and they haven't got any hair on their head – I get very uptight about that.'

Warming to his theme, he went on to expand on his feeling of alienation from them all. 'They talk about Negroes and they talk about black and white and they talk about colours of red and blue and yellow. Man, I just don't see any colours at all when I look out. I've read history books. I've never seen one history book that tells how anybody feels. I've found facts about our history, I've found out what people know about what goes on but I never found anything about how anybody feels about anything happens. It's all just plain facts and it don't help me one little bit to look back.'

The 1,400 guests started to get very uneasy and there was an outbreak of booing when he likened himself to Kennedy's assassin Lee Harvey Oswald. 'I don't know exactly what he thought he was doing but I got to admit honestly that I too ... I saw something of myself in him. I don't think it would have gone ... I don't think I could go that far, but I got to stand up and say I saw things that he felt, in me.' As an outraged chorus of boos and hisses grew, he brought his rambling thoughts to an end. 'I accept this Tom Paine award on behalf of James Forman of the Students Non-Violent

Coordinating Committee and on behalf of the people who went to Cuba.'

The reverberations went on for a long time afterwards. His reference to three students arrested for trying to travel to Cuba in direct contravention of a US ban were probably acceptable enough, and even the ageist personal insults about baldness induced nervous titters of amusement, but America's grief over the assassination of President Kennedy was still palpable and such seemingly glib references to his killer Lee Harvey Oswald couldn't be stomached. Dylan had not only elevated himself to a figure of infamy in American establishment eyes but with it he'd inadvertently accelerated his own unwanted status as a messiah of youth. On the back of it, *Life* magazine profiled him as 'The Angry Young Folk Singer' and Dylan had achieved the last thing he wanted – he had become a spokesman for a generation.

Dylan wrote an apology of sorts to the Emergency Civil Liberties Committee in the form of a long and rambling explanation of his misunderstanding of the occasion, his feeling of alienation whenever under public scrutiny, the general confusion in his head and his philosophy as a songwriter and a person. 'My life runs in a series of moods in private and in personal ways, sometimes I, myself, can change the mood I'm in to the mood I'd like to be in. When I walked thru the doors of the Americana Hotel I needed to change my mood … for reasons inside myself. I am a restless soul. Hungry. Perhaps wretched.'

He hinted at the discomfort of his own celebrity. 'I perform rarely and when I do there is a constant commotion burning at my body and at my mind because of the attention aimed at me. Instincts fight my emotions and fears fight my instincts….' On the Lee Harvey Oswald issue he said 'When I spoke of Lee Oswald I was speaking of the times, I was not speaking of his deed, if it was his deed. The deed speaks for itself. But I am sick, so sick, at hearing "we all share the blame" for every church bombing, gun battle, mine disaster, poverty explosion, and president killing that comes about. It is so easy to say "we" and bow our heads together. I must say "I" alone and bow my head alone….'

Bob with trademark ciggy and harmonica.   © Daniel Kramer

The 'Angry Young Folk Singer' clearly wanted out.

Returning to the US in June 1965, after his UK tour, Dylan was mixed up and confused. He didn't know what it was he wanted to do, he just knew something had to change. And, above everything else, his days as a folk icon were over. He has since said (in Martin Scorsese's *No Direction Home* documentary [2005]) that it was never his intention to upset or insult the folk establishment. He continued to revere Alan Lomax, Pete Seeger and the other respected denizens of the American folk firmament, but it felt irrelevant and held little interest to him any more. Further still, it was lumbering him with unwanted symbols of leadership, conscience and morality that he was determined to shift at all costs. The madness of the British tour and the emotional upheaval of his private life blurred the edges even more and, with The Byrds unwittingly making a rock svengali out of him, Dylan's mind was ablaze.

The signs were already there about the sort of album Dylan would make next. The more insular songwriting style that had emerged on *Another Side Of Bob Dylan* had been corroborated by the more upbeat settings on the rockier half of *Bringing It All Back Home*, and he was obviously not about to go back to making an acoustic folk album full of clear message songs.

'Half-wracked prejudice leaped forth / 'Rip down all hate' I screamed / Lies that life is black and white / Spoke from my skull. I dreamed / Romantic facts of musketeers / Foundationed deep, somehow. / Ah, but I was so much older then / I'm younger than that now …'. 'My Back Pages' on *Another Side Of Bob Dylan* was as clear a message as any that there were to be … well, no more messages.

And despite Irwin Silber's open letter in response to Dylan's 1964 Newport appearance, the idea of outraged folk purists pulling their hair out at the notion of drums and electric guitars didn't really seem an issue. After all, nobody batted an eyelid when Brownie McGhee and other authentic blues icons of the era amplified their guitars at Newport and elsewhere. And at that 1964 Newport festival, they'd found a new hero to fight the good fight in words and song in the shape of Phil Ochs. Far more in tune with political issues and world events than Dylan ever was, Ochs's calling card was topicality and, one of the first songwriters to rail against the escalating military exercise in Vietnam with a nice line in sardonic humour, he had anthems-a-plenty. As he did with so many of those in his inner circle of friends, Dylan habitually baited Phil Ochs, but he should not have done – Ochs was his means of escape.

The 'folk rock' tag had already been brought into currency as a result of journalists urgently seeking a label to explain the new style propagated by The Byrds, but nobody seemed to place too much importance to it. 'My biggest concern,' Irwin Silber told the journalist Richie Unterberger nearly 40 years later, in the book *Turn! Turn! Turn!*, 'was not with the electricity or the category but with what Dylan was saying and doing about moving away from his political songs … he was the most exciting person I'd heard since Woody Guthrie and he combined a great artistic feel with a political sense that was poetic, that moved people. To find him turning his back on it at a time when the civil rights movement was at its height, there were the beginnings of the protest against the Vietnam War and the new left was developing a whole new sense of politic … to have Dylan deliberately, consciously, moving away from it at that time, I really felt bad about it.'

Of course, there were more cynical suggestions about Dylan's changing path. With Al Grossman's hand on the tiller, the more commercial opportunities availed by the rock world weren't about to be overlooked. Grossman's loud, aggressive, hard-headed business style was always at odds with the exaggerated idealism of the folk movement. Grossman had helped jazz impresario George Wein organize the first Newport Folk Festival in 1959, but as his entrepreneurial career escalated, he scarcely disguised the fact that his main motivation was profit. Newport was built on alternative values and left-wing commitment, but in the burgeoning folk scene of the early 1960s Grossman clearly saw dollar signs rather than the tools to change the world.

He became Dylan's manager – earning 20 per cent of his royalties and 25 per cent of his publishing – in May 1962. It was a deal that suited them both. Few looked twice at Dylan at the time, while Grossman already handled Peter, Paul & Mary, a tuneful trio that he had put together precisely to tap into the commercial potential of folk music in the same way The

Weavers had done a decade earlier, before the McCarthy blacklist scuppered them. Peter, Paul & Mary signed to Warners and Grossman quickly figured that if they sweetened Dylan's songs for mainstream consumption he could make stars out of both of them. It worked like a charm. Peter, Paul & Mary initially broke through with 'If I Had A Hammer' (written in 1949 by Pete Seeger and Lee Hays) and 'Puff The Magic Dragon' (set to music by the group's own Peter Yarrow from a children's poem written by his friend Leonard Lipton – and not, as some assume, a song about marijuana). In 1963, they hit No. 2 with 'Blowin' In The Wind' – at the time the fastest-selling single in Warner Brothers history – and followed it into the Top 10 with another Dylan song, 'Don't Think Twice, It's Alright'. They also took Dylan's 'The Times They Are A-Changing' into the UK charts and recorded various other Dylan covers, including 'When The Ship Comes In', 'Too Much Of Nothing' and 'It Ain't Me Babe', although their biggest ever hit came in 1969 when they had a worldwide smash with a John Denver song, 'Leaving On A Jet Plane'.

'Bobby Dylan's writing put us on another level,' said Peter Yarrow. 'We went into the studio and released "Blowin' In The Wind" as a single. We didn't wait for an album, we just put it out. Instinctively, we knew the song carried the moment of its own time. I remember Albert Grossman asking me if he should manage Dylan. We're walking in the Village and I said "Yeah, I think so." And Albert said "Yeah, I think so too. He's too good not to happen." In the beginning, Bobby was a Woody Guthrie imitator, he didn't have his own identity. Albert really shepherded him through those early years.'

Born in Chicago to Russian Jewish immigrants in 1926, Albert Grossman gained an economics degree from Roosevelt University and set off to make his fortune from the entertainment industry. His early reputation was partly built on his success running Chicago's famous Gate of Horn folk club, which he set up in a basement at the Rice Hotel. Here he discovered Odetta, an Afro-American singer from Alabama who had been championed by Pete Seeger and Harry Belafonte.

Grossman guided Odetta to national attention with a live album recorded at the Gate of Horn and a 1959 appearance with Belafonte on the network show *TV Tonight*. He procured her a prestigious headlining spot at Newport, promoted a sell-out show at New York's Carnegie Hall and even got her a part in a movie, an adaptation of William Faulkner's *Sanctuary*. By 1963 Grossman had transformed Odetta into one of the biggest stars of the day and her album *Folk Songs* became one of the year's bestsellers. The young Dylan was somewhat in awe of her, describing her as 'a goddess'.

In 1959 Grossman set up the Newport Folk Festival with George Wein and saw huge dollar signs latent in folk music. 'The American public is like Sleeping Beauty waiting to be kissed awake by the prince of Folk Music,' he pronounced grandly to writer Bob Shelton. In part, his instincts were spot on. If folk music was the prince, Albert Grossman was the kingmaker. He saw market opportunities and moved swiftly to fulfil them – creating Peter, Paul & Mary out of what he saw as a gaping void left by the likes of sweet-voiced singing groups such as The Weavers and Kingston Trio (initially offering one of Dylan's Greenwich Village mentors Dave Van Ronk the place of 'Paul', which ultimately went to Noel Stookey). Grossman took an increasing interest in Dylan as his reputation among other singers grew – signing him in 1962 and providing the muscle to escort him from the clubs in Greenwich Village to the world's biggest concert halls.

Grossman found that his aggressive marketing technique produced results and cared little about who he upset on the way – his eyes were firmly set on the bigger picture. Yet for all his faults, he recognized one thing – he had little aptitude for music. When his artist was playing he never interfered … and he didn't see why record companies should, either. Even when he was back in Chicago running the Gate of Horn club long before he ever met Dylan, he would throw out any punters who talked through the performers' acts. One of his most significant legacies was to gain complete artistic control for the artists he represented – a particularly vital factor in the case of someone as wilfully individual as Dylan.

Grossman's uncompromisingly brutal willingness to make enemies for the greater good of profit and profile provided exactly the lever that Dylan needed in order to lift him from the folk bearpit.

However, Grossman did not always best serve his artist's interests. While Dylan recoiled from the endless 'spokesman for a generation' epithets garlanded upon him, describing himself in his 2004 autobiography *Chronicles* as 'more a cowpuncher than a pied piper', it was actually Grossman who had prompted a lot of these descriptions in his hype to the press. In the end the two men probably used one another, and each got what he wanted from a partnership that always seemed more one of mutual convenience than genuine bond. But Grossman was no Colonel Tom Parker, and Dylan was no Presley either. Dylan may have turned a blind eye to Grossman's more obnoxious traits and he may even have winced a bit at some of the yelling and bullying that went on in his name, but he was too shrewd and involved in his own destiny not to clock what was going on every inch of the way. For his part Grossman knew when not to cross the line. He recognized Dylan's genius and had genuine respect for his talent and sensibility. He saw his job as making as much money for the both of them as he could in the quickest way possible, but he knew that with an artist as single-minded as Dylan this could not be done at any cost, and the artistic career path would always have to be driven by Dylan himself.

In *Chronicles*, Dylan does not paint a pretty picture of Grossman, describing his gangster-like lifestyle in Chicago. 'He had an enormous presence, dressed always in a conventional suit and tie, and he sat at a corner table. Usually when he walked his voice was loud, like the booming of war drums. He didn't talk as much as growl.' Yet while he may now suggest he didn't much care for Grossman, Dylan acknowledges that he knew at the outset what Grossman could do for his career and went into business with him with his eyes wide open. 'He (Grossman) had seen me around before but paid me little mind. After my first record on Columbia had been released, there was a noticeable shift on his part to represent me. I welcomed the opportunity because Grossman had a stable of clients and was getting all of them work.'

Dylan and Grossman were never ever especially close, but they spent a lot of time together in the early years. Dylan often stayed with Grossman, both at his apartment in New York and his house in Woodstock, and Grossman remained at Bob's side during this crucial period of his career, bigging him up, giving outsiders the hard sell and defending his corner. Grossman did the deals, plotted the commercial path and was the much-feared and frequently reviled presence making a nuisance of himself in board rooms and record company offices, but he went to great lengths never to upset Dylan's muse. The idea that Grossman was standing behind Dylan, urging him to forsake his artistic principles and chase rock stardom, is wide of the mark. Dylan himself had been ruthlessly ambitious from the start and in Grossman he had found exactly the right catalyst to make it all happen. David Braun, who was Dylan's attorney for a number of years, describes Grossman as 'smart as anyone I met regarding business, the man who invented personal full-time management ... he was the first person to realize there was real money to be made in the music business.'

Almost inevitably, the hitherto symbiotic relationship between Dylan and Grossman ended messily. There had been a mutual respect between them, but Dylan's semi-retirement after his motorbike crash in 1966 gave them the time and opportunity to think about each other's shortcomings and altered the nature of their relationship. Grossman was frustrated that Dylan's break hindered his earning potential and Dylan in part blamed Grossman for some of the pressures that had been heaped on him, and paradoxically may also have been jealous of the time Al was now spending on other artists. Dylan certainly wasn't the only one of Albert's clients who had become disenchanted with his management style. Odetta was furious about the way that she was neglected when Grossman found bigger fish to fry, and Mary Travers of Peter, Paul & Mary resented the fact that he appeared to make more money than all three of them. Grossman in turn began to fall out of love with management, which caused more friction with Dylan. They were never to live in each other's pockets again, the way they did through those early years, and as their working relationship neared its end they barely spoke, both sides seething with resentment. Dylan told Robert Shelton it was he who pulled the trigger, sacking Grossman in 1971 and calling the lawyers to move in. Grossman responded by suing Dylan for unpaid royalties. The interminable legal arguments rumbled through the courts for years, with Grossman finally winning the case.

At the time his association with Dylan was coming to an acrimonious end, Grossman built the Bearsville Recording Studios near Woodstock, in due course adding a restaurant and theatre complex and founding Bearsville Records. He remained married to former New York waitress Sally Bueler, the girl in the red dress on the cover of *Bringing It All Back Home*, for 22 years until a sudden heart attack killed him on a Concorde flight to London in 1986.

Released to coincide with Dylan's 1965 European tour, 'Subterranean Homesick Blues' became a Top 10 hit in Britain (it had peaked at No. 39 in the US), its frenzied rhythmic stanzas taking him to a broader audience from the one that had bought his only previous UK single 'The Times They Are A-Changin'' (which had reached No. 9 earlier in the year), yet baffling the hell out of everyone who heard it. Partly based on a Woody Guthrie/Pete Campbell collaboration 'Taking It Easy', which Pete Seeger had also recorded with the Weavers, it also owed plenty to the rock'n'roll riffs of Chuck Berry's 'Too Much Monkey Business', while the machine gun couplets alluded to the style of Jack Kerouac and the beat poets. It was almost a precursor to rap, while the drug allusions of the opening line ('Johnny's in the basement mixing up the medicine / I'm on the pavement thinking about the government') was an indication that LSD had become a recreational pastime, a fact later confirmed by the producer Paul Rothchild, who claimed to have been with Dylan when he tried acid for the first time after a concert at the University of Massachusetts in the spring of 1964.

By anybody's standards, 'Subterranean Homesick Blues' was an extraordinary record and, at a time when the most popular records of the day in the UK charts included the crooning likes of 'The Minute You're

Gone' by Cliff Richard, 'Where Are You Now (My Love)' by Jackie Trent and Roger Miller's 'King Of The Road', it might as well have come from outer space. It certainly put Dylan into a new sphere. If he could get a major hit with *this*, then Dylan must have felt that he had carte blanche to go off and do any damn thing he wanted. This was before anyone had seen the famous footage of Dylan – with a cameo appearance by Allen Ginsberg – holding up cue cards offering keynote words and phrases from the song as it played at the opening of D. A. Pennebaker's *Don't Look Back* documentary. Shot in a back alley outside London's Savoy Hotel and still seen regularly on music TV stations, the sequence was voted No. 7 by *Rolling Stone* magazine in its Top 100 list of the greatest videos ever made.

There were dissenters against the shock of the hyped-up rhythmic assault and crazed lyricism of 'Subterranean Homesick Blues', of course, but buoyed by the positive reaction of British audiences to the song, Dylan paid them little heed. 'I didn't want to do that by myself, I thought I could get more power out of it with a small group behind it. I didn't understand what the gripe was all about. I'm a musician not a critic, I don't self-analyze my own work,' he said later in the *No Direction Home* documentary. 'I read that Stravinsky had negative responses, Coltrane and Charlie Parker had lots of negative responses – people are always emotionally charged up if some artist they feel is not doing what they used to do in a previous time.' He acknowledged the success of the single in Britain had encouraged him greatly. 'British audiences were the first to accept what I was doing at face value. To that crowd it wasn't different at all, it was right in line with everything they've read in school, from the Shakespearean tradition to Byron and Shelley. The British audiences were the first ones who accepted it.'

However, when he finally reached the end of the dark tunnel that constituted that 1965 European tour he was shattered by the banal questions being fired at him all the time, the acolytes hanging on his every word, the strain of going on stage on his own to satisfy an adoring crowd who thought he had all the answers, the inevitable parties that followed, the press hounding him, the flashbulbs, the constant travelling, the expectation, the demands, the responsibility, the emotional pressures, Pennebaker's bloody camera following him everywhere he went. And then he got sick, and he snapped.

He and Sara took time out for a short holiday in Portugal and, exhausted and dispirited, Dylan decided enough was enough. Stop the world, he wanted to get off. Bob Dylan resolved that his music career was over. He was quitting.

Chapter 3

LIKE A COMPLETE UNKNOWN

'You said you'd never compromise / With the mystery tramp /
But now you realize / He's not selling any alibis ...'
Bob Dylan, 'Like A Rolling Stone'

'**I**'d quit…I'd literally *quit* singing and playing …'
Talking to Martin Bronstein for the Canadian Broadcasting Company
in February 1966, nine months after the event, Dylan was still stunned by
the venomous muse that unexpectedly overtook him and shook him out of
the torpor that engulfed him as he sunk to his lowest ebb.

He had returned to the States physically and mentally exhausted by
the stresses of his European tour and the wall-to-wall partying that went
with it. He was sick, both literally and metaphorically. His last
performance on that tour was a BBC TV recording in front of a live
audience at Shepherds Bush BBC Theatre on 1 June, when his set
included 'Mr Tambourine Man,' 'It Ain't Me Babe' and 'It's All Over
Now, Baby Blue'. Following this, he took a short time out in Portugal, and
while there he decided that something had to change. He had made five
albums in just over three years, and in the flood of extraordinary songs
that occupied them he had outgunned all of the songwriting factories
churning out hits for record companies at that point.

It had brought him much of the fame and adulation he had craved back
home in Hibbing, Minnesota, but it didn't make him feel good. The cost to

his prized personal freedom and need for privacy felt too great. The critical sniping, the idiotic press conferences, the rapt, expectant audiences, the drudge of planes, hotels and concert halls, the whole gruelling irrelevance of stardom that devoured him when he wasn't singing or writing. And all the while, the world's youth seemed to be staring at him, apparently hanging all its hopes and expectations on his every utterance. At the age of 24, Dylan had reached burnout. That was it, he decided, time to retire.

Not that he told anyone, or had any other plans. He thought he might write books or plays or something … *anything,* as long as he could pursue his art at a safe distance away from that suffocating, soul-eating radar.

He escaped with Sara Lownds, the woman he described as 'holy'. Dark and stylish, Sara was sometimes likened by those to who knew her to a young Sophia Loren and was very different to any of the other women Dylan had previously had serious relationships with – Suze Rotolo, Joan Baez and Echo Helstrom. He later waxed lyrical about her 'flesh like silk' and 'saintlike eyes' in 'Sad Eyed Lady Of The Lowlands', the epic song about her that took him an age to perfect and was clearly inspired by a natural character with little taste for the trappings of celebrity or a glamorous lifestyle. The 'Lowlands' of the title was a play on her name.

Born Shirley Noznisky, she changed her name to Sara, apparently at the insistence of her first husband, magazine photographer Hans Lownds, who championed her brief career as a cover girl. Still a teenager when she had arrived in New York and set up home with Lownds, she lived with him on the East Side and was enjoying some lucrative assignments until she fell pregnant with their daughter, Maria. After her split from Hans, she worked as a secretary for a film production company and lived in an apartment in MacDougal St in Greenwich Village. It was then that she first met Dylan, after being introduced by Sally Grossman, a close friend. She knew film-maker Donn Pennebaker from her work at the production company and may well have been the key to Grossman agreeing to Pennebaker's *Don't Look Back* movie.

As Sara's relationship with Dylan blossomed early in 1965, both were keen to keep it quiet. Relishing her down-to-earth sensibility and air of inner peace, Dylan was keen to prevent it being sullied by Village gossip ... not to mention the wrath of Baez should she ever find out. This softly-softly approach also suited Sara, who had no taste for personal attention or the celebrity life. Throughout their entire relationship – they married later that year – Sara fiercely protected their privacy and has still never agreed to be interviewed about their time together.

After the madness of Europe, Sara represented to Dylan a peaceful haven. They went to Woodstock in upstate New York and rented a cabin from the mother of Peter Yarrow (of Peter, Paul & Mary). And without any particular plan or motivation, he picked up a pen and paper and ... exploded. All the frustration, anger, bitterness, indignation and excitement that had accumulated in the previous four years or so, since his arrival in New York had been met largely with a mixture of indifference and ridicule, erupted in an adrenaline overload that produced a vicious torrent of words and ideas which, before he knew it, had rambled across 20 scruffy, handwritten pages. It had no real form or purpose, it had no plan or message, it had no story and it certainly wasn't intended to be a song at all. It was just a stream of consciousness; a *manic* stream of consciousness.

Sitting at a piano, he picked up that long piece of vomit and started mouthing the phrase 'how does it feel?' as a rhythm took shape in his head and he played around with the tune of 'La Bamba'. Somehow, out of that charged, unyielding onslaught, emerged 'Like A Rolling Stone'. It was unlike anything he had written before – or, indeed, anything anybody else had written before.

It is odd that, in the context of the flood of bile and vitriol that follows, the opening words should be the traditional fairy story introduction 'Once upon a time ...', so redolent of gentle scene setting and childhood innocence. But Dylan quickly follows it with his snarling, spiteful put-down of an anti-heroine, once full of grand ideas and self-regard, clearly being set up for a fall. 'How does it feel to be without a home, like a complete unknown ...'.

As the verses roar on, the rage intensifies and the dismantling of a false pride becomes ever more brutal and cruel, the singer relishing every word of his vicious character assassination. Every line feels like a knife plunging into his helpless victim. Blood spurts with each new wound as other characters are drawn into the action to watch the carnage and destruction. The mystery tramp, the frowning jugglers, the clowns, the chrome horse and the diplomat with the Siamese cat, who 'really wasn't where it's at' and took everything he could steal.

It is a cautionary message to high society, a particularly twisted and evil morality tale full of invective aimed at the privileged and proud. 'When you got nothing, you got nothing to lose / You're invisible now, you got no secrets to conceal …': it's a song of revenge, Dylan has said, in which case that is a hell of a vengeance.

There is a theory that the seeds of 'Like A Rolling Stone' had been planted during the UK tour, when Dylan, Bobby Neuwirth and Joan Baez had been in a hotel room singing an old Hank Williams favourite 'Lost Highway' (written by Leon Payne), which opens with the line 'I'm a

© Daniel Kramer

The not at all flamboyant Bob Neuwirth proudly shows off his paintings. And tricyle.

rolling stone all alone and lost / For a life of sin I have paid the cost …'. Dylan was also closely familiar with Muddy Waters' 1950 tune 'Rollin' Stone', which had become part of the blues holy grail for young British bands, not least The Rolling Stones themselves, and would have been at the back of Dylan's mind in his chosen imagery.

Much speculation has arisen around the unfortunate being that incurred Dylan's wrath to such a degree as to inspire such a fiendish outpouring of bile and hatred. And who were the bit-part characters who dipped into the action with such colour, intriguing, unexplained cameos: Napoleon in rags? Miss Lonely? Princess on the steeple? Or, best of all, the Mystery Tramp? Are they one and the same? Are they real people or figments of the frantic Dylan imagination? Questions, always with Dylan there are questions.

The most obvious conclusion is that it was written about Joan Baez, from whom he'd recently split and who had already been mercilessly baited and ridiculed when they were together in Europe, until she had finally had enough and decamped. Baez, the former queen of folk music, a reminder of the world and the culture Dylan wanted to escape with such finality, certainly ticked several boxes. The daughter of a physicist, granddaughter of a minister, she had a moneyed background and had lived in exotic parts of the world and was so righteous and indignant that she, far more than Dylan ever did, involved herself in demonstrations and uprisings and personified the whole protest ethos.

Her voice was pure and her conviction was absolute – not for her the diversion of rock or the camouflage of cryptic poetry. 'I had a purist upbringing,' she said, 'and when I was 18 I literally thought that if you added bass and drums you became wicked and vile.' Her political drive and her need to march and campaign and protest and do things was always much more real than Dylan's, giving rise to the 'St Joan' epithet that came to be interpreted as a damnation. 'My political drive is stronger than my musical drive,' she conceded, and right there in that sentence lay the roots of the deep chasm between the two of them.

Serious Dylanologists, however, discount as far too glib the theory that 'Like A Rolling Stone' was inspired by Dylan's scorn for Baez. Baez herself has suggested it is about her old nemesis, acid-tongued Bobby Neuwirth. Dylan's brother in arms, he was all over Pennebaker's *Don't Look Back* film, seemingly goading Bob all the way. Painter, road manager, sidekick, confidante, henchman, poet, underground cult hero, womanizer, party organizer, self-appointed king of cool and baiter-in-chief of Baez, Donovan and any other unfortunate who wound up in the line of fire of his sledgehammer jibes, Neuwirth went on to become a film-maker and a credible singer-songwriter in his own right, co-writing the wonderful 'Mercedes Benz' with his friend Janis Joplin. He was even immortalized – waist down at least – standing behind Dylan on the *Highway 61 Revisited* sleeve. The bile that came tumbling out of Dylan on the song certainly has a mark of Neuwirth about it.

Another victim often put in the frame is Edie Sedgwick, the beautiful 22-year-old Californian socialite, heiress, model, actress and Andy Warhol acolyte with a history of anorexia and mental problems. She had been close to the Dylan camp since meeting him at a club – the Kettle of Fish - in Greenwich Village at Christmas 1964, and had an intense sexual relationship with Bobby Neuwirth (she later described herself as his sex slave). Sedgwick's head was filled with dreams of stardom and she talked to Al Grossman about appearing in a movie opposite Dylan. It never happened and Sedgwick descended into drug dependency, dying of a barbiturate overdose in 1971. 'Leopard Skin Pill Box Hat' and 'Just Like A Woman' on the 1966 album *Blonde On Blonde* are usually thought to have been about Edie Sedgwick, so it is perfectly feasible that Dylan foresaw her fate in 'Like A Rolling Stone'. Some have tried to implicate Dylan in the demise of Edie Sedgwick, suggesting that he and Grossman strung her along about the movie idea and had a lot of amusement at her expense, treating her as a plaything.

The 2007 movie *Factory Girl*, based on her life, features a thinly disguised Dylan (who threatened legal action to stop the film when it became apparent that the movie suggested Edie had an affair with him that helped to precipitate her death) as a character called Quinn. Andy Warhol certainly seemed persuaded by others to believe that 'Like A Rolling Stone' was about Edie and, furthermore, that he was the diplomat referred to in the line 'You used to ride on a chrome horse with your diplomat'. In his book *The Philosophy of Andy Warhol* (1975) he wrote 'I'd get answers like "I hear he (Dylan) feels you destroyed Edie" or "Listen to 'Like A Rolling Stone' – I think you're the diplomat on the chrome horse, man." I didn't know exactly what they meant by that – I never listened to the words of songs – but I got the tenor of what people were saying, that Dylan didn't like me, that he blamed me for Edie's drugs.'

Given the personal tribulations that acted as the backdrop to the song's creation, however, the theory is also sometimes voiced that it is a harsh, autobiographical self-assessment targeted by Dylan at his old self. Writer Mike Marquese certainly thought so, referencing 'Napoleon in rags' – ridiculed in the song for 'the language that he used' – as a self-description. 'The song only attains its full poignancy when one realizes it is sung, at least in part, to the singer himself – he's the one with "no direction home,"' writes Marquese in his book *Wicked Messenger* (2003). This fits, too, in a tangled fashion, although it is easy to over-think motive and meaning when analyzing Dylan lyrics, and the Sedgwick/Baez theories carry as much weight.

Rock critic Greil Marcus has written a whole book about the song, (*Like A Rolling Stone*, 2005) but even he does not wade too deeply into analysis of the central characters populating the narrative. According to Marcus it is a song of freedom about being liberated from your old hang-ups and your old knowledge and the fear, the frightening part of facing that, particularly when hc gets to scrounging for your next meal. He talks passionately about the 'fear' in the line 'Do you want to make a deal?' and figures that 'Once upon a time you dressed so fine …' isn't so much about a rich person falling apart as cold reality dawning on someone.

'I see it as being about a *comfortable* individual,' writes Marcus, 'or a comfortable society, suddenly discovering what's going on in Vietnam – the society we're taught about, and you realize, as you become aware, drug aware, socially aware, the disaster of the commercial society. The key line,' he continues, 'is "You've got no secrets to conceal." Everything has been stripped away. You're on your own, you're free now. You've gone through all these levels of experience – you fell, someone you believed in robbed you blind, took everything he could steal and finally it's all been taken away. You're so helpless and now you've got *nothing left*. And you're invisible – you've got no secrets – that's so liberating. You've nothing to fear anymore. It's useless to hide any of that shit. *You're a free man*. That to me is the message. You know: "Songs of Innocence and Experience."'

Dylan himself has never fully explained it. 'I used to know what I wanted to say before I used to write the song. But now I just write a song like I know that it's going to be all right and I don't really know exactly what it's all about, but I do know layers of what it's all about,' he told Ralph Gleason obliquely later in 1965.

The following year he was scarcely any clearer. 'It was just a rhythm thing on paper all about my steady hatred directed at some point that was honest,' he said. 'In the end it wasn't hatred, it was telling someone something that they didn't know, telling them they were lucky … I never thought of it as a song until one day I was at the piano and on the paper it was singing "How does it feel?" in slow motion. It was like swimming in lava. You see your victim swimming in lava. Hanging by their arms from a birch tree. Skipping, kicking the tree, hitting a nail with your foot. Seeing someone in the pain they were bound to meet up with.'

It changed everything. As he completed 'Like A Rolling Stone' it opened his eyes to a new direction, completely obliterating everything that had gone before, totally reviving his spirit and reawakening his soul. The rush he had got from it was so exciting and life-affirming that he wanted to record it immediately – all thoughts of abandoning songwriting in favour of literature or drama went up in flames.

'It was the most honest and straight thing I put across that reached popularity,' he said in *No Direction Home*. 'I'd literally quit singing and playing and I found myself writing this long piece of vomit that turned into "Like A Rolling Stone". I'd never written anything like that before. *Nobody* had written anything like it before. Anybody can write a lot of the things I used to write, it was just that nobody thought of writing them – but that's only because I was hungry. I'm not saying it's better than anything else, but after that I wasn't interested in writing a novel or a play. I just wanted to write songs. Now there was this whole new category.'

A new album had been the last thing on his mind when he had returned to the States at the start of June. He had no material and he had no appetite to write any. Just a couple of weeks later, he knew he'd written the best song of his life.

Initially there was no plan to record 'Like A Rolling Stone' as a single – Dylan still wasn't perceived as an artist likely to make any significant dent in the charts. But, newly energized, Dylan wanted to tap into this unexpected new phase of creativity and get it into the studio. Tom Wilson, who had overseen most of *The Times They Are A-Changin'*, *Another Side Of Bob Dylan* and *Bringing It All Back Home* so successfully was again enlisted and Dylan was booked into Columbia Records Studio A in New York on 15 June to start work on his new album.

Al Aranowitz and Tom Wilson at the scene of the crime as 'Rolling Stone' falls to earth.

As virtually the only black producer working in the mainstream at the time, Wilson was an unlikely character to have become such a formidable influence in the American music industry. A tall, slim, imposing figure from Waco in Texas, he became involved in music while studying at Harvard via the university jazz society and, in the early 1950s, the radio station WHRB – it was this experience that he later credited as giving him the grounding for his latest triumphs in the music industry. He was obsessed by modern jazz and a year after graduating from Harvard he set up his own label, Transition, and among his triumphs were Cecil Taylor's *Jazz Advance* and Sun Ra's first LP, *Jazz By Sun Ra*, later retitled *Sun Song*. But he couldn't sustain it and sold out to the Chicago label Delmar. He became jazz A&R director for Savoy Records, produced jazz radio programmes and was also assistant to the director of the New York State Commission for Human Rights.

In 1963 he joined Columbia Records as a staff producer and replaced John Hammond as producer on the final sessions for Dylan's *Freewheelin'* album when Al Grossman fell out with Hammond. Unimpressed by the label's handling of his charge, Grossman was trying to get Dylan out of his Columbia contract on the grounds that Bob was under 21 when he had signed it. Clive Davis, who was general attorney at Columbia at the time, conceded Grossman had a point and counselled an appalled Hammond to pull out the stops to placate him. Uneasily, they made their peace, but in the fall-out Hammond left the studio and Wilson was at the controls for four Dylan cuts on *Freewheelin'* – 'Girl From The North Country', 'Masters Of War', 'Talking World War III Blues' and 'Bob Dylan's Dream'. He was retained to look after Dylan's next three albums.

It was Wilson who came up with the title *Another Side Of Bob Dylan*, to the consternation of Dylan himself. 'I begged and pleaded with him not to do it,' Dylan said in the *Biograph* liner notes. 'I thought it was overstating the obvious. It seemed like a negation of the past, which in no way was true. I know Tom didn't mean it that way, but that's what I figured that people would take it to mean. But Tom meant well and he had control, so he had it his way. I guess in the long run he might have been right....'

Choosing titles apart, Wilson's input at this stage was distinctly limited. Dylan was still playing solo and acoustic and Wilson's role was primarily confined to rolling the tapes and putting his thumbs-up at the end of it. Dylan himself had little interest in the technicalities of recording or the subtleties of sound, and there was little artistic interplay between the two of them. Essentially what Dylan wanted, Dylan got. 'With Dylan you have to take what you can get,' Wilson told Nat Hentoff.

Wilson, the jazz man, was himself somewhat bemused to find himself working with a folk singer, even one as individual as Dylan. 'I'd been recording with Sun Ra and Coltrane and I thought folk music was for the dumb guys. This guy played like the dumb guys, but then these words came out. I was flabbergasted. I said to Albert Grossman, "If you put some background to this you might have a white Ray Charles with a message."'

He held that thought and subsequently came to play a key role in the genesis of Dylan's emergence as a folk-rock pioneer. Indeed, he would later claim the credit for the electrification of Dylan. Six months after finishing the *Another Side Of Bob Dylan* sessions, Wilson went back into the studio and started playing around with some of his old cuts. The Animals had just topped the charts both in Britain and the States with their impassioned rock take on the old blues howler 'House Of The Rising Sun' and Wilson went back to the solo version Dylan had recorded for his debut album in 1961. Inspired by The Animals, Wilson brought in session musicians to play a powerhouse R&B arrangement, which he then dubbed on to Dylan's original vocals.

Dylan evidently heard it and was not impressed. In addition to being an experiment to see how Dylan would sound with a rock band behind him, Wilson had wondered about the track's potential as a single. Dylan's negative reaction quickly buried that suggestion, but it gave those involved plenty of food for thought. 'That was where I first consciously at Columbia started to try to put these two different elements together,' he later told writer Clinton Heylin.

Not that this was the first time Dylan had been party to an electric experiment. There were three sessions during the *Freewheelin'* recordings in 1962 when, at John Hammond's suggestion, he used a band to work on the bluesier material. A small backing band was deployed on his adaptation of an old blues song 'Corrina Corrina', once recorded by Joe Turner and released on *Freewheelin'*, albeit with a much-changed lyric that borrowed lines from Robert Johnson. 'Mixed-Up Confusion' – a song Dylan wrote in the back of a taxi on the way to session – was given a full-on rock arrangement.

The idea was to reflect Dylan's pre-Guthrie influences, specifically Elvis, and 'Mixed-Up Confusion' was to be the single that took him to a new place. At three different sessions there were numerous attempts to nail the song, variously with Dick Wellstood (piano), Howie Collins, Bruce Langhorne and George Barnes (guitars), Herb Lovelle (drums) and Leonard Gaskin, Art Davis and Gene Ramey (bass). There was even talk of an attempted Dixieland arrangement, but it has never seen the light of day even as a bootleg, and we can only assume this was one of Tom Wilson's notions that was never indulged. It is said that a frustrated Dylan stormed out of the session at one point, suggesting that some of Wilson's more outlandish ideas might have been already causing friction between him and Dylan.

In December 1962 'Mixed-Up Confusion' was released as a single, making an argument for it to be regarded as the first ever folk-rock record, but focused as it was on Dick Wellstead's pounding, Jerry Lee Lewis-style piano, it sounded more like a homage to early rock'n'roll. The fact that Dylan also recorded a cover of 'That's All Right', Elvis Presley's first single, supports this theory. In the event, none of it mattered. Backed by 'Corrina, Corrina' on the B-side, the single failed to make any sort of ripple and sank without trace. It was omitted from the *Freewheelin'* album and was only dredged up when people became curious in the wake of his 1965 success.

So when Tom Wilson started dubbing a rock backing to 'House Of

The Rising Sun' it was not the alien concept that it might have appeared at a time when Dylan was the undisputed king of folk song. Wilson was a wilful and dynamic character who could clearly see Dylan's crossover potential and played a big part in making it happen on *Bringing It All Back Home*. He hired the session musicians, acted as a go-between for a nervous Dylan and the quizzical musicians, and interpreted Dylan's wishes. He was a lively, upbeat character with a vigorous sense of humour – the sound of Wilson giggling wildly at the beginning of 'Bob Dylan's 115th Dream' is an endearing feature captured on one take of the *Bringing It All Back Home* sessions.

They weren't working in a void, either. Some of Dylan's Greenwich Village contemporaries were thinking along the same lines. Fred Neil – who had befriended Dylan when he first arrived in New York and invited him on stage to play harmonica during his regular spots at the Café Wha? in MacDougal Street – was trying out various line-ups for a band project. It resulted in his 1965 album *Bleecker & MacDougal*, which featured Pete Childs playing electric guitar and vigorously energizing his folk songs on tracks like 'Country Boy' and 'Travelin' Shoes'. John Sebastian, who played harmonica on the album, was putting together his own electric band, the Lovin' Spoonful, around the same time.

More important on the road to *Highway 61*, however, was his friend John Hammond Jr, the blues singing son of the Columbia legend who had signed Dylan – and many other classic acts – to the label. By 1963, Hammond Jr was playing with a black four-piece electric band and he would later link up with Levon & the Hawks, a Canadian R&B band he had seen backing Ronnie Hawkins, who were now ploughing round the New York bar circuit. The result was the trailblazing 1965 LP *So Many Roads*, which stoked up classics by Muddy Waters, Willie Dixon and Bo Diddley into an R&B fervour and effectively introduced into the folk-rock melting pot the guitarist Robbie Robertson, drummer Levon Helm and organ player Garth Hudson. Dylan saw them rehearsing and was greatly impressed. They were to play a massive role later in Dylan's evolution, reinventing themselves as the Band. Another guitarist recruited by Hammond, Mike Bloomfield, was to play an even more immediate role in Dylan's future.

'I thought Mike would be great alongside Robertson,' Hammond told *Mojo*. 'But when he heard Robbie, suddenly he didn't want to play guitar. Robbie was really intense. He had this Telecaster sustain-note reality that was phenomenal ... a real gunslinger. So Bloomfield decided he'd rather play piano. Dylan was there checking it out and you could tell he was really digging it.'

Announcing him as a guest on stage at one of his concerts in 1980, Dylan claimed he remembered Bloomfield introducing himself and playing him Big Bill Broonzy and Sonny Boy Williamson licks at a club in Chicago around 1960. Bloomfield's own memory was that the encounter occurred much later. Dylan was playing in Chicago and, after deciding the one Dylan album he'd heard was 'lame', he had gone along as a sceptic to put him in his place. In the event he found a 'nervous, crazy guy', who was disarmingly nice and deeply knowledgeable about the blues. Bloomfield reassessed his opinion of Dylan.

Up in Woodstock working on 'Like A Rolling Stone', Dylan decided he needed a strident guitarist to put the boot into the song. He remembered the encounter in Chicago and thought Mike Bloomfield might be the man.

Bloomfield had impeccable credentials. Born in Chicago in 1943, his boyhood idols were Chuck Berry and Presley's original guitarist, Scotty Moore. He got his first guitar at 13 and was in the right place to absorb the vibrant Chicago blues scene first hand, becoming a regular at various South Side blues clubs, learning at the feet of legends such as Muddy Waters, Otis Spann, Howlin' Wolf and Magic Sam. On occasion, he would even leap onstage to join them, plugging in and aping their riffs. Far from being offended, the blues cognoscenti happily indulged him, amused by the blues passion of a young white boy and impressed by the fact that he could actually play. He came from a moneyed background – his father was a restaurant supplier who owned the patent on many commonly used restaurant items, including the classic diner coffee machine and the glass sugar dispenser – but Bloomfield (who also had a little-known talent for fire-eating) had rebelled against his privilege to play the guitar and live in relative squalor, immersing himself totally in the mores and culture of the Chicago blues set.

By the age of 18, Bloomfield was running his own blues club, the Fickle Pickle, and was at the centre of a circle of emergent young white blues players including Paul Butterfield, Elvin Bishop, Charlie Musselwhite and Nick Gravenites. He sought out some of the older, forgotten blues masters, like Sleepy John Estes, Little Brother Montgomery, Yank Rachell and Big Joe Williams, backing them at his club. He became close friends and a regular touring partner with Williams, who wrote a song 'Pick A Pickle' in his honour ('You know Mike Bloomfield will always treat you right … come to the Pickle every Tuesday night …').

In 1964 John Hammond Snr flew to Chicago and signed Bloomfield to CBS, and he recorded a series of tracks with Nick Gravenites and Charlie Musselwhite as the Group. But CBS didn't quite know what to do with a collection of white boys playing Chicago blues and declined to release anything. So they went back to playing clubs in Chicago until Bloomfield got a call from producer Paul Rothchild early in 1965 inviting him to play piano and slide guitar with the Paul Butterfield Blues Band.

Bloomfield was nervous about linking up with the temperamental Butterfield, who had a fearsome reputation on the blues circuit, not only for his stomping harmonica playing and howling voice but as a man with a vicious tongue who didn't take prisoners. Their paths had crossed many times – most regularly at the club Big John's, where they both played – and Bloomfield freely admitted he was scared of Butterfield and had great reservations about joining his blues band. 'I didn't like him … he was just too hard a cat for me,' he told *Rolling Stone* later. 'I think he thought of me as a folkie Jew boy – a white kid hanging around and not playing the shit right, but Paul was *there.…*'

The band was signed to Elektra, which saw their multi-racial line-up and modernistic approach as the perfect vehicle to sell authentic blues to a crossover audience. Bloomfield and Butterfield weren't friends and had little in common apart from music – but they made their partnership work superbly. The domineering Butterfield contained his ego sufficiently to allow Bloomfield to fully express his brilliant guitar playing and share the spotlight.

They were working on their first album when Bloomfield received the call from Dylan to play on some new tracks he was putting together. He arrived at the house in Woodstock armed with a brand new Telecaster to find out what he could do for the guy he had set out to ridicule in Chicago a couple of years earlier. 'I didn't even have a guitar case,' said Bloomfield, 'I just had my Telecaster. Bob picked me up at the bus station and took me to this house where he lived.'

Dylan sat him down and played him 'Like A Rolling Stone'. Uncertain what was expected of him, Bloomfield started to jam along, playing his trademark blues licks, but Dylan stopped him. 'Hey man, I don't want any of that B. B. King stuff, I want you to play something *else*,' he said. Dylan, who was playing the piano ('All the weird keys which he always does, all on the black keys of the piano,' observed Bloomfield), didn't give Mike much indication what he *did* want. 'I figured he wanted blues, string bending, because that's what I do,' Bloomfield told *Hit Parader* in 1968. 'I fell apart … but we messed around with the song and I finally played something he liked. I played the way that he dug and he said it was groovy.'

And so they gathered a few days later at Columbia Studio A, New York on 15 June 1965 to record it. In addition to Dylan, Tom Wilson and Mike Bloomfield, there were Bobby Gregg and Paul Griffin, drummer and pianist respectively from the *Bringing It All Back Home* sessions, Roy Halee as studio engineer and Pete Duryea as assistant engineer. A few others had also been called in by Wilson – guitarist and 'tambourine man'

Bruce Langhorne, Al Kooper hoping to play some guitar and Joe Macho Jr on bass guitar.

The engineers Roy Halee and Pete Duryea were both starting out on their careers. Duryea's time behind the desk was destined to be shortlived as he appears to have swiftly disappeared off the recording radar after the album was completed, but Halee was here to stay.

A Long Islander, Halee (whose father, also called Roy, had been the singing voice of Mighty Mouse in the 1940s Terrytoons cartoons) was a cameraman at CBS Television working on game shows such as *The $64,000 Question*. Laid off when CBS decided to move all their game shows to Hollywood, Halee simply walked out of CBS, crossed the street to the Columbia building and asked if they had any work. They did, and stuck him in a cubicle editing tapes of mainly classical recordings. After 18 months of feeling very claustrophobic, Halee finally succeeded in persuading Columbia to let him try something different, and they gave him the chance to work on his first studio session – engineering 'Like A Rolling Stone'. By Halee's own admission, he was terrified and hadn't a clue what he was doing or what was expected of him, but he clearly made a good fist of it, going on to become a production icon in his own right, indelibly associated with Simon & Garfunkel.

There is much conflicting evidence about who exactly played on those sessions. Researcher Michael Krogsgaard was given permission to search through the Sony archives in New York, examining recording files, original tapes and Columbia's own diaries of sessions, and concluded that the pianist was Frank Owens (rather than Griffin) and that there was another guitarist, Al Gorgoni.

If he was there, Gorgoni – who later played the memorable electric guitar overdubbed so dramatically on Simon & Garfunkel's 'The Sound Of Silence' – doesn't seem to remember it. In his own painstakingly detailed list of sessions, he recalls his work on *Bringing It All Back Home* – as well as a string of No. 1 hit singles for the likes of Connie Francis, the Four Seasons and Ruby & the Romantics – but no mention of 'Like A

Rolling Stone', or any other *Highway 61* cut, so we can probably safely rule him out.

It is unlikely that Owens was there either with plenty of testament – from Al Kooper among others – that after initially playing organ, Paul Griffin was the one who played all the piano parts on 'Rolling Stone'. Griffin was a good friend and a big fan of Owens' playing, and it is likely his name was in the frame when Wilson was suggesting names for the session. Indeed some of the documentation unearthed by Krogsgaard may have listed Owens (and Gorgoni too) in advance of the session, but they were ultimately omitted either due to prior bookings or Wilson's ultimate preference for the other names on the list.

Clinton Heylin also sifted through the Columbia files with a fine-tooth comb for his book detailing Dylan's recording sessions *Behind Closed Doors* (1995) and this seems the most reliable reference, although he does have Russ Savukus playing bass on 'Like A Rolling Stone' when most other evidence points to Joseph Macho Jr. The latter keeps popping up on the various bootlegs that have emerged from the period and Greil Marcus's book *Like A Rolling Stone* is unequivocal that Macho was the man on bass.

It certainly suited Wilson's desire for continuity and a safe pair of hands on the bass to have Joe Macho back on the team, as he had done a sterling job when called in to help out on *Bringing It All Back Home*. Macho was not only a fine technical player, he was flexible and adaptable too, happy to switch from upright string bass to electric bass guitar without asking too many questions. Joe Macho – his real name, though he also used the name Joe Mack on many sessions – was 44 at the time and a seasoned veteran of the New York jazz fraternity, with enough experience not to be fazed by the whims of the artist or the vagaries of the recording industry. If including Bloomfield had been Dylan's call, the other session musicians were called in by Wilson, who mostly thought it best to go with those who had served previously on *Bringing It All Back Home* and knew Dylan's modus operandi.

A seasoned session drummer, Bobby Gregg had worked with Tom Wilson at various times since his jazz days in the 1950s. Admired for his disciplined, metronomic, rhythmic style Gregg had done plenty of studio work and had sat behind the mixing desk to produce a single – 'Marlene' – for an apparently drunk Richard 'Popcorn' Wylie. In 1963 Gregg even released his own album, *Let's Stomp And Wild Weekend*.

Sandy Nelson had been riding high in the charts with 'Let There Be Drums' and with jazz drummer Buddy Rich was getting much attention fronting his own band, the hugely proficient rhythm master Gregg was being lined up as a star in his own right – but it did not happen. His album failed to capture public imagination, plans for a touring band never materialized and Gregg retreated to session work, more than equipped to handle anything Dylan had to throw at him.

Paul Griffin, too, had been round the block enough times not to fret about Dylan's ramshackle approach to the session. Raised by a single mother in Harlem in the 1940s, in a neighbourhood full of pimps and junkies, Griffin was both streetwise and a natural musician. Taken by his mother to Paradise Baptist church, he sat directly behind the church pianist each week, studying the keys and sneaking back into the church after the service to teach himself how to play. Eventually, when the pianist died, he took her place. It stood him in good stead and Griffin went on to have a long career in music. In demand as a session pianist, he played with a variety of R&B, soul and jazz artists including King Curtis (with whom he made 10 albums), Cissy Houston, the Shirelles, Mickey Baker, Jimmy Lewis, Panama Francis and Aretha Franklin.

Dylan liked Griffin. He was polite and good-natured with a placid temperament and an easy-going personality, well equipped to roll with the inevitable punches in a sometimes fraught studio situation. More importantly, he was a superb keyboard player with an intuitive sense of when and how to adapt his style to match Dylan's mood. He had been a serene presence during the flurry of activity on the third day of sessions at Columbia Studios in January which had produced 'Maggie's Farm', 'It's

All Right, Ma (I'm Only Bleeding)', 'Gates Of Eden' and 'It's All Over Now, Baby Blue' – and at which the musicians had finally nailed the problematic 'Mr Tambourine Man'.

Hardly noticed, at first, Al Kooper was also in the studio, desperate for a chance to play. A Brooklyn-born guitarist, Kooper joined his first band at 15 – The Royal Teens, who had a novelty hit in 1958 with 'Short Shorts', a daft song also recorded by the Hollywood Argyles and covered in the UK by Freddie & The Dreamers.

Kooper dropped out of the University of Bridgeport, took on casual work at various studios and linked up in a songwriting partnership with Bob Brass and Irwin Levine, who wrote a No. 1 hit 'This Diamond Ring', for Gary Lewis & The Playboys. By his own admission he was not a great guitarist but he got plenty of work playing on pop records, partly because of his gregarious personality and because people liked having him around, and partly because producers felt he represented a more authentic sound for teen bands.

'People would hire me because their only alternative was to hire these jazz players to play this teenage music. These guys were smoking cigars, emulating what kids would play. So they'd hire me to get that "dumb kid sound". I assume that's why I was hired because I really couldn't play anywhere near as well as those other guys.'

Most of the records he played on were no-hopers, destined never to be heard again once they left the studio, but the experience served Kooper well. 'It was very educational,' he says. 'I learned how to read and write music for the studio. I made friends with the players. They were all nice to me with some exceptions. I didn't claim to be up to their musicianship but it was a great university. The difference between the first time and the fifth time I was on a session was immense. The first time they should have thrown me out, but I was lucky.'

He was 21 and living in Greenwich Village when he met Tom Wilson, who offered to show him the ropes of studio production and engineering. Wilson invited him along to Columbia Studios on 15 June to absorb the

Dylan session merely as an observer, to further this education. But Kooper, an irrepressible, livewire character, had brought his guitar and was itching to get involved – though he put his guitar away the second he heard how good Mike Bloomfield was.

They finally got around to attempting some music at around 2.30 pm, initially in desultory fashion, with Dylan vague about what he wanted to do. There was no masterplan, no time schedule, nothing pre-arranged. A light-hearted Dylan just started playing riffs and the others played along as best they could, when they thought it appropriate. Nobody had a clue where it was leading, but Dylan seemed to be enjoying himself.

Eventually Bob worked himself up into a fierce R&B groove that transmuted into a rough song of sorts and was dutifully recorded by Wilson and noted in the records as 'Phantom Engineer Cloudy'. There were 10 takes, each getting faster and more furious with Dylan belting out seemingly random extracts from vaguely remembered old blues songs as they played. Nobody considered it a serious effort and having heard some of the new material in Woodstock a few days earlier, Bloomfield was in no doubt this was merely a warm-up for the main event. It was, although the frantic riffs of 'Phantom Engineer Cloudy' did provide the bones of a track that was later re-worked as 'It Takes A Lot To Laugh, It Takes A Train To Cry'.

As the afternoon wore on, Dylan changed tack and started playing another unidentifiable bluesy number, again appearing to make up words as he went along. 'Of course, you're gonna think this song is a riff / I know you're gonna think this song is a cliff / Unless you've been inside a tunnel / And fell down 69, 70 feet over a barbed-wire fence – alright!' he sang gleefully. The musicians were more relaxed now and the track really began to swing – Mike Bloomfield started to dig into his considerable box of tricks while Paul Griffin pounded away on the organ. It was fast and furious and great fun for all involved, not least Dylan himself, spilling out his makeshift nonsense lyrics: 'Well this woman I've got, she's filling me with her drive / Yes this woman I've got she's thrilling me with her hive /

She's calling me Stan / Or else she calls me Mister Clive …'. The track became known as 'Sitting On A Barbed Wire Fence', and though it was ultimately shelved, it did finally see the light of day on *The Bootleg Series Vol. 1-3*, released in March 1991.

There was a brief return to 'Phantom Engineer Cloudy', three more takes of 'Sitting On A Barbed Wire Fence' and then, with the assembled personnel relaxed, happy and fired up, Dylan decided they'd have a go at 'Like A Rolling Stone'.

Mike Bloomfield, who knew what was coming, recognized the other two tracks they'd been working on were merely the entrée for the main course. Dylan played it through and Bloomfield dabbled along with him, just as he'd done at the cabin in Woodstock a few days earlier. Dylan said nothing to the other musicians and it was left to Bloomfield to talk them through the arrangement required.

The initial play-throughs of 'Like A Rolling Stone' were relatively genteel; Dylan sat at the piano playing it almost in waltz time, completely at odds with its vicious lyrics, but as he got into his stride the tempo rose and the playing became more intense. They worked it into a blues and there were five takes that afternoon, but by 6.30 pm they decided to call a halt and reconvene the next day.

Back at Columbia Studios the next afternoon, things began to get more serious as the musicians launched into 'Like A Rolling Stone' again. More familiar with it the second time around, they approached it with greater energy and intent and the session gathered momentum as the sound began to take shape.

Al Kooper watched it all in excitement and wonder as Dylan and the other musicians blasted out their early assaults on 'Phantom Engineer'/'It Takes A Lot To Laugh' and 'Sitting On A Barbed Wire Fence'. He yearned to join them with his guitar, but he also knew that in this company he was out of his depth. His frustration reached boiling point as he watched the first run-throughs of 'Like A Rolling Stone', but he remained realistic, watching in awe of Mike Bloomfield's licks and acknowledging his own guitar playing wasn't in the same league.

He still gleefully recounts the story of how he bluffed his way on to 'Like A Rolling Stone'. Paul Griffin was playing Hammond organ when Tom Wilson suggested he tried the piano instead to lighten the sound. Sitting in the control room, Kooper tried to persuade Wilson to let him have a go on the organ, saying he had an idea for the part, but the producer would not hear of it, quite reasonably pointing out that he was a guitarist, not an organ player. But when Wilson took a phone call, Kooper saw his chance and wandered over to the organ.

The rest has become part of rock legend. Barely noticing Kooper had commandeered the organ, Wilson returned to signal the musicians to play another take. Wilson briefly glanced at Kooper in surprise, Al looked back at him and laughed and before anybody could do anything about the uninvited guest, the band was away into another take.

'I *had* played organ before,' says Kooper now, 'but just on my own demos. The song was a very long one, and the band was playing so loud I couldn't hear the organ. I put my hands on the keyboard, and not hearing what I was playing but knowing enough about music to know that if I played a C it would fit into an F chord, I waited for the band to make a chord change before I played. It was the first complete take of the day, and when they went to play it back, Dylan said, 'Turn up that organ.' Tom Wilson said, 'That cat's not an organ player.' Dylan said, 'Don't tell me who is an organ player. Just turn up the organ.' That was the take of 'Like a Rolling Stone', and that is how I became an organ player.'

Clearly it worked. Kooper's stilted but striking fills as the first verse gets underway are a key element in the groundbreaking released version of 'Like A Rolling Stone'. He is the first to admit that his work on the song is hardly innovative or brilliant in any way – indeed, it is basic in the extreme – but the rooted rumble Kooper supplied intertwined so profoundly with Bloomfield's guitar and Paul Griffin's piano that it is hard now to imagine the track without it.

Kooper was oblivious that he was playing such a crucial role in a landmark recording. He describes the session as 'general chaos' without anybody calling the shots or dictating the order with all the musicians effectively left to work out their own parts. Dylan himself was so preoccupied with his own performance – his singing, his enunciation, the harmonica he carelessly grabbed at one point late in the action – that he seemed to pay little attention or even interest in what the others were doing.

There were 15 takes of 'Like A Rolling Stone' that day and the whole thing became more charged and dynamic the longer it went on. The song itself gradually intensifies as it unfolds its poison, the band raising the temperature with each verse, the messy sounds of the different instruments fighting for space unconsciously adding to the tensions of Dylan's barked vocals and vituperative lyrics. Everyone involved got caught up with an ugly jungle of words and music that incongruously collided somehow to make perfect sense, bombarding the senses from all directions.

Nobody had ever created anything quite like it before and everybody there that day knew it. They grouped together to hear the fruits of their labour as Wilson pushed the playback button and giggled between themselves. They knew it was special.

Chapter 4

HOW DOES IT FEEL?

'Ain't it hard when you discover that / He really wasn't
where it's at / After he took everything he could steal ...'
Bob Dylan, 'Like A Rolling Stone'

The party went on long into the night. Buoyed up by the successful completion of 'Like A Rolling Stone', Dylan, Al Grossman and Bobby Neuwirth were in the mood to party and went straight from the studio to Grossman's apartment at Gramercy Park to do just that. They had with them an acetate of the track that Tom Wilson had made up for Dylan to listen to and approve before the record was cut to vinyl. It didn't look like much – just a metal plate covered in a layer of acetone – but Dylan clutched it proudly. He knew how precious it was. They cracked open the wine and played it, whooping and giggling with delight. Then they played it again. And again.

They called other friends to come and listen; they would arrive to find Dylan and Neuwirth playing the acetate over and over and dancing with delight at what they heard, getting more and more wasted, laughing at one another's expressions of wonder as the threshing mesh of sound exploded out of the speakers. Paul Rothchild, a friend of Dylan's from the Village who was house producer at Elektra and had already been producing The Butterfield Blues Band album, was one of the first arrivals at the impromptu celebration going on at Grossman's apartment. He was instantly stunned by what he heard.

'They told me they'd already played it 25 times before I got there,' he told writer Bob Spitz. 'Dylan just sat in a chair with a smile plastered on his face and his leg going a mile a minute. He was grooving on the knowledge that he'd made a great record. Then they played it through for me and I was practically blown out of my seat. I couldn't absorb it all and made them play the thing five times straight before I could say anything.'

It was, Rothchild told Spitz, an almost evangelical moment and he had no doubts about the monumental importance of what he was hearing.

'I realized while I was sitting there that one of *us* – one of the so-called Village folk singers – was making music that would compete with all of *them* – The Beatles and The Dave Clark Five – without sacrificing any of the integrity of folk music or the power of rock'n'roll. As a producer, this was an awesome revelation for me. I knew the song was a smash and yet I was consumed with envy because it was the best thing I'd heard any of our crowd do and knew it was going to turn the tables on our nice, comfortable lives.'

Dylan's music publisher Artie Mogull was also there, seemingly unable to comprehend what he was hearing. Dylan's grin got bigger with each play. *This* was the breakthrough he had been seeking. It was another way of approaching his new style of songwriting, but one with discernible roots in the blues, R&B and the dirty rock'n'roll firmament that had brought him to this point. Without The Animals, without The Beatles, without The Byrds, without John Hammond (father or son) he may never have reached this musical landmark, but the escape hatch from folk music had been opened and he was suddenly away in a far distant place that made perfect sense.

Word soon got out that Dylan had recorded something extraordinary and some of the more visionary of the old Greenwich Village crowd felt that, at a stroke, Dylan had made what everybody else was doing sound pointless and outdated. Frank Zappa said the first time he heard 'Like A Rolling Stone' he felt like throwing in the towel, because he knew there was nothing he or anybody else could do to top it.

Dylan, Grossman and everybody else connected with the song just wanted to get this new masterpiece in the shops as quickly as they could.

At over six minutes it should have been far too long to be a single, but having already torn up the rule book of songwriting and reinvented arrangements, recording techniques and musical genres at the same time, length was hardly a major concern.

The musicians had gone into the sessions with an open mind, to start recording a new album. But once the deed was done there was little dispute that 'Rolling Stone' *must* be a single that should be in the shops at the earliest possible opportunity. That, at least, was the thinking of Dylan and Grossman and a lot of other people who heard the edited tape at Columbia in the days immediately after the recording. Not everyone else agreed. The wheels tend to turn slowly in major record corporations and company procedure had to be followed. And with procedure came dissenting voices....

Shaun Considine, co-ordinator of new releases at Columbia, immediately agreed they had a huge hit single on their hands and played it to the A&R and promotion departments, who were equally excited by the thrilling new sounds they were hearing. But before any release could be ratified, it had to go before Columbia's weekly sales meeting. That's when the proposed release hit trouble. The sales and marketing people didn't like it.

'Their objection came on two levels,' said Considine. 'The unstated reason was that they just didn't like raucous rock'n'roll. Sales and marketing had made Columbia a winner by selling mainstream American music – pop, jazz, country, gospel, the best of Broadway and Hollywood. But rock? No way.'

There was historical evidence to support Considine's assessment. The label had turned down Elvis Presley in 1955 and the first American album by The Beatles in 1963 and, given its successful track record, it was deeply suspicious of something as brazen as a righteous protest folk singer suddenly reinventing himself as an embittered rock'n'roller. Old traditions died hard at Columbia, a company that knew what it liked, understood how to sell it and was reluctant to upset the status quo.

These objections, however, were initially put on the back burner as the big guns of sales and marketing recoiled against the idea of single lasting six minutes. Three minutes was the upper limit for singles in 1965 and to release anything longer than that was deemed to be the kiss of death for radio play. Their suggested compromise was to cut the song in half – three minutes on one side of the single and three minutes on the other. Predictably Dylan and Grossman were apoplectic at the very notion.

Dylan had been here before with 'Talkin' John Birch Paranoid Blues', a biting satire on right-wing paranoia about Communism, which he had recorded in 1963 and wanted to include on *The Freewheelin' Bob Dylan*. He caused some outrage when he attempted to include a verse about Hitler in rehearsals for *The Ed Sullivan Show*. 'Now we all agree with Hitler's views / Although he killed six million Jews / It don't matter much that he was a Fascist / At least you can't say he was a Communist / That's to say like if you've got a cold you take a shot of malaria …'

Wholesome American TV wasn't ready to stomach that and nor were the men in suits at Columbia Records, which refused to release it despite Dylan's most indignant protests. In the end he remodelled the song as 'Talking World War III Blues' ('Some time ago a crazy dream came to me / I dreamt I was walking into World War III'), and it was several years before 'Talkin' John Birch Paranoid Blues' ever saw the light of day. Dylan conceded defeat on that occasion but he was not happy and a couple of years of success down the road he was ready to take on Columbia over 'Like A Rolling Stone'.

The waters were further muddied by Columbia's relationship with its parent company CBS. Dylan had once played for the CBS bigwigs at a sales conference and failed to impress, either on stage or, probably

Thinking of the dollars…the formidable Al Grossman.

more importantly, off it. He simply would not play ball, declining to go through the glad-ragging motions of handshakes, fake smiles and small talk regarded as *de rigueur* at such functions. The arguments over 'Like A Rolling Stone' coincided with Columbia moving offices into a new corporate building – later known as Black Rock – on Sixth Avenue, where releases came under much closer scrutiny from its CBS masters. Worse, one of the primary Dylan sceptics from sales and marketing was promoted to a position of major prominence and influence at CBS. Suddenly, Columbia's priority release of 'Like A Rolling Stone' was shuffled sideways with no scheduled release date and no prospect of getting one any time soon.

The Irish-American Shaun Considine – who later became a respected author – remained one of Dylan's most vociferous champions at Columbia. In the process of junking old demos and memorabilia to facilitate the move to the CBS headquarters, he found a studio acetate of 'Like A Rolling Stone', took it home and played it to death. 'The effect,' he explained later in the *New York Times*, 'was the same as it had been the first time I had experienced it. Exhilaration. Heart pounding. Body rolling – followed by neighbours banging on the walls in protest. Then, on Sunday evening, it came to me. I knew exactly where the song could be fully appreciated.'

He took it to Arthur. Arthur was a painfully hot and fashionable new club on East 54th St in Manhattan, co-owned by the likes of Mike Nichols, Stephen Sondheim, Leonard Bernstein … and Shaun Considine. Ironically Dylan had recently been refused entry when he tried to get in looking scruffy and drunk, accompanied by a bunch of noisy, anti-social mates.

Considine gave the acetate to the house DJ and asked if he would play it, without telling him who it was by. When the DJ put it on the effect was electrifying. The whole dance floor was suddenly full as people threw themselves around to the rhythms. It consumed them for the full six minutes and received such a reaction that the DJ – who had collared Considine while it was playing to find out who it was by – simply announced that it was the new Bob Dylan single and played it again.

Among those transfixed by it that night were DJs from two influential

New York radio stations WABC and WMCA. The next morning they both called Columbia to demand copies of 'Like A Rolling Stone'.

Suddenly the song which had been shunted to the back of the queue on the 'unassigned release' list became the subject of urgent meetings as Columbia mobilized its forces to get the record into stores as quickly as possible. Again, the question of the length of the song became an issue and enemies within continued to insist the song would somehow have to be reduced to three minutes to have any chance at all of success.

Goddard Lieberson, the mighty president of Columbia who rarely got his hands dirty over such trifles, was called on to mediate. Lieberson, a remote figure to most at Columbia, had met Dylan once, during his UK tour earlier that year when legend has it he was harangued by Joan Baez about his label's 'exploitation' and 'commercialization' of her then boyfriend's music. If Lieberson bore a grudge he didn't show it. He had, after all, shown enough vision to guide Columbia towards introducing the concept of the long-playing vinyl disc to the record industry after years of painstaking development by a team led by Columbia's Hungarian-born studio engineer Peter Carl Goldmark. Lieberson's decree on the matter was unequivocal. Artistic quality and integrity was paramount when applying rules and values. The command was made – 'Like A Rolling Stone' should be released as nature and Dylan intended.

Columbia went into overdrive to turn around the single in double-quicktime to capitalize on the word-of-mouth anticipation already building at a frantic pace. Promotional copies were pressed on red vinyl and shipped out to DJs on 15 July, just a month after it was recorded. Incredibly, sales and marketing still put the spoke in: it arrived on the DJs' turntables chopped in half: after three minutes, the song simply faded out and you had to flip the disc over to hear the rest.

In the end, DJ power won the day. Radio stations simply played one side, then the other immediately afterwards. Some DJs took the initiative of splicing the two sides together on tape, then playing the whole thing as Dylan had recorded it. Those who did not think the world was ready for a six-minute single had egg all over their faces and copies were rapidly pressed up that had the full version on one side, backed with 'Gates Of Eden' from *Bringing It All Back Home* on the other.

The response was the same as Dylan and the others had when they got so excited listening to the playbacks in the studio four weeks earlier; when they played it over and over again and danced through the night at Al Grossman's apartment; when they first played it to the Columbia A&R department. The same reaction they saw at Arthur. Everyone went mad for it.

Officially released on 20 July, it entered the *Billboard* chart the following week, although it proved to be a slow burner and took three weeks to reach the Top 10. Columbia's sales and marketing team had been partly right in their gloomy assessment that a song this long and this brutal would struggle for airplay, but those DJs who did go with it got a huge response. Due to public clamour to hear it, radio gradually and very reluctantly fell into line and started giving the six-minute beast mainstream airtime. The monster gathered its own momentum and remorselessly trundled over pop convention to take its place in music industry history.

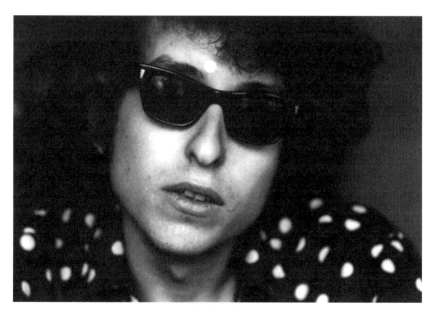

Once upon a time you dressed so fine…'Rolling Stone'-era Bobby.

On 11 September, more than seven weeks after its official release, it peaked at No. 2, kept off the top spot by The Beatles' 'Help!', the title track of their new movie. It caused waves through Europe, too, reaching No. 4 in the UK, where The Rolling Stones had just taken up residency at No. 1 with 'Satisfaction'. It remains Dylan's biggest hit single.

With one extraordinary six-minute rant, Bob Dylan had blown away all notions of himself as a folk or protest singer – together with all conventions of what constituted the entire pop/rock industry. He had redefined the art of songwriting and brutally dismantled all the standard edicts of structure, lyricism, commerciality and marketability. Even The Beatles, the dominant commercial world force of the time, had largely adhered to the familiar pattern of simple chords, boy-meets-girl lyrics and short, sharp songs that seldom broke the three-minute ceiling.

Dylan had constructed a howling gale of sound that was almost demonic in its intensity while he waged a complex, raging verbal assault on a person, or persons, unknown. It sounded angry, ugly and bitter and, nothing like it had ever been done before in the pop music sphere, at least not anything with credibility or which had been taken seriously by anybody who counted. But here was 'Like A Rolling Stone' in all its pent-up, scary rage being taken *very* seriously indeed by the people who mattered most – the buying public.

A sense of shock ran through the industry as it realized the significance of what Dylan had done – and more importantly the public's positive reaction to it. Nothing could ever be quite the same again. John Lennon and Paul McCartney listened in awe to it together at Lennon's mansion in Weybridge, Surrey, and a teenage Bruce Springsteen was inspired to such a degree that he no longer had any doubts about what *he* wanted to do with the rest of his life.

Dylan scarcely had time to bask in the glory. There was the rest of the new album to be made, not to mention a significant live appearance. Four days after 'Like A Rolling Stone' hit the stores, the 1965 Newport Folk Festival opened....

Chapter 5

FORGET THE DEAD YOU'VE LEFT, THEY WILL NOT FOLLOW YOU

'Praise be to Nero's Neptune / The Titanic sails at dawn /
And everybody's shouting / "Which Side Are You On?"'
Bob Dylan, 'Desolation Row'

Newport Folk Festival represented an almost sacrosanct symbol of the ideals of folk music. The Rhode Island town provided an atmospheric, colonial setting for the annual gathering of the clans, with its surrounding beaches and harbour and a strong sense of history. This was the flagship event of the folk movement – at least, it was for those primarily involved in crafting Newport's cherished spirit of purity and independence: the likes of Pete Seeger, Theodore Bikel, Oscar Brand and George Wein (with a little help from his less idealistic-minded partner Al Grossman).

The Newport Folk Festival had been founded in 1959, a time when there was some justification for considering folk song to be a cultural force that could change the world. Johnny Horton had a No. 1 hit with Jimmy Driftwood's 1941 song 'Battle Of New Orleans', covered in Britain by Lonnie Donegan, whose pioneering skiffle performances of American folk songs helped trigger the British folk revival.

The folk singers were keenly aware they could have a role to play in shaping opinion in a world where the political climate was shifting fast.

Charles De Gaulle took power in France in November 1958 after a landslide defeat of his Communist opponent; Fidel Castro overthrew the dictator Batista to take power in Cuba; the Dalai Lama fled to India to escape Chinese oppression in Tibet; the death occurred of John Foster Dulles, the US Secretary of State primarily responsible for waging the Cold War against Communism; racism raged in the southern states of the US while 50,000 blacks rioted in South Africa; and US Vice President Richard Nixon, in Russia for the American National Exhibition, had an impromptu 'kitchen debate' with Nikita Krushchev as American paranoia about 'reds under the bed' continued to pervade all aspects of society.

The American folk scene was also buoyed by the return, in 1958, after nine years in England, of one of its foremost folklorists, Alan Lomax, described by Pete Seeger as 'more responsible than any other single individual for the whole revival of interest in American folk music.' In charge of the Archive of American Folk Songs in the Library of Congress in the late 1930s, Lomax also undertook a series of influential field trips collecting folk songs in America and, indeed, the rest of the world. 'He left the USA as an *enfant terrible* and he returns a legend,' said Seeger.

These were some of the world events colouring the background to the first Newport Folk Festival in 1959. Jazz impresario George Wein had launched the successful Newport Jazz Festival in 1954 with huge success, presenting many of the greats, including Miles Davis, Louis Armstrong, Count Basie and Duke Ellington. The film *Jazz On A Summer's Day* had been shot at the 1958 festival, by which time Wein was exploring ways of extending the range of the festival, to incorporate special blues and gospel shows. Aware of the growing popularity of folk music after meeting Odetta and Joan Baez, he investigated the possibility of including a folk afternoon at the 1959 jazz festival, with Odetta, Pete Seeger and The Weavers earmarked to perform.

Yet the more Wein looked into it, the more he realized that a single afternoon of folk music at Newport was barely sufficient to scratch the surface of what was emerging in the genre's fast-moving community.

Eventually he decided that folk music merited its own festival. He recruited Odetta's manager, Al Grossman, as his partner to produce the new festival, which was rapidly put together in six months and opened by Pete Seeger singing 'Bells Of Rhymney'. Others who played at the new festival included Odetta, Leon Bibb, Sonny Terry & Brownie McGhee, John Jacob Niles, Frank Hamilton, New Lost City Ramblers, Earl Scruggs, The Kingston Trio and Bob Gibson. Yet the hit of the festival turned out to be an 18-year-old Joan Baez, in an unscheduled guest slot after being invited by Bob Gibson to join him on stage.

That year there were 28 performers, it poured with rain and the organizers lost a significant amount of money. But it was still decreed a success and Vanguard released three live albums from the event.

Wein was delighted with the new addition to his festival roster. 'The folk world was not as defined as the jazz world,' he concluded. 'There was not much of a machinery in place to handle the business of folk music. There was no sense that the critics were out there sharpening their claws and waiting to pounce. There was less backbiting, complaining and carrying on. The performers believed not only in their music, but in a message: the message of their songs as well as the message of simply being there, in Newport, together.'

The following year Wein and Grossman extended and broadened the folk festival to embrace ever wider elements of the folk community, with performers from Africa, Scotland, Spain and Israel, as well as the States. Pete Seeger, the acknowledged father of the movement, welcomed the all-embracing ideals of the event:

'Newport Festival has tried to put on one stage as many different varieties of what could be called folk music as possible,' wrote Seeger in *The Incompleat Folksinger*. 'It's not easy; in our rainbow-patterned country there are many kinds of folks. What is a good song in one idiom may be bad in another.'

The festival, he said, was all about integrity. 'The audience respects the basic integrity of each performer. No singer is singing a song because it happens to be on the Top 40. Each is making the kind of music he or she thinks is the best in the world, even though only a small corner of the world may agree. Also, all the music shares certain basic qualities. Even the most age-old and anonymous songs once rose out of the lives of hardworking people and even the newest songs drew upon traditions handed down by generations of unknown musicians.

'Singers come to Newport not for riches, because no performer at Newport, but nobody, gets paid more than a small standard fee, slightly above the Musicians Union minimum, plus their travelling expenses and hotel.'

The festival attracted a mainly young audience – primarily students – that dragged their tents to the beach after each evening's formal entertainment had finished, where they lit bonfires and sat together swapping songs long into the night.

'This scene,' said Wein, 'reflected the true spirit of the folk revival and stood at the very heart of the festival.'

In 1960, however, trouble struck the Newport Jazz Festival when fighting drunks wrecked the event, scared off the audience and virtually bankrupted Wein and Grossman, who dissolved their partnership. While Grossman chased big bucks with Peter, Paul & Mary, the folk community became increasingly alarmed by the commercial implications and there were no folk festivals in Newport in 1961 or 1962.

The hardcore folkies, however, were keen to revive it. Pete Seeger approached Wein and proposed a non-profit-making, musician-run Newport Folk Foundation to ensure the ideals and integrity of the folk movement were upheld. Seeger himself had foregone his fee for the 1960 festival with the proviso that it be used to bring the French-Canadian fiddler Jean Carignan to play. One of Seeger's conditions for the revised festival was that every performer, irrespective of fame or box-office power, would receive $50 plus expenses to play there. Any profits accrued from the festival were to be ploughed back into the movement through folk library endowments, fieldwork, research and other musical endeavours.

In the end, a board was established involving Seeger and his Japanese wife, Toshi, Theodore Bikel, Bill Clifton, Clarence Cooper, Erik Darling, Jean Ritchie and Peter Yarrow of Peter, Paul & Mary. Other board members inducted on to the committee included Oscar Brand, Judy Collins, Ralph Rinzler, Alan Lomax, Ronnie Gilbert and Mike Seeger, all charged with preserving the festival's integrity and, by implication, the unassailable ideology of folk music per se. George Wein was producer.

The avowed aim of the Folk Foundation was a new Newport festival, presenting 'folk music in a situation free of the usual economic necessities and [to] help preserve the traditions on which the current revival is based'. The unimpeachable principles painstakingly established as the 1963 Newport Folk Festival was put in place had a large bearing on the subsequent events when Bob Dylan came to perform.

That 1963 festival – held at Freebody Park, a former baseball stadium built in 1897 – was a rallying call for folk singers to rise up, embrace the civil rights movement and identify itself as a political force. A month before the festival, Peter, Paul & Mary had crashed

Peter, Paul & Mary, Joan Baez, Pete Seeger, Theodore Bikel, The Freedom Singers and Dylan at the grand finale of Newport, 1963.

into the charts with their version of 'Blowin' In The Wind' and the group was the big crowd-puller, the star attraction of the weekend. George Wein, naturally, recognized their popularity and planned to use them as one of the climaxes of the festival, earmarking them to close the show on the Friday night. Al Grossman, though, had other ideas. As manager of both Peter, Paul & Mary and Bob Dylan, he called the shots and insisted Peter, Paul & Mary should be the last act on before the interval and that Dylan – still not widely known by the casual festival-goer – should be the night's closing act.

Dylan had made a low-key Newport debut earlier that day with Joan Baez in front of a small crowd at a discussion and song session; Pete Seeger and Theodore Bikel were also on the stage. When he reappeared on the main stage to close the concert that night, the atmosphere was intense and the audience attentive as Dylan delivered his bombs, including 'With God On Our Side', 'Bob Dylan's Dream', 'Talkin' John Birch Paranoid Blues', 'A Hard Rain's A-Gonna Fall'. To the background of the civil-rights struggles, an uprising of social concern throughout the country and a spirit of youthful rebellion and self-awareness, Dylan's lyricism cut through the night with razor sharpness.

Newport 1963 was to prove a key catalyst of the growing civil-rights uprising as 600 members of the festival audience marched through Newport behind Baez and members of the Student Nonviolent Coordinating Committee, a movement that had spawned its own vocal group, The Freedom Singers, led by Cordell Reagon and Bernice Johnson (who later founded Sweet Honey In The Rock). The song they marched through Newport singing was 'Blowin' In The Wind'.

When Dylan closed his set that year, Peter, Paul & Mary came on to lift the roof with 'Blowin' In The Wind'. They were then joined by Baez, Seeger, Bikel and the Freedom Singers for an emotive encore of 'We Shall Overcome', a song that Seeger had already taken on protest marches as a beacon of protest and hope. At the centre of it all that night in Newport, the legend of the sallow-faced young Bob Dylan as the torch-bearer of that symbol of rebellion was cemented.

By 1964, Newport had assumed an almost sacred significance in the minds of the folk-music revivalists, aligning it closely with the political ideals and spirit of rebellion inspiring America's new left. Now that the festival was firmly established as a non-profit enterprise, the Newport Folk Foundation stringently protected its integrity and went out of its way to donate funds to various projects, from Guy Carawan's work reviving interest in the folk styles of the Georgia Sea Islands to Ralph Rinzler's field-research expedition through eight American states. Rinzler subsequently returned with a string of artists who played the opening night of the 1964 festival, including Mississippi Fred McDowell, Frank Proffitt, Cajun musicians from Louisiana and Sacred Harp singers from Alabama.

Record crowds of 64,000 swarmed to Newport in 1964, where the undisputed stars of the event – Peter, Paul & Mary, Judy Collins, Joan Baez and, by now, Bob Dylan – appeared alongside the unknowns, and were paid exactly the same. Blues legend Muddy Waters shared a guitar workshop

The answer my friend… Peter, Paul & Mary at Newport, 1963.

with Elizabeth Cotten, the black maid from North Carolina employed as a home help by Pete Seeger's musicologist father Charles and stepmother Ruth Crawford Seeger. One day, the Seegers heard her playing guitar and softly singing 'Freight Train', a song she had written when she was 12. The family decided this was something the world deserved to hear and persuaded her to perform on stage. Johnny Cash was there too, sharing a stage with old-time fiddler Clayton 'Pappy' McMichen, and the Delta blues was represented by legends Skip James and Son House, rescued from obscurity to share a bill with one of Dylan's muses, Dave Van Ronk, and Jose Feliciano.

Despite the huge success of the 1964 event, the festival came under great threat the following year as local residents reacted angrily to the chaos caused by the fans who descended on the town, blocking streets and sleeping on the beaches, in cars, gardens, shop doorways, anywhere they could find. The council voted unanimously to ban both the folk and jazz festivals from Freebody Park.

The epochal events of 1965 would never have had the opportunity to take place if the Newport community had their way, and, once again, the festival was only rescued by the resilience and commitment of the committee, who were determined to keep it alive, come what may. After intense politicking they finally got the council to consent to the 1965 festival being held a few miles out of town on the Cornell Highway, at what became known as Festival Field. Once used for drying fishing nets, it was larger than Freebody Park and lent itself to a wider array of events. Mini-stages were set up on the perimeter of the grounds to host workshops before the evening concerts.

By now, folk music was big news. The Byrds and others had alerted the mainstream and fans flocked to Newport. To those for whom Newport represented a precious symbol of integrity, idealism, principle and unity – essentially, most of those involved in running it – the chart attention it was now enjoying was considered so irrelevant that it barely caused a ripple in their world. The festival organizers had tunnel vision in the belief that folk music, *their* music, was not connected to the commercial world. They had a conviction, an unerring belief in the music as a political tool with a social importance that rode high above the normal tenets of the music industry; they could only assume that Bob Dylan still shared that belief.

Prior to the main event on Sunday night, Dylan made a brief solo acoustic appearance at a songwriting workshop on the Saturday afternoon, which gave a clue to the circus building around him that weekend. It was intended as a low-key fringe event, akin to numerous other low-profile fringe sessions going on around the festival. But as soon as Dylan appeared, wearing a bizarre polka-dot shirt with fluffy sleeves, and started singing 'All I Really Want To Do', there was a surge to see him. The crowd was so big it threatened to spill all over the small stage and there was so much noise when Dylan appeared the surrounding events were disrupted. Those at the back trying to see Dylan loudly complained that the music being played on other stages meant they couldn't hear him. The co-operative principles of the festival were under threat from the cult of the personality; Dylan was ushered away after just about getting through his allotted 30 minutes.

Al Grossman, having dumped his short haircut and conservative suit and tie, now resembled 'a freaked-out Benjamin Franklin', in Newport promoter George Wein's words. 'He looked less like a member of the folk community and more like a Greenwich Village con man – which, some might argue, he was,' said Wein. Already regarded with grave suspicion in this environment, Grossman was accused of opportunistically perpetuating the hype around Dylan. There were mutterings, too, among members of the festival committee that Grossman was turning the event into a drug orgy, as the pungent smell of marijuana filled the Newport air.

Simmering resentment towards Grossman exploded in unexpected fashion. Partly due to the blessing of Newport's resident blues expert, Sam Charters, partly due to Peter Yarrow's enthusiasm and partly due to the muscle of their new masters at Elektra Records who'd released the well-received *Born In Chicago* album featuring them, The Paul Butterfield Blues Band were due to appear at the festival. There was much interest in the band's brilliant guitarist Mike Bloomfield and they were booked to play at a Friday afternoon blues workshop alongside the likes of Rev. Gary Davis, Willie Dixon, Memphis Slim, Lightnin' Hopkins and Son House. 'It seemed harmless enough to present them as an example of one of the many tributaries which flowed from the wellspring of the blues,' said Wein.

Instead of the usual couple of hundred enthusiasts who gathered at these fringe events, the Butterfield factor attracted around five thousand noisy fans. A few eyebrows were raised when the Butterfield band thrashed out their own raucous interpretation of Chicago blues – not least from the workshop's compere, the revered Alan Lomax, who introduced them with acidic disregard. 'We've got these guys and they need all this fancy hardware to play the blues. Today you've heard some of the greatest blues players in the world playing their simple music on simple instruments. Let's find out if these guys can play at all.'

In his autobiography, *Myself Among Others*, George Wein contends that this relatively low-key set itself almost caused a riot as an outraged Albert Grossman, in the process of taking over the management of the Butterfield band, berated Lomax for his sour introduction. Suddenly they were having a full-scale fight. 'Grossman snapped at him, Lomax snapped back,' said Wein. 'The next thing we knew, the folk world's most venerable fieldworker and its most powerful businessman were physically brawling. Lomax and Grossman: two middle-aged, un-athletic men literally rolling in the dust. They had to be separated by onlookers. It was quite a scene.'

Butterfield drummer Sam Lay eventually pulled the two grey-haired combatants apart but news of the Lomax-Grossman brawl spread around the festival like wildfire. Right there in that cameo was a microcosm of the furore that was to explode later when Dylan stepped on the concert stage. Lomax was the protector of the old, intently aware of the music's role as a social statement and determined it should remain that way. Immensely proud of his fieldwork in the southern states, where he had discovered many great musicians and singers, Lomax took the view that white men shouldn't play the blues.

Grossman was the face of a ruthless, changing world, keen to spread the music as fast, as far and as profitably as it would go, with no care for the delicacies of the folk tradition or the sanctity of Newport. To Lomax and most of the others on the Newport committee, Grossman was the anti-Christ. That night an outraged Lomax called a meeting of the festival board demanding Grossman should be banned on the grounds that he was wilfully destroying the festival's ideals, and was introducing drugs into the equation to boot.

The board, minus an absent Peter Yarrow, initially voted in favour of a ban, but George Wein pointed out that the likely consequence was a retaliatory walk-out by Grossman's charges: Bob Dylan, Buffy Sainte-Marie, Jim Kweskin, The Paul Butterfield Blues Band and Peter, Paul & Mary. Considering these artists also happened to be the festival's biggest attractions, Wein didn't think it was a smart idea to cancel the very artists who had attracted most of the audience to Newport in the first place. Reluctantly, the committee reinstated Grossman.

There was tension everywhere as the idealism of the event so fiercely guarded by Seeger and Lomax came under intense pressure from the march towards commercialism that had resulted from the music's own success. The festival may have been non-profit making, but folk music had infiltrated the mainstream and there were profits to be made from the music being played there. Divisions arose, even among those who had been at the heart of events. New takes on folk music were emerging and the old guard could not control it.

While Peter, Paul & Mary took out a full page ad in the programme thanking Pete Seeger for all he had done for folk music, Robert Shelton – whose enlightened *New York Times* review in 1961 had done much to trigger initial interest in Dylan – wrote a contentious piece in the same programme, urging the folk world to open its eyes to the developing music around them.

Elsewhere, the traditionalists and the reformers were lining up against one another. The core collegiate audience was encouraged by Lomax and Seeger, the fathers of the folk revival, to adhere to the principles that it held so dear; to use music as a positive force that could change the world for the better. Populism, chart records, mainstream radio, music for profit: these were the enemies who should be fought at all times. But with the music breaking its borders at such a spectacular rate, this hard-line, intellectual stance was getting more difficult to maintain and some important voices were beginning to question it.

'The middle-class collegiate audience of folk music is only part of the music scene,' wrote Shelton. 'The tastes, interests and social attitudes of the high school student or drop-out, the working class kid, must also be appreciated.'

Despite Peter, Paul & Mary's praise of Pete Seeger, group member Peter Yarrow fought the Newport formula. He wanted a Sunday afternoon showcase of new artists from the cities and threatened to pull out of the festival completely if he didn't get his way. The committee let him have his concert.

The fight between Al Grossman and Alan Lomax was the physical manifestation of a much graver divide suddenly afflicting the folk music dream. 'We didn't realize it at the time but the message of the backstage spectacle was larger than the incident itself,' said George Wein. 'Lomax symbolized the hallowed traditions of folklore; Grossman was the power broker whose very existence threatened to corrupt those traditions. For the first time the tension that had lurked beneath the placid surface of the folk revival erupted in plain sight. The conflict was personified there in the flesh.'

Little of this undercurrent of tension would have been evident to the audience that gathered at Newport in solidarity with the Seeger/Lomax vision of a unified counter-culture. Among the guests they'd tempted to Newport that year were a group of prison inmates who had been granted temporary parole so they could sing their work songs at the festival. Spokes Mashiyane journeyed to the festival under his own steam from South Africa and became an instant hero with his penny whistle *kwela* music – jazz-style street tunes. Already a hero of the anti-apartheid movement, Mashiyane established his own legend throughout the weekend, perfectly fulfilling the Seeger/Lomax ideals of Newport as a symbol of the fight against oppression.

Higher profile sets included Joan Baez, singing with Donovan, and her younger sister, Mimi, with her husband, Richard Fariña. Among the blues icons and the likes of Irish travelling singer Margaret Barry, bluegrass innovator Bill Monroe, English folklorist and singer Bert Lloyd, and up-and-coming Canadians Ian & Sylvia and Gordon Lightfoot, they reflected an enlightened cross-cultural and all-encompassing view of the folk-music world. Seeger and Lomax were making a statement of international and cultural unity that could scarcely be overlooked.

What could go wrong? Who could possibly upset such a proud and united expression of unity? Not Bob Dylan, surely? Nobody anticipated the sort of set Dylan was preparing for his bill-topping Sunday night concert. Dylan himself doesn't appear to have given it too much thought in advance. He turned up at Newport on his own, apparently prepared to play a solo acoustic set with no thought of going on stage with a band, electric or otherwise.

Yet, still basking in the glow of recording 'Like A Rolling Stone' and excited by the possibilities opened up by the track, the prospect of going out alone to do his acoustic set with the old 'spokesman for a generation' aura weighing him down cannot have seemed remotely enticing. 'Maggie's Farm' was already a hit and 'Like A Rolling Stone' had just hit the stores, but here he was stepping back into an old world he'd already – mentally at least – left behind long ago.

Dylan had given little clue of what was in his head when he arrived. The way he has told it since – notably in the *No Direction Home* documentary – it was the last thing on his mind to offend the likes of Alan Lomax or Pete Seeger, for whom he retained the profoundest admiration, or betray the principles of the festival. Looking back from a time when spontaneity and instinct are rarely entertained on any kind of stage, it seems incredible now to even countenance the suggestion, but Dylan appears to have been telling the truth when he claimed he only assembled the band for that fateful concert during the course of the weekend. If he *had* planned to perform with a band, he certainly hadn't told any of the other musicians he roped in to help him. Al Kooper was hanging out and when Dylan saw Mike Bloomfield at the festival with The Paul Butterfield Blues Band the notion of playing 'Like A Rolling Stone' on stage during the weekend must have seemed irresistible. After all, he had already done it in the studio, hadn't he?

Dylan was among those entertained by the behind-the-scenes Lomax/Grossman scrap and The Paul Butterfield Blues Band's subsequent set. He marvelled again at the intensity of Mike Bloomfield's guitar playing and the sheer gut power generated by the band. If he was still unsure about the wisdom of trying to put an electric set together at such short notice, watching the Butterfield band kick up dust convinced him that it could and should be done.

Afterwards, Dylan approached Mike Bloomfield and asked him to put together a band to reproduce the 'Like A Rolling Stone' sound later at the festival. Bloomfield didn't have to look far. He asked the Butterfield rhythm section – Sam Lay on drums and Jerome Arnold on bass – along with another friend from Chicago, pianist Barry Goldberg. Al Kooper wasn't scheduled to play at all at Newport (although he did play acoustic guitar with Richard and Mimi Fariña in a workshop spot), but was hanging out minding his own business on the Friday afternoon when he bumped into Grossman, who told him Dylan was looking for him. When he went backstage, Dylan simply said: 'I wanna play electric on Sunday.' By implication rather than by direct request, Kooper ascertained he was expected to join him.

Dylan was holed up in one of the many mansions scattered around Newport not far from the festival site and that is where Lay, Arnold, Goldberg, Bloomfield and Kooper joined him on the Saturday night, in order to thrash out a set to play the next day. 'It was a tough night,' recalls Kooper. 'It was complicated and ugly.' The chemistry between Dylan and the Butterfield band members was all wrong and tempers became frayed as they tried to knock a set into shape with minimal warning. Kooper wasn't the only one thinking it was a bad idea.

In theory, it was a band fully equipped to blow preconceptions apart. Bloomfield had known Barry Goldberg since they were in rival teenage bands in Chicago and the two were full of mutual respect. Goldberg was a highly rated pianist and organ player with a great pedigree – he had once sat in for Otis Spann and played with Muddy Waters. Both he and Bloomfield had played with Howlin' Wolf on Chicago's West Side. 'Nobody shakes a string like Michael Bloomfield,' said Goldberg. 'His intensity was unbelievable.'

Already 30, the burly Lay had been around the block a few times, and prior to linking up with Butterfield, he had spent six years working with Howlin' Wolf. He had developed a distinctive 'double shuffle' style of drumming based on the handclaps he'd heard as a child from the congregation at churches back home in Birmingham, Alabama. It was a style that he created in empathy with the bluesmen he found himself backing. 'The way I play I could guide people like Lightnin' Hopkins and

John Lee Hooker,' he said. 'My style was to fit them. For some unexplained reason, I can hear it coming before they get there. People can follow me.'

In 1959, he had moved to Chicago to back harmonica king Little Walter and became part of the furniture on the music scene there. Butterfield first spotted him playing with Little Smokey Smothers at the Blue Flame club and, in the process of forming his own band, invited Lay to join. Lay's rhythm partner with Wolf, Jerome Arnold was, at 28, a highly experienced bass guitarist who had started out with his brother, the harmonica player Billy Boy Arnold, which led to an invitation to join Otis Rush's band. His reputation as an accomplished, flexible bassist grew during two years with Wolf, before the effusive Lay sang his praises loudly enough to trigger a meeting with Butterfield, resulting in a place in his band.

Lay had never heard of Dylan. As the oldest in the band, he was designated driver of the rented station wagon that took the Butterfield entourage from Chicago to Newport, Everywhere they went, 'Like A Rolling Stone' seemed to be blaring out of a radio somewhere and with each play, Bloomfield's pride at his own contribution grew and grew. It was, decided Lay, the greatest thing he'd ever heard.

After working with various blues legends, neither Lay nor Arnold were fazed by the invitation to back Dylan at Newport and Lay wasn't above gently mocking his idiosyncratic ways. He was particularly amused by Dylan's unruly hair, serenading Dylan with a Muddy Waters song 'I Found A Bird Nest On The Ground' in its honour.

With the exception of Al Kooper, the makeshift line-up was a hardy, experienced unit well used to living by the seat of their pants and, given the instinctive, homespun approach of some of the blues stars they had accompanied, ought to have been capable of turning Dylan's fanciful, eleventh-hour decision to turn his new rock recording direction into an accomplished live reality. They were good ... but they weren't miracle workers. Dylan naively expected that one night together knocking out a few tunes in a mansion in Rhode Island would equip them to put in a show-stopping performance the next day.

Lay and Arnold, in particular, found it hard to fathom what was on Dylan's mind as they attempted to thrash out a meaningful sound. As they grew tired and tetchy trying to bring cohesion and clarity to Dylan's vague instructions, Lay, Arnold, Bloomfield, Goldberg and Kooper could all see they might indeed stop the show, but not for the reasons Dylan had in mind.

None of them gave a thought to the crowd's likely reaction on ethical grounds or considered they might be shattering some unwritten law of the festival. These were all passionate advocates of the blues, well used to the cut-and-thrust and charged excitement of Chicago clubs where power, intensity and soul were everything and nobody worried too much about musical finery or the subtlety of lyrics. The scrap between Grossman and Lomax had scarcely endeared the complicated ideologies of the folk world to the Butterfield band members; they knew little and cared even less about the cherished values that they were rampaging all over. They were getting off on their supercharged blues rock and if they were getting up the noses of the stuffy old folkies when they were doing it, so much the better. And Dylan seemed too consumed by his new direction as a born-again rocker to give the matter any thought.

As he had participated at the 'Like A Rolling Stone' sessions, Bloomfield certainly recognized where Dylan's head was and drove the rehearsals with trailblazing zeal, though the logistics of knocking a proper set together in such a limited time weighed heavily. Dylan seemed to think he'd just get up on stage, sing a few songs, the band would join in behind him and all would be well. It's a philosophy that has suited him on many tours since, but the guys in the band knew it was never going to be that simple.

Lay and Arnold knew the blues inside out and kept trying to play twelve-bar. But Dylan was inventing a style that had no precedent and Arnold in particular had trouble mastering the fluidity demanded to make Dylan's vigorous cascade of words work. Dylan relied on his musicians to mould their instruments around him and, away from the safety net of a pure blues root, Lay and Arnold struggled to meet his expectations.

Hanging out at the house at the same time, Odetta and Mary Travers of

Peter, Paul & Mary watched and listened in some horror as the tempers frayed and the rehearsals frequently teetered on the verge of complete meltdown, the musicians striving vainly to weld some sort of unity out of the mess. If Dylan felt frustrated, Mike Bloomfield winced at the prospect of this debacle transferring to a large stage in front of thousands of expectant people the next day. The guitarist could only see it all ending in tears.

In the event, they managed to get a handle on just three songs that night – the singles 'Maggie's Farm' and 'Like A Rolling Stone', plus a ramshackle treatment of 'It Takes A Lot To Laugh, It Takes A Train To Cry', which was still evolving out of the 'Phantom Engineer' track that had emerged from the warm-up jam Dylan and Bloomfield had presided over at the 'Like A Rolling Stone' sessions six weeks earlier.

When they dispersed at dawn, the band members all had grave reservations about the wisdom of going out on stage that night. Kooper was convinced the Butterfield band was the wrong vehicle for such a sea-change move and feared it could irreparably damage Dylan's new style. But Bob had a statement to make and wouldn't be diverted. He had made up his mind to play with an electric band at Newport and play with an electric band he would.

It seems almost inconceivable that Dylan didn't understand how what he was doing would affect the folk community. The baggage of rock had been used at Newport before: Muddy Waters had turned up with amplification and a heavy rhythm section the previous year and the festival had not spontaneously combusted. And while some may have disapproved, The Paul Butterfield Blues Band and Mississippi's Chambers Brothers had already played with electric instruments at Newport in 1965 without causing a riot.

Dylan said he had no idea what to expect of the Newport rock experiment and had no particular aspirations as to where it would lead him, but felt so frustrated and worn by the European tour and so rejuvenated by the 'Like A Rolling Stone' sessions that he was compelled to march through the doors it was opening for him. He was in the charts, he was reaching people who had never heard of him before and, for the first time in ages, he felt artistically inspired and fulfilled. The fall-out on the audience awaiting him now was the last thing on his mind. It really wasn't his problem or concern.

Besides, he thought, it was all music – just music. Who could possibly object to that? What he might have underestimated was the enduring magnitude of his own iconic status within this environment, despite his own best efforts to shake it off. He had never shared the religious zeal with which so many of those at Newport still regarded the folk movement as a political weapon of change. He followed his intuition, he refused to co-operate in the press's games, he made life difficult for anyone attempting to canonize him and at every turn he tried to rid himself of his own legend. With 'Like A Rolling Stone' already unleashed on an unsuspecting world, he may even have thought he'd already managed to escape it. He was wrong.

The first clue the Newport hierarchy had that Dylan intended to use the festival to break out of his folk straitjacket was during the soundcheck at the end of the Sunday afternoon new artists' concert, when he ambled on stage with Kooper, Bloomfield and the others. Scheduled to play in the afternoon, the Butterfield band had to pull their set due to a storm that caused fears of electrocution. After Mimi and Dick Fariña closed the afternoon show, the festival committee – under pressure from Al Grossman – hastily rescheduled Butterfield band's set to open the evening concert.

So the stage had already been set up for the Butterfield band as Dylan, Kooper and the others shuffled around, tried out their instruments and loosely ran through the three numbers they had rehearsed the night before, stopping only to ask for the volume to be turned up. Backstage, the alarm bells started to ring.

Pete Seeger introduced the climactic final concert on Sunday 25 July 1965 by playing a tape of a newborn baby crying and asked the audience what sort of a world they thought the baby would grow up in. All the artists performing that night, said Seeger, would be singing for the world they wanted that baby to grow up in. 'Tonight,' he said, 'let's sing for this child. Let's show her a world of peace.'

Closely involved with the festival since its inception, Seeger held a deep affinity with Newport, regarding it as a vital refuge from what he described as the 'fakelore' infecting the industry. He cherished Newport and believed electric instruments had no place there, glorying in telling the story of a guy trying to plug an electric guitar in at an English folk club and being stopped by an irate club owner. 'If you can't play it yourself, you're not going to play it with my electricity!', he told him firmly.

Apart from Dylan and The Paul Butterfield Blues Band, the bill for that Sunday night's concert consisted of standard Newport fare, covering most of the bases embraced by the folk revival, including Appalachian dulcimer player and singer Jean Ritchie; topical songwriter Len Chandler; 70-year-old Texan blues singer Mance Lipscomb and activist/campaigner Fannie Lou Hamer. Booking Hamer, especially, was seen as a bit of a coup for the festival. The granddaughter of slaves, the youngest of 20 children, Hamer was vice chair of the Mississippi Freedom Democratic Party and arrived at Newport fresh from a high profile civil-rights campaign in Mississippi.

To Seeger, the concert represented the perfect Newport mix of radical thought and solid folk-music values that held little regard for the commercial world. Like Lomax, Seeger had grave reservations about the inclusion of the Butterfield band, but figured that once they had left the stage, the precious soul of Newport would not be threatened.

The downpour that had brought a premature end to the afternoon concert had passed, leaving the early evening air clear as the Butterfield band duly went on stage. Many filtering into the field to be greeted by the disconcertingly raucous thunder of Chicago blues assumed that they were hearing a record over the PA. The starting time had been brought forward to 6.30 pm to accommodate them, and the field was relatively empty as the band started to let rip.

As the field filled up some of the audience pointedly shielded their ears from the barrage and others marched to the sound deck, demanding that the sound should be turned down. But there were no boos or clenched fists, more a sense of irritated confusion for the festival's sudden lunge into an alien loudness and unwelcome aggression. There were sporadic outbreaks of dancing from pockets of blues fans who were getting into the music, but mostly the performance was received in glowering silence and cold applause.

The concert then dutifully reverted to type, followed the concerned tone set by Pete Seeger at the outset. Ronnie Gilbert, Seeger's old colleague from his days in The Weavers, was certainly a safe pair of lungs. In 1947 Gilbert had co-founded The Weavers with Pete Seeger, Lee Hays and Fred Hellerman, and her soaring contralto vocals had been the key ingredient in seducing the American public and making The Weavers the first commercially successful folk group. Their smash hits included 'Tzena Tzena Tzena', 'Kisses Sweeter Than Wine', 'On Top Of Old Smokey' and, most crucially, Leadbelly's 'Goodnight Irene' and Woody Guthrie's 'So Long, It's Been Good To Know You', before Senator Joseph McCarthy started flexing his muscles and The Weavers found themselves blacklisted out of existence.

Staying true to Seeger's call for the night's artists to send a message to the world, Gilbert delivered Dylan's 'Masters Of War' to a standing ovation. There was a terrific reception, too, for another Alan Lomax discovery, Georgia's Moving Star Hall Singers, a vibrant gospel group who had been Newport heroes since 1959.

Immediately preceding Dylan was Cynthia May Carver, better known as Cousin Emmy, an extraordinary banjo picker from Kentucky, who had been discovered by Alan Lomax on one of his field trips and represented the very essence of traditional American folk music. A radio star in West Virginia in the 1930s, she had also appeared in a couple of movies, *Swing In The Saddle* and *The Second Greatest Sex*, and went on to tour with The New Lost City Ramblers.

The 62-year-old Emmy danced, sang, milked the crowd and played flailing eastern Kentucky banjo as if her life depended on it. With her little blonde bob and cheery smile, she even played a tune by slapping her cheeks. She finished with a wild version of 'Turkey In the Straw', a rip-roaring country song that gained currency after being played by minstrels with their faces blacked up in the 1820s. 'Turkey in de straw, turkey in de hay / Roll 'em up an' twist 'em high tuck-a-haw/An' twist 'em up a tune called Turkey in the Straw', sang Emmy and the whole place went wild, stomping and whistling and vainly demanding more. Newport could not have found a more extreme contrast to what Bob Dylan was cooking up if it had tried.

There followed a long delay as the festival prepared for Dylan's entrance. A buzz of anticipation went through Festival Field as the fans awaited the return of their hero. They knew he had left Baez and many of his other old sparring partners behind; they knew his songwriting had become more oblique and more personal of late, and that he was experimenting with folk rock; they had heard the Byrds' chart-topping rocked-up version of 'Mr Tambourine Man' and the electric side of *Bringing It All Back Home*; some may even have heard *Like A Rolling Stone*. They knew he was moving on, but he was Bob Dylan, and this was Newport – he wouldn't let them down.

On stage, checking the amps to make sure everything was switched on, were Joe Boyd, sound manager for the weekend, and Paul Rothchild, who had been recruited to take charge of the mixing desk on the grounds that he was one of the few who had ever twiddled knobs for an electric band before (he later went on to greater fame as The Doors' producer). Satisfied that all was well, they crept off and waited for the fireworks to start.

Eventually, Peter Yarrow appeared. The man around whom Al Grossman had built Peter, Paul & Mary, Yarrow was part of the furniture at Newport and a guy who had many reasons to thank Dylan, whose songs were the most popular part of his group's repertoire. They had won a Grammy in 1963 for 'Blowin' In The Wind', which was only kept off the top of the US charts by Little Stevie Wonder's 'Fingertips Part 2'. There were persistent rumours (always denied) that Peter, Paul & Mary had paid half the $10,000 it had taken Grossman to buy out Dylan's contract from his old manager, Roy Silver, and they had a stake in his future.

Despite the sweetness of his group's sound, Yarrow considered himself a Modernist and was not about to be sceptical about Dylan's new direction. Peter, Paul & Mary had just had a torrid night of their own, flying out of Newport to play a gig for 15,000 fans at Forest Hills Tennis Stadium the night before and then flying straight back to Newport for the rest of the festival. Yarrow was thus testament to the commercial fruits of folk music while avowing total faith with the cherished ideals of Newport.

In an interview with the *Saturday Evening Post* the previous year, he had claimed that Peter, Paul & Mary could 'mobilize the youth of America in a way that nobody else could,' even going so far as to suggest they could have a direct influence on the upcoming election between Lyndon Johnson and Barry Goldwater if they were so minded (they weren't, apparently). A couple of decades later, he offered a more measured view. 'In no way did I think folk music alone was going to do it, but I did think it was more than simply the window dressing or the accompaniment to events that were changing the concept of Americans as to who they were and what they might be on a day-to-day basis.'

Far from being the climactic finale, Dylan's set was scheduled halfway through the evening following a decree from Seeger that the festival would be more egalitarian if it eschewed the well-worn pattern of shows building up to the appearance of the so-called stars at the end of the night. It was not an idea that gained much favour with Dylan, who had originally even been pencilled in to play during the afternoon. Egalitarian or not, the scheduling left Dylan feeling even more sour and alienated by the festival.

Privy to the apprehension backstage and Dylan's own dark mood, and perhaps anticipating the problems looming ahead, Yarrow opted for a low-key introduction which made it clear Bob would not be on stage very long. 'One-two … can I have some volume on this microphone?' said Yarrow, before addressing the audience. 'Cousin Emmy's a gas, right?' The audience, in good humour, laughed and applauded.

'There's someone coming on the programme now …' waffled Yarrow 'As a matter of fact the entire programme tonight was designed to be a whole group of small performances. You know, I will be performing later with the group that I'm a part of, you know … and we're all limited in the time that we can be on stage for a very specific reason. The concept of the programme tonight is to make a programme of many, many different points of view that are together and yet without the huge expanse of the performing of any group. We will be very limited in time and so will each person who comes up. The person who's coming up now …'

A single note of an electric guitar from behind briefly stopped Yarrow, who looked momentarily irritated when it was followed by another couple of random notes as Mike Bloomfield tested his tuning.

Yarrow ploughed on. 'The person who's coming up now is a person who has in a sense …'. The sound of feedback again halted Yarrow. 'This person has changed the face of folk music to the large American public because he has brought to it a point of view of a poet. Ladies and gentlemen, the person that's going to come up now [long, dramatic pause] has a limited amount of time.' Another pause as a chorus of boos went up with shouts of 'Nooooo.'

'His name is Bob … Dylan.'

The audience started cheering, though a few of the cheers stuck in their throats as the full five-piece band came into view. There were gasps of recognition as Dylan came to the front fully armed and defiantly wearing the uniform of rock'n'roll – a loud, garish green polka-dot shirt, black leather jacket, black pants, Ray-Ban shades, pointy boots with Cuban heels and, most sinister of all for those in front of him, a Fender Stratocaster. It was the first time he had played electric guitar on stage since the Golden Chords, his High School band in Minnesota.

The audience strained to take in the scene. With his bushy hair, lean physique, button-down shirt and sports coat, Bloomfield, standing next to Dylan, could have been his brother. Sam Lay and Jerome Arnold were wearing gold shoes for the occasion. Newport had never seen anything quite like it before. And they had certainly never *heard* anything like it.

A few random snatches of conversation were heard between the sounds of instruments being checked while the audience, hushed now, watched intently in rapt fascination. 'Maggie's Farm,' mumbled Dylan, swinging round to turn his back on the audience to check on the rest of the band. 'Ready?' he asked as Bloomfield fiddled with his guitar. Bloomfield nodded.

What happened next has become the stuff of so much legend it is hard to differentiate the myth from reality. Bloomfield struck up the first chords of 'Maggie's Farm' and they were off and running. Well, they were off at least.

As instructed, Paul Rothchild whacked the sound up to – by 1965 standards – deafening levels. The audience started howling as the sound distorted and Dylan's voice was largely lost in the volcanic charge of Bloomfield's guitar while the rhythm section seemed to be playing something else entirely. In a sense they were. Nobody on stage could hear what the others were playing, and the rhythm that cranked into action at the back was out of sync with the melody line going on at the front. They were all out of tune and it was as if everyone on stage was playing something completely different, while the mixing desk had gone completely haywire. They were playing 'Maggie's Farm', but they might as well have been playing 'Dixie'.

Dylan waded on as pandemonium broke out around him. Not everyone was appalled; the way Joe Boyd tells it, the boos of the audience merged with a far greater number of cheers and yelps of excitement, as the unexpected surge of power ripped through them and lifted them to their feet.

Peter Yarrow, too, was thrilled by the jagged fury of the sound, as indecipherable as its components were. 'They didn't have sophisticated monitor systems,' he said. 'People couldn't really hear themselves. It wasn't technologically set to do a well-integrated, precise show. You couldn't hear Bobby's voice properly on stage. There was a lot of leakage of the electric instruments, but "Maggie's Farm" kinda worked 'cos it's so *direct*.'

Maria Muldaur, singing at the festival as a member of the Jim Kweskin Jug Band, also got into 'Maggie's Farm', accusing those booing Dylan of hypocrisy. 'We all loved Muddy Waters, we'd all listened to early

R&B, not to mention Elvis and Chuck Berry,' she told Dylan biographer Bob Spitz. 'The music Bob played that night wasn't any different except that it was folk-type lyrics put to an incredible beat. They just needed something to be pissed off about and Bob provided them with an earful.'

Pete Seeger and the others didn't see it quite like that. Happily bopping away to 'Maggie's Farm' and enjoying the tumultuous reaction it was having in the audience, Joe Boyd suddenly found himself yanked backstage to be confronted by the thunderous faces of Seeger, Lomax and Theodore Bikel telling him to turn the sound down. 'And that's an order from the board!'

With barely a pause and not a word to the audience, the band had launched into 'Like A Rolling Stone', which was no more coherent nor any quieter. Al Kooper, at least, was enjoying himself. 'I thought we did "Like A Rolling Stone" real good,' he said.

The audience were howling louder as Boyd returned to the mixing desk to relay the orders from Lomax, Bikel and Seeger to drop the sound. 'Grossman, Yarrow and Rothchild were sitting behind the board, grinning like cats,' wrote Boyd in his book *White Bicycles*. The three of them were clearly in no mood to obey the orders from above. 'Tell Alan the board is adequately represented at the sound controls and the board member here thinks the sound level is just right,' said Yarrow, who told Boyd he had one more message he would like him to pass on to Alan Lomax and the rest of the fellow board members – he raised his middle finger in their direction as Grossman and Rothchild laughed.

From here on the stories get more convoluted. The most popular – though sadly untrue – myth is that Pete Seeger suddenly produced an axe, with which he attempted to cut the electricity cables. One hysterical account even has an axe-wielding Seeger running amok backstage while an ashen-faced Peter Yarrow tried to reason with him.

'I *was* very upset,' says Seeger, 'but only because the sound was so loud and distorted you couldn't hear the words. I just wanted them to turn the sound levels down so we could hear the song. I just told them to get the distortion out of his voice so people could hear.'

So he didn't try to chop the cables with an axe? 'No. I may have said something like, 'If I had an axe I'd cut the cable myself', but that's all.'

As 'Like A Rolling Stone' blitzed on, Seeger stormed out with tears in his eyes. George Wein went after him and found him sitting alone in a parked car in a field behind the stage with his hands over his ears. 'That noise is terrible,' he said, 'make it stop!' But nobody made it stop and without pausing at the end of 'Like A Rolling Stone', Dylan led the band straight into 'It Takes A Lot To Laugh, It Takes A Train To Cry' – or 'Phantom Engineer' as it was still called then – as the uproar continued both in front and behind the stage. 'It seemed,' said Paul Rothchild at the mixing desk, 'that everybody on my left wanted Dylan to get offstage and everybody on my right wanted him to turn it up. So I turned it up.'

'It Takes A Lot To Laugh …' was probably the most successful of the three songs they played that night: Bloomfield cut loose playing boogie guitar, the more orthodox blues template allowed Lay to feel more at home, and the rhythm at last gelled with the rest of the band. It was still raw, it still enraged as many as it delighted, it still left poor Pete Seeger desolate, but it started to make sense.

And then, suddenly, the song was over. 'Let's go man, let's go,' said Dylan and, as dramatically as it had swept through the park, the rage of noise disappeared and the band was gone. The most infamous stage performance in rock history lasted less than 20 minutes.

The repercussions started immediately. A volley of boos greeted the band's departure. It might have been, as Al Kooper vociferously insisted, frustration by the audience at the brevity of the set. Or it could have been anger at the appalling quality of sound that had rendered so much of the set unlistenable. Or perhaps, as was the popular assumption of the day, it was the sound of outraged purists registering their dismay at the introduction of what Pete Seeger described as 'machines' at an event that prided itself on being a healthy, honourable alternative to the commercial world.

There was no doubt Dylan himself was shaken and upset by the reaction of the crowd. He looked shell-shocked as he came offstage, boos ringing in his ears. He did not know if they were booing him because he had played electric or because he had left the stage so early, but all he could hear was booing. It was not a reaction that he had ever experienced before and his expression showed he did not like it.

'I did this very crazy thing,' he said. 'I didn't know what was going to happen, but they certainly booed, I'll tell you that – you could hear it all over the place.' No, he said, he didn't think the boos reflected reaction to the performance. 'I had no idea why they were booing … I don't think anybody was there having a negative response to those songs, though. Whatever it was about, it wasn't about anything they were hearing.' Even interviewed in the *No Direction Home* documentary four decades later he still seemed nonplussed by the experience, making respectful noises about Seeger, Lomax and the rest.

It could be that Dylan's own emotions may have been chemically fuelled. 'As soon as he came on it was obvious he was stoned,' admitted the Irish folk singer Liam Clancy – an old friend from the Greenwich Village days whose girlfriend Cathy had a fling with Dylan. 'He was bobbing around on the stage, it was very Chaplinesque actually.' Clancy, though, also described it as the night he saw 'the butterfly emerging from the caterpillar'.

Peter Yarrow walked back out on stage to an increased chorus of boos, not knowing quite what to do or say. 'Yes, he will do another tune, I'm sure. We'll call him back. Would you like Bobby to sing another song?' It was a fair question. This was new territory and Yarrow genuinely didn't know if they did or not.

More cheers than boos now seemed to be filling the air. 'Listen, it's the fault of the … er … he was told he could only do a certain period of time,' burbled Yarrow. He looked apprehensively to the side of the stage. 'Bobby can you do another song, please?' He turned back to the audience. 'He's going to get his axe.' Yarrow retreated. He really didn't know if Bobby had gone to get his axe or if Pete Seeger had gone to get *his* axe.

Backstage, frantic negotiations were going on to get Dylan back on stage. He said he couldn't because they had only rehearsed three songs as a band. Peter Yarrow reasoned with him, Bobby Neuwirth cajoled him, George Wein pleaded with him and even Al Grossman tried to persuade him. But, said Bob, the band had only rehearsed three songs. Then *play solo*, they chorused. 'I can't,' said Bob, 'I don't have a guitar.' The most commonly held memory is that it was Johnny Cash who then came up to Dylan, presented him with his Gibson acoustic guitar and told him to get back out on stage. Dylan reluctantly agreed.

A triumphant Yarrow announced that Dylan was returning with an *acoustic* guitar and the crowd went wild. Dylan rc-appeared with the Gibson to huge cheers, shuffled around with the mic for a minute or so, turned to the side and called for a harmonica. Harmonicas appeared from everywhere. Peter Yarrow duly brought one. Dylan put it around his neck and then played – pointedly – 'It's All Over Now, Baby Blue', a choice widely perceived to be a personal message that the set he had just played marked his departure from this scene forever.

'You must leave now, take what you need, you think will last,' sang Dylan poignantly. 'But whatever you wish to keep, you better grab it fast / Yonder stands your orphan with his gun, crying like a fire in the sun / Look out the saints are comin' through / And it's all over now, Baby Blue.' If it was a loving farewell, the fans didn't seem to interpret it that way, cheering as loudly as they had booed earlier.

Those in the crowd who had decided to be enemies of the rock'n'roll Bob saw it as their own personal victory over evil forces. They had forced the horrible electric band offstage after three numbers and now they had got the old Bob back. There were cheers of triumph as the song ended.

There were shouts for 'Mr Tambourine Man' as 'It's All Over Now, Baby Blue' ended and Dylan instantly said 'Okay, I'll do that.' A slight pause as he tuned up, a few mumbles from the audience, and he was away into the track that was still riding high in charts all over the world courtesy of The Byrds and was effectively the catalyst of his move into the big, bad mainstream.

At the end, ecstatic applause was again replaced by boos as Dylan sauntered off at around 9.30 pm, to be replaced again by the hapless Peter Yarrow's attempts to introduce the next act, the black gospel group The Moving Star Singers. Order was restored as a trail of artists who perfectly fitted the Seeger-Lomax profile took the festival sedately to its anti-climactic climax ... Oscar Brand, Len Chandler and Peter, Paul & Mary went through the motions, lamely parading ideals that suddenly looked irrelevant and outmoded. For many of the artists, audience and board members it seemed like the sad death throes of a dinosaur.

The evening ended with an ensemble performance of 'When The Saints Coming Marching In' and then, as the audience quietly filed out of Festival Field, Mel Lyman, a big player on the Boston folk circuit and a member of the Jim Kweskin Jug Band, appeared in front of a microphone at the side of the stage. Over and over he played the melody of 'Rock Of Ages' on harmonica, so slowly and mournfully that it sounded like a ghostly lament to the emptying arena. Indeed, it was a consciously provocative coda to the revolution witnessed earlier; perhaps even an epitaph for the entire folk-music movement. Or maybe it was a personal statement by Lyman, who had told Jim Kweskin earlier that day he was quitting his band (he was later to establish a hippy commune and religious cult at Fort Hill, near Boston and claim, among other things, to be Jesus Christ).

Perhaps surprisingly, Dylan hung around at Newport for the traditional après-festival party, although he remained non-communicative while a sober mood prevailed and various parties assimilated the significance of the night's events. At one point, Maria Muldaur approached him and asked him to dance, but he merely said: 'I would, but my hands are on fire.'

The arguments raged on afterwards. Still deeply hurt, Pete Seeger put the blame squarely on Al Grossman and described Dylan as 'a corpse'. He would resign from the festival committee, cease to write his column for *Sing Out!* magazine and effectively abdicate from his role as the benign father of American folk song. *Sing Out!* editor Paul Nelson wrote a passionate piece defending Dylan's performance at Newport and promptly resigned, while the debate raged in the folk press for a year afterwards. Dylan himself received a volley of mail accusing him of everything from being a 'sell-out' to a 'fascist'.

'There are a lot of occasions when you can look back and say, "Well after that night, things were never the same",' said Joe Boyd. 'But it's very rare that you're in a moment where you know it is at the time. You knew, as it was happening, that paths were parting.'

Paul Rothchild, the man at the mixing desk, was equally certain this was the night that changed everything for Dylan and for contemporary music generally. 'To me, that night at Newport was as clear as crystal. It's the end of one era and the beginning of another. There's no historical precedent. This is a folk festival, *the* folk festival, and you couldn't even say it's blues and the blues has moved to an electric format. This is a young Jewish songwriter with an electric band that sounds like rock'n'roll. There were two very big passions happening here. It was an election. You had to choose which team you were going to support.'

They did hold the Newport Folk Festival again the following year with the board voting to 'eschew show business presentation' – with Phil Ochs, the Lovin' Spoonful, Richie Havens and Jack Elliott on the bill. Al Kooper even made a return visit playing organ again as part of the electric Blues Project, a Greenwich Village-based blues/rock band formed by guitarists Danny Kalb and Steve Katz, who were signed to Elektra and pioneered long impromptu jam sessions on stage. But, re-designed with a large crafts area to reflect its new incarnation as a massive organic workshop of folk life, it was a commercial disaster. Audiences slumped and the event that had made an $80,000 profit in 1965 lost $15,000 a year later.

In 20 minutes at Newport, Rhode Island, on 25 July 1965, Bob Dylan had effectively killed the folk revival. Within four days, he was back in the recording studio.

Chapter 6

LOOKIN' FOR
THE FUSE

---

*'Now I wish I could write you a melody so plain / That could hold
you dear lady from going insane / That could ease you and cool you
and cease the pain / Of your useless and pointless knowledge ...'*
Bob Dylan, 'Tombstone Blues'

Dylan didn't dwell on the events of Newport. He just got the hell out
of Rhode Island and wrote a collection of vicious new songs.

In the studio the previous month to record 'Like A Rolling Stone', Dylan
had virtually no other fresh material. The long, painful process as he
grappled with the rumbling blues 'Phantom Engineer Cloudy' before
turning it into 'It Takes A Lot To Laugh, It Takes A Train To Cry', and tried
to get some sense out of the garbled mesh of 'Sitting On A Barbed Wire
Fence' showed that he was a long way short of having a complete album in
his head, let alone on paper. Given the incredible volume of his output and
the number of concerts he had played in the preceding couple of years, it was
hardly surprising that Dylan's cupboard was bare. Yet, within weeks, he
would miraculously conjure up a new album's worth of new songs. Many of
them just happened to be among the best material he would ever write.

While the aftershock of Newport had the folk community in hot
debate, Dylan was soon out partying again. The exhilaration he had
experienced recording 'Like A Rolling Stone' had not been jolted by
replicating it on stage and he was eager to get back into the studio at the

earliest opportunity. In the days immediately after the festival, he spent almost every waking moment writing on anything that was to hand – lyrics found their way on to scraps of paper, the backs of cigarette packets and menus. The reaction to 'Like A Rolling Stone' had galvanized him once more, triggering a torrent of confused and angry creativity.

One man who wouldn't be there with him, however, was Tom Wilson. The amiable jazz man from Texas had been Dylan's benign studio guide for over two years, leading him from the unbridled social commentaries of 'Masters Of War' and 'Talking World War III Blues' on *Freewheelin'* through the hoops of his rampaging imagination, right through *Bringing It All Back Home* to the Pandora's Box of 'Like A Rolling Stone'. (Contrary to the sleeve notes of *Freewheelin'*, which credit only John Hammond, my research has convinced me that Wilson had taken over the role of producer by the time Dylan came to record 'Masters of War' and 'Talkin' World War III Blues', on his return from his UK in April 1963.) Wilson had been an astute accomplice. He had none of the baggage of a folk background and was only too keen to encourage Dylan in his ambitions to go beyond the beyond. By his own admission a man mystified by the mores of folk music, Wilson at times seemed perplexed to find himself so embroiled in what he saw as the straitjacket of folk, and was keen to get Dylan out of it.

Not that Wilson played any obviously proactive role in the artistic process. To many eyes, all he did was book the studio, check to see if the engineers had set up the microphones correctly, press the right buttons, hold the stopwatch and lie back to wait for Dylan's genius to do the rest. He had a say in the selection process of takes and tracks to be used, and came up with the title for *Another Side Of Bob Dylan*, but his was not a creative role in the manner of a Phil Spector or George Martin. Wilson himself freely conceded his role was more practical than creative, which was how Dylan – never given to fret over technical perfection or production niceties – seemed to like it. It was generally accepted that Wilson had plenty of ideas of his own and was entirely sympathetic to

Dylan's rock ambitions. It was he, after all, who – unsolicited – had spent an afternoon playing with tapes of recordings Dylan had made in 1961 and 1962, including overdubbing a rock backing on to 'House Of The Rising Sun'. In 1966, his similar experiment with Simon & Garfunkel would achieve spectacular results.

'My main difficulty has been pounding mic technique into him,' he said of Dylan in 1964, in an interview with Nat Hentoff. 'He used to get excited and move around a lot and then lean in too far, so that the mic popped. Aside from that my basic problem with him has been to create the kind of setting in which he's relaxed. For instance, if a screen should bother him I'd take it away, even if we lose a little quality in the sound.'

Wilson may have been foisted on Dylan by Columbia after Al Grossman fell out with John Hammond, but the producer recognized Dylan's genius and the need to bend to his whims and instinct, and the two had a perfectly convivial working relationship. He took his own lead from Dylan and certainly did not feel inclined to push him too far, even if the sound engineers were not happy with any of the few takes Dylan was prepared to provide. 'With Dylan you take what you can get,' said Wilson emphatically. 'You don't think in terms of orthodox recording techniques when you're dealing with him. You have to learn to be as free on this side of the glass as he is out there.'

There is little doubt that Wilson helped to ease Dylan on to his electric path, facilitating the electric setting in which he envisioned his songs. Dylan did not have a lot of experience of recording with other musicians and would have found the transition prickly without Wilson's practical help and easygoing nature. He put Dylan's aspirations and peace of mind above all other considerations – a policy that disgruntled and frustrated those who urged more precision, planning and recording takes but suited the impetuously restless young Dylan down to the ground. Wilson was professional, organized and technically sound, but was open-minded enough, too, to accommodate Dylan's bouts of whimsy. And he was perfectly prepared to accept the unexpected.

The results of the 'Like A Rolling Stone' sessions were there for all to see, and nobody was aware of any big falling out with Dylan or even Al Grossman. Yet when the musicians reconvened at Studio A, Columbia Studios, New York, on Thursday 29 July 1965, Tom Wilson was absent.

The reasons largely remain shrouded in mystery. There had been a row between Dylan and Wilson, but it was behind closed doors and neither party ever divulged what it was about. Interviewed by Jann Wenner in 1969, Dylan said he had no recollection of why they'd split, feigning surprise to find Johnston in his place on 29 July. In another interview in 1974 he credited Wilson as one of the most important people he'd ever worked with. Wilson was certainly a man with his own opinions and was not afraid to voice them. He had his own take on the folk-rock beast he had helped to create, so tensions may have arisen between them, with the producer perhaps not even aware he had upset a silently seething Dylan. Perhaps Dylan or Grossman thought that, after playing the role of passive facilitator, Wilson was getting ideas above his station.

The only clue Wilson left was an interview with *Melody Maker* in 1975, when he intimated that Dylan's preference at the time was to get Phil Spector involved, a notion that never got off the starting blocks. Indeed, the mind boggles at what sort of an album *Highway 61 Revisited* might have become had Spector been installed behind the controls.

Others have suggested Wilson's offhand approach to recording meant quality was sacrificed in favour of a fast turnover and his ramshackle production policy did not find favour among many of the musicians with whom he worked. However, this seems an unlikely reason to dump him given Dylan's own aversion to spending long periods seeking perfection in the studio. In fact, given Dylan's well-documented subsequent dislike of long recording sessions, Wilson's eye-on-the-clock approach was probably viewed as a plus. If Dylan liked to record in the moment, Wilson was his perfect foil.

Asked what Wilson contributed to sessions, Bruce Langhorne spoke of him 'hanging out in the control room saying "Oh we got a take – that's really cool."' According to Langhorne, Wilson offered little creatively but was the catalyst for a lot of things that happened in Dylan's recording career. 'A lot of production,' he told writer Richie Unterberger, 'is putting the right people together for the right projects. Then they'd just step out of the way and let the project take over and have its own life. I think that's the kind of producer Tom Wilson was.'

It is more likely that Dylan associated Wilson with the old world from which he wanted a complete break. Wilson held no truck with folk, but he was still indelibly associated with Dylan the protest singer and spokesman for a generation. It wasn't as if Dylan felt indebted to Wilson; he had been a political appointment by Columbia to pacify Al Grossman when Bob's manager was trying to extricate Dylan from his contract on a technicality.

But now Dylan was a very different artist and a much-changed character who, with the drama and raw power of 'Like A Rolling Stone' and Newport still surging through him, felt that he needed a clean break and a fresh face in front of him to ride that wave. It is easy to see that, in the excitement of the moment, he might well have thought of Phil Spector as the producer to ride it with him. Spector had been one of the most successful producers of the early 1960s, with his Wall Of Sound productions turning girl groups The Crystals and The Ronettes into huge stars, while his 1964 signings, The Righteous Brothers, were on their way to a record-breaking eight million airplays with his production of 'You've Lost That Lovin' Feelin''. Of *course* Dylan and Grossman sat up and took notice.

Apart from Spector, various other names were touted to take over the new Dylan album, among them Terry Melcher, the man behind The Byrds' smash version of 'Mr Tambourine Man', and Don Law, Columbia's veteran head of country, who had produced records by the blues legend Robert Johnson.

Equally, though, it surely wouldn't have taken them too long to reject the notion, given Spector's propensity to be the star of the show and forcibly stamp his style on the proceedings. At a time when Dylan was taking such a positive grip on his destiny, it is unthinkable that he would have willingly risked relinquishing it by unleashing the one producer whose trademark was the creation of his own signature sound. A few years later, Spector said he would love to work with Dylan, claiming Bob had never been properly produced because 'nobody has the guts, balls or ambition' to stand up to him. He wanted, he said, to work with Dylan on an *opera*. Sadly, that project never got out of the pipedream stage.

The speed at which things were happening encouraged a complete re-examination of the recording process and Dylan and Grossman may well have seen Wilson as part of the rickety furniture they associated with the old regime. Tensions would certainly have arisen and it wouldn't have been difficult for Wilson – who 'took no shit from no one', according to his friend, Wally Amos – to rub either or both of them up the wrong away. Despite the fact that they had apparently been working together quite amicably since 1963, Dylan and/or Grossman's goodwill towards Wilson might simply have been exhausted. Perhaps they just didn't *like* the guy. Bob Johnston, Wilson's replacement, told Greil Marcus that Al Grossman 'hated' Tom Wilson, though he was at a loss to know why.

On the rare occasion Dylan was cornered on the topic he played ignorant. 'I don't know how it happened,' he once said, in typically offhand fashion. 'One night Wilson was there and the next night Johnston was there.'

Wilson went quietly. He had enough ideas of his own not to worry unduly about the end of his association with Dylan. He, too, had been inspired by 'Like A Rolling Stone' and went back in the studio immediately afterwards to tinker with 'The Sounds Of Silence', an acoustic track he had produced for the then-unknown duo Simon & Garfunkel for the *Wednesday Morning 3A.M.* album.

Written by Paul Simon the previous year as a lament in response to the assassination of John F. Kennedy, the song – or the album on which it appeared – barely created a ripple and Simon and Garfunkel went their separate ways. But Wilson believed in it and, fired up by Dylan's amalgamation of folk and rock, he brought in Al Gorgoni to play an electric guitar part, with Bob Bushnell on electric bass and 'Like A Rolling Stone' drummer Bobby Gregg. Unknown to Paul Simon, by now working his way round the European folk circuit, and to Art Garfunkel, it was released as a single and a few months later started to climb the US charts, reaching No. 1.

Tom Wilson went on to work with The Mothers of Invention and The Velvet Underground, so getting the bullet from Dylan did his career no harm. He got on with his life and never badmouthed Dylan at any point. He died suddenly from a heart attack at his home in LA in September 1978.

Hello darkness my old friend… Simon & Garfunkel after the Tom Wilson treatment in 1968.

The search was on for a new producer, but one man already installed at Columbia was determined to get the gig. Bob Johnston was a longstanding Dylan fan who had watched him playing in the Village and followed the twists and turns of his career, convinced he was a genius. A staff producer at Columbia, he had long coveted the chance of working with him in the studio.

'He was freaky to me … because I still believe that he's the only prophet we've had since Jesus,' Johnston told Richard Younger in an interview for *On The Tracks* magazine. 'I don't think people are gonna realize it for another two or three hundred years when they figure out who really did help stop the Vietnam war, who did change everybody around and why our children aren't hiding under the damn tables now worrying about an atomic war. One day they'll wake up and they'll realize what they had, instead of asking what kind of album he did and is it as good as the last one? That was always bullshit to me.'

When the word had gone round that Wilson was for the chop, Johnston had been in like a shot. Friendly with Wilson, he sought his blessing and then went straight to John Hammond and the other Columbia heavyweights to pitch for the job. Neither Dylan nor Grossman knew the 33-year-old Johnston, but he was an engagingly persuasive, ebullient character who wanted to work with Dylan so badly that he was determined not to let the opportunity slip away.

And he had a lot going for him. His technical efficiency won him a lot of admirers at Columbia and his enthusiasm, knowledge and likable, infectious personality were impossible to deny. More importantly, the artists both warmed to him and respected him. He may have been house producer at Columbia but he was no company man and left nobody in any doubt that his role in the studio was to represent the artist not the record company. Here was a musicians' producer – a guy who had seen it all and done it all on the other side of the control booth long before he ever got involved in production.

A long, tall Texan, born in Hillsboro on 14 May 1932, Donald Robert Johnston came from a family steeped in music. His great-uncle was a concert pianist and his grandmother, Mamie Jo Adams, was a songwriter of some regard. Johnston was later fond of claiming she co-wrote 'When Irish Eyes Are Smiling', although her name doesn't appear in the credits. His mother, Diane Johnston, was also a professional songwriter who, in the 1950s, had some success when a couple of her songs – most notably 'Can't Shake The Sands Of Texas From My Shoes' – were recorded by The Singing Cowboy, Gene Autry.

A member of the US Navy, Johnston claims he was singing in a servicemen's club in Boston one night when Frank Sinatra walked in. He stopped singing, but Sinatra indicated to him that he should continue and applauded enthusiastically at the end. 'I saw him with his entourage and some great-looking women and thought: "That's a great way to make a living."'

After leaving the navy, he returned to Texas and started writing songs with his mother. In 1956 and 1957, Mac Curtis, a young rockabilly pioneer picked up some of their early songs, such as 'You Ain't Treating Me Right', 'I'll Be Gentle, You Are My Very Special Baby' and one of Curtis's most popular hits, 'Blue Jean Heart'.

Johnston had a stab at solo stardom after a studio engineer in Fort Worth had sent one of his songs to producer Clyde Otis, who was impressed enough to get him into the studio in November 1956 to record 'Born To Love One Woman'. Otis also introduced him to New York publishing heavy hitter Bobby Mellin. Bob – or Don Johnston, as he was known then – subsequently signed to the Dot label.

He started playing gigs, but concluded he was on the wrong side of the microphone while opening for Ricky Nelson one night in Los Angeles; halfway through his set an hysterical mob of teenage girls rushed at the stage screaming Nelson's name, leaving Johnston in no doubt his presence was no longer required and forcing him to beat a hasty retreat. The idea of being torn limb from limb by an army of marauding teenage girls in the name of Ricky Nelson led Johnston to conclude he was not cut out to be a pop star. 'It was embarrassing,' he said later, with some understatement. 'I looked like shit 'cos I didn't have any money and he looked like four million dollars.

Instead, Johnston became attracted to the studio side of the industry. He got a job as staff producer at Kapp, a largely MOR New York label set up in 1955 by David Kapp. Hearing a new Aretha Franklin record in 1964, he contacted the arranger, Bob Mercy, who had been responsible for the string arrangements and asked him if he could provide something similar for an album he was working on by Helena Troy. It transpired that Mercy, who worked at Columbia, was also in the process of producing new albums for Barbra Streisand and Andy Williams and asked Johnston if he had any material that might be suitable for either of them. He did. Mercy was so impressed that he invited Johnson to work for Columbia and installed him in a makeshift office that doubled as a broom cupboard.

One of Johnston's first projects at Columbia was Patti Page. An American icon from Oklahoma, Page had crossed into pop from the country music scene and had spent 13 weeks at No. 1 in 1950 with 'Tennessee Waltz'. She had 26 Top 10 hits and four No. 1s, and helped to pioneer double-tracking vocals (originally because she could not afford backing singers). All of her biggest hits had been with Mercury, but her career had been on the slide since the end of the 1950s – she had not had a hit since 'Left Right Out Of Your Heart' in 1958 – and in 1963 she joined Columbia. The problem for Columbia was how to revive the profile and fortunes of a passionate singer who had been left forlornly behind by the irresistible march of rock'n'roll, becoming, in most people's perceptions, a relic of the past. The problem was re-directed to Bob Johnston's broom cupboard.

Johnston found the answer in Hollywood. Bette Davis was starring in a new horror movie called *Hush … Hush, Sweet Charlotte*, which told the story of a mad, wealthy spinster living in a big house in Louisiana, tortured by the memory of the gruesome murder of her fiancé. It was a big movie and Johnston had the inspired idea of Patti Page recording a cover of the Frank De Vol/Mack David title song, performed in the movie by Al Martino. It worked – Patti Page found herself back in the charts, and Johnston's reputation at Columbia went sky high.

So when Johnston put himself in the frame for the Dylan production gig, those at Columbia who called the shots – John Hammond, Bill Gallagher (president of Columbia) and Bob Mercy – readily agreed. After his success with Patti Page, his overtures were well received, although Mercy was baffled by his enthusiasm. 'Why do you want to work with him? He's got dirty fingernails and he breaks all the strings on his guitar.' Still, without asking Dylan or Al Grossman if they had any opinions on the matter, Hammond informed Johnston he was the new Dylan producer.

He had not been involved in the recording of 'Like A Rolling Stone', but Johnston's first duties as Dylan producer were to protect it from the people at Columbia that were keen to smooth its rough edges. One executive wanted Dylan to re-record the vocals and it was down to Johnston to fight Dylan's corner from a technical side. Johnston, was openly scathing about the lack of musical understanding of the men in suits who worked at Columbia and talking bitterly of executives tapping their feet out of time and whistling out of tune whenever they were played some new record; he relished the challenge – and won the argument.

Sometimes his damnations extended to other producers at the company who had got their positions without any real musical background. 'Anyone who can't write songs, can't sing, can't produce, can't perform, really shouldn't be working with an artist. You need to relate on their level, if for no other reason than you can stay out of their way when you need to. All the other staff producers at Columbia were picking songs based on what their boss liked last week so they could keep their jobs for three months.'

From day one, Johnston's sole priority was the personal wellbeing and artistic satisfaction of the artists. Given the chance to work with somebody he considered a genius, he was perfectly prepared to fight anybody he needed to fight on the artist's behalf – one reason alone why Dylan would have taken to him. At the time, producers were still mostly record company pawns, an adjunct of the corporate machine and very much part of 'them' in an 'us-and-them' situation. Johnston was a father of three young kids and sought security as much as the next man, but nevertheless was unusual in the way he lined up proudly alongside the 'us'.

Dylan and Johnston met for the first time at Columbia Studios on West 52nd Street on 29 July, as work began again on the album that would be *Highway 61 Revisited*. A grinning Johnston marched up to Dylan in his usual affable manner. 'Hi, I'm Bob Johnston.' Dylan shook his hand, smiled back and said: 'Hi, I'm Bob too…' From this point the two Bobs got on well, and Johnston later said proudly they never had a cross word throughout their working relationship – although that may have been something to do with Johnston's eagerness to accommodate Dylan's every whim.

Shortly after arriving at the studio on the first day, Johnston sacked one of the staff engineers in the studio, a German who clearly did not want to be there and dissed Dylan. That was totally unacceptable to Johnston, who got rid of him immediately. He replaced him with Mike Figlio, himself a singer who had already left his own minor footnote on recording history as the man who mixed Tony Bennett's 'I Left My Heart In San Francisco', a song for which Bennett had so little enthusiasm that it was the last track he attempted in a full day of recordings in 1962, and it was hurriedly knocked out in three takes.

Johnston made no bones about his own role in the process. He was there simply to facilitate Dylan's recording and, as far as he was concerned, Dylan could spend an hour blowing his nose and he would tape it. He had no delusions of grandeur himself, had no interest in being the star of the show or making his own mark on the recordings: it was Bob Dylan's album and his job was simply to make it as easy as he could to record the album he wanted with as little pressure and as few hassles or complicationsas was humanly possible. As far as Bob Johnston was concerned, what Dylan wanted, Dylan got.

'I never cared what he did in the studio,' Johnston told *On The Tracks*. 'I was trying to get down anything he was doing next, so we could have a record of it – so people could hear it all over the world. I figured that was my job.'

He wasn't fazed, either, by murmurings about Dylan's 'difficult' reputation in the studio or the spectre of the formidable Al Grossman looming over him. He knew all about the dispute with John Hammond and the falling out with Tom Wilson, but had no fears about his own ability to keep them happy. 'My attitude was, if Dylan wanted to record under a palm tree in Hawaii with a ukulele, I'd be there with a tape machine, I'm an artist's producer. I give my artists lots of freedom and if they fuck up – it's their life.'

Apart from Bob Johnston there was a familiar look about the musicians who gathered in Studio A on 29 July. Mostly it was the same personnel from the 'Like A Rolling Stone' sessions. Mike Bloomfield, Al Kooper, Paul Griffin, Bobby Gregg and Russ Savakus knew the score now (Frank Owens arrived later). Information from the main man would be sparse and they would be expected to slot in when and how they saw fit.

There was no blueprint for recording with Bob Dylan, no test card or rulebook. The experience of recording 'Like A Rolling Stone' and playing with him at Newport had taught the musicians that patience and spontaneity would be requisites of this session.

Initially, he got the band warmed up with the same process that had worked so well on 'Like A Rolling Stone' – a few run-throughs of 'Phantom Engineers', [sic, on session sheets] which had by now almost fully completed its transmutation into 'It Takes A Lot To Laugh, It Takes A Train To Cry'. And then he turned his attention to 'Tombstone Blues', another blitz of surreal poetry that had been germinating for a while as he had attempted to turn it into song form. The momentum of 'Like A Rolling Stone' had given him the impetus to try it within an unblinking rock framework and he saw the Chicago blues element provided by Mike Bloomfield as its perfect foil. It was one of Dylan's favourites. 'I felt like I'd broken through with this song, that nothing had been done like it before … just a flash really,' he said in the sleeve notes to *Biograph*.

In a manner that was to become frustratingly familiar to the session musicians, he played them through the song once or twice on piano and guitar and then expected them to somehow tap into the energy of the moment and deliver their parts in sympathy with his vocals and the song's essence. The rest was down to instinct – on all sides. Dylan knew the sort of sound he wanted but he couldn't articulate it, expecting those around him somehow magically to tune in to his wavelength and feed off his energy and passion until they arrived at the same point.

So they listened intently as he played them 'Tombstone Blues', with its raggedy, raucous structure and another tumbling torrent of words that made no clear or obvious sense to anyone hearing them for the first time. With its blatant disregard for conventional structure built over two incessant chords, Dylan fans were later to claim 'Tombstone Blues' as the first punk song.

While the folkies wailed about Dylan's perceived betrayal, the ironic thing about 'Tombstone Blues', his wildest, hardest, heaviest song to date, was that he had secreted inside it one of his most political messages.

> 'Well, John the Baptist after torturing a thief
> Looks up at his hero the Commander-in-Chief
> Saying, "Tell me great hero, but please make it brief
> Is there a hole for me to get sick in?"
> 'The Commander-in-Chief answers him while chasing a fly
> Saying "Death to all those who would whimper and cry"
> And dropping a bar bell he points to the sky
> Saying, "The sun's not yellow, it's chicken."'

With disquiet about the Vietnam War growing by the day, Dylan's sideways allusions during a complex, confusing, colourful assault on jingoism and national pride, were veiled but sharp.

Certainly the anti-war campaigners had no doubts about Dylan's intent when he wrote:

> 'The king of the Philistines his soldiers to save
> Puts jawbones on their tombstones and flatters their graves
> Puts the pied pipers in prison and fattens the slaves
> Then sends them out to the jungle.'

References to Jack the Ripper ('who sits at the head of the chamber of commerce'), Belle Starr ('she hands down her wits'), Jezebel ('the nun she violently knits') and the mother of the blues Ma Rainey unwrapping a bed roll with Beethoven – among various images of Galileo, Delilah, Gipsy Davey and Cecil B. DeMille – suggest a rampant disillusionment with the American dream and the useless facades of those who held it dear.

And as much as it was a track conceived, born and delivered in an exclusively rock-orientated firmament and owing much in format to Chuck Berry, 'Tombstone Blues' did have powerful echoes of the blues. The title had been used in blues songs of the 1920s, notably by Lillian Miller, Lonnie Johnson and, in 1928, one of the *Highway 61* reference points, Bessie Smith.

Dylan tinkered with 'Tombstone Blues' throughout what was – for most of the band – a frustrating morning in the studio. It was a work in progress and Dylan made no bones about it, sitting at the piano, rehearsing and urging the others to join in, only to stop short suddenly, trying out different ideas, switching the words and then having another crack. A silently absorbed Bob Johnston let him get on with it. He was learning fast about Dylan's unorthodox, insular way of running a recording session. 'You always had to keep your eye on him,' the producer said. 'He came in and played a song to the band once and that was how they learned it. He never counted off, just launched right into it, so you always had to keep the tape rolling.'

The recording set-up at Studio A was primitive and problematic. Sitting at the console, Johnston put everything on to a four-track tape machine that, bizarrely, was in another room along the hall and somebody, usually Mike Figlio, had to yell 'Roll tape!' to an engineer. Then there would be a succession of further yells of 'Is the tape rolling?' to establish whether everything was ready for the recording process.

'God, it took twenty minutes to get those damned machines going,' said Johnston. 'It was like a Three Stooges short. So I got into the habit of using several machines with Dylan so as not to lose anything. He would start a song on the piano and if the musicians dropped out during it, he'd go to the guitar and start playing another one. I lost one song that way and never again, so I always used multiple machines.'

Johnston had quickly deduced that he needed three microphones to record Dylan properly 'because his head spun around so much' and settled him in front of the big classic Neumann U47, grand old king of the vocal tube microphones, large, imposing and solid, with its distinctive curved grill at the top.

Founded by Georg Neumann in 1928, the Berlin based Neumann company had provided microphones for many of the public events and rallies leading up to the Second World War. After the war, it had adapted the Telefunken V14 tube designed for field radios, condensing the sound to create a sharper quality on a new super microphone to use for broadcast and recording. It came to change the smooth sound of recordings from the old 'ribbon' mics designed to pick up sounds from both sides of the mic popular with pre-war dance band crooners. The Neumann condenser system enabled concentration on the voice, creating an immediate tone, which came to be the benchmark for pop recordings and was used for some early classical stereo records.

Realizing Dylan's habit of moving around as he sang could affect clarity, Johnston left nothing to chance. He wanted to make sure that all of Dylan's lyrics were clearly audible and used a sound 'baffle' mechanism to deaden reverberation on his guitar and prevent it from muffling his voice. He also boosted his voice using an audio equalizer to make sure nothing was lost as he shifted positions.

Dylan paid little heed to the growing frustrations of the band as they waited on him to firm up an idea. Nothing moved until Dylan had sorted things out in his own mind and gave the nod, at which point it became all systems go as the musicians tried to second-guess what was in Dylan's head and deliver the sounds he might be looking for. Once he had got the basic elements of a song figured out, Dylan did not hang around; he wanted the track to be completed as swiftly as possible, and those around had to be ready to deliver. None of them were used to working this way. They looked to Bloomfield to offer guidance and show them how to interpret Dylan's vision, but the process was neither easy nor, at this stage of the game, satisfying.

Dylan's attitude was anathema to the older musicians gathered at Studio A, who had been raised on sheet music and traditional recording routines. For Dylan, 'Tombstone Blues' was all about spirit and energy. He did not care if the instruments were out of tune, or if the sound wasn't perfect or technically correct. Or if he hit a few bum notes. Or if the words changed. Or if nobody else knew what the hell he was trying to achieve. They tried take after take of 'Tombstone Blues' but Dylan invariably stopped them to shift his phrasing around or introduce a different lyric. 'It was,' observed Al Kooper, 'totally disorganized, totally punk. There was no sheet music, it was totally by ear. It just happened.'

Dylan – and all the others – were, in effect, making it up as they went along. None of them had ever worked in quite this way before and while Kooper relished the anarchy and Bloomfield responded to the challenge, some of them reacted badly. As they tussled through most of the morning with 'Tombstone Blues', bass player Russ Savakus, began to get increasingly agitated and started to lose the plot. They eventually nailed 'Tombstone Blues' to Dylan's satisfaction, but it took 12 takes to do it and Savakus's nerves were seriously frayed.

Savakus considered himself an adaptable musician. In the 1950s he had played several sessions with the notoriously unpredictable and wayward jazz trumpeter Chet Baker – by then in his twenties and regarded as one of the world's greatest talents, but already in the grip of the heroin addiction that ultimately destroyed him. But Savakus had got on well with the wayward Baker and had come through it with his reputation enhanced and his pride intact. After Baker, Savakus felt equipped to handle anything. But Dylan's ultra-loose modus operandi was something different again and he made no secret of his displeasure at the apparent disorganisation of the session. Snappy and grumbling, he threatened to walk out.

Not that Dylan noticed Savakus's brewing tantrum. Bob remained ebullient and focused, seemingly oblivious to the consternation that his haphazard working practice was creating among his fellow travellers. His creative juices were in full flow and he had no mind for the delicate sensibilities of Russ Savakus or anyone else.

When they broke for lunch, a chain-smoking Dylan went back into the studio alone. He was still not content with the blitzkrieg blues treatment of 'It Takes A Lot To Laugh, It Takes A Train To Cry'. The track had already gone through many incarnations since its loose beginnings – including the torrid, ramshackle live outing at Newport – but in Dylan's mind it remained a country blues song to the core.

His lyrics drew heavily on classic blues imagery, with the train as a metaphor for life and references to the 'good-looking moon', 'brakeman' and 'my gal' placed it as a variant on familiar old blues warhorses such as 'Shotgun Blues', 'Alabama Woman Blues' and 'Milk Cow Blues', a landmark blues track originally recorded in 1934 by Kokomo Arnold, which inspired different variations by Robert Johnson, Leadbelly and Elvis Presley and which Dylan had originally performed in 1962.

'It Takes A Lot To Laugh, It Takes A Train To Cry' had moved a long way from that original source and Dylan felt it had lost some of its essence. So, while the others were taking a break, Dylan sat at the piano for over an hour trying to restore the song's original character. By the time the others returned he had cracked it, slowing it down to a rumbling swagger with an elegant piano arrangement. The musicians were barely back in the studio when Dylan was playing them the new arrangement. No doubt surprised to find themselves confronted with yet another new version of a track they thought had been already put to bed, they were asked to shoulder arms and deliver.

Paul Griffin had been booked into another session that afternoon and reluctantly left them to it, but Frank Owens, the replacement Griffin had recommended, took his place at the piano and slotted seamlessly into the session. Owens had arrived early and watched in fascination as Dylan had reworked It 'Takes A Lot To Laugh, It Takes A Train To Cry'. Fully briefed by Griffin on the studio world of Dylan, Owens had plenty of experience playing with jazz artists and was not fazed at all by the sympathetic spontaneity that Dylan expected of his musicians.

Owens was braced for a long afternoon battling with 'It Takes A Lot To Laugh' but four takes later, the track was done and dusted. The slower trawl Dylan wanted had revealed an unexpected beauty in the song and melody. Frank Owens' decorative piano lending a seductive delicacy to the chugging rhythm, with a restrained contribution from Mike Bloomfield leaving the canvas clear for Dylan's elongated and atmospheric wailing harp interlude and fade-out. After all the grief, anger and frustration that Dylan had put into getting the song into the sort of shape he felt worked and the painstaking effort the musicians had applied into helping him get there, a beguiling calm had prevailed and the track re-emerged as a relatively simplistic, unblemished homage to the blues heroes of old. Everybody involved knew it had been worth all the sweat. It was back to basics and it was crystal clear to them all that it was right.

On fire now, Dylan unveiled a new song, entitled 'Black Dalli Rue'. 'You got a lotta nerve / To say you are my friend, / When I was down / You just stood there grinning … You got a lotta nerve / To say you got a helping hand to lend / You just want to be on / The side that's winning,' he sang, and he was off on the blistering barrage of scattergun bitterness that would be re-titled to become 'Positively 4th Street'. It was earmarked as the natural successor to 'Like A Rolling Stone' in spirit, form and commercial appeal, but keeping faith with the working practice that had done the trick on 'Like A Rolling Stone', Dylan initially held it back in order to work on a couple of other tracks.

Written immediately after the Newport debacle, it is impossible to think the song could have been driven by anything else. 'You say I let you down / You know it's not like that / If you're so hurt / Why then don't you show it / You say you lost your faith / But that's not where it's at / You had no faith to lose / And you know it …'.

The world thought 'Like A Rolling Stone' was a volcano of searing bile, but it seemed tame in comparison to the vicious, calculated attack of 'Positively 4th Street'. If 'It's All Over Now, Baby Blue' was his melancholic, slightly regretful farewell to his old world, he got out of town in an explosion of hate, fury, disgust, scorn and ridicule. There were no cryptic references, no names to decipher, no oblique passages to unravel, it can be interpreted as a full-on assault on the narrow-minded hypocrisy he had been subjected to the previous weekend. It remains one of the most cogent, potent and brilliant songs Dylan has ever written – not least for the barbed parting verses: 'I wish that for just one time / You could stand inside my shoes / And just for that one moment / I could be you / Yes, I wish that for just one time / You could stand inside my shoes / You'd know what a drag it is / To see you ...'.

The title is presumed to refer to West 4th St in Greenwich, where Dylan shared an apartment at No. 161 with Suze Rotolo. It also housed Gerdes Folk City and other folk joints where he had played. He had, however, also lived at 4th Street in the bohemian Dinkytown district of Minneapolis during his short sojourn at the University of Minnesota, stayed at East 4th Street in New York and would have known well the 4th Street Drug Store in Clarksdale, on Highway 61 – the focal point of much of the early civil-rights activities, involving Aaron Henry, who ran the store, and Medgar Evers, the black campaigner whose murder in 1963 by the Ku Klux Klan inspired Dylan's 'Only A Pawn In Their Game'. Whichever way you look at it, however, the lyrics always seem to point back to the Greenwich Village old guard and others who considered that Dylan had betrayed them.

'Positively 4th Street' was immediately considered by all who heard it to be a natural follow-up single to 'Like A Rolling Stone' and Greenwich Village was a den of gossip when word got out about the specific identity of Dylan's targets in the song. There was no shortage of candidates. *Sing Out!* editor Irwin Silber had been on Dylan's case for a long time, famously writing him an open letter in the magazine in November 1964, decrying his new direction, and he was one of those most vocally dismayed by the Newport set.

Izzy Young at the Folklore Center, who had had his run-ins with Dylan, was also put in the frame. 'At least 500 came into my place and asked if it was about me,' he said later. 'I don't know if it was, but it was unfair…. Dylan comes in and takes from us, uses my resources, then he leaves and *he* gets bitter. He writes a bitter song. He was the one who left.'

Some people assume it is a knock-back at Suze Rotolo, while a finger of suspicion also latched on to two Greenwich Village contemporaries: Phil Ochs, now being hailed as the folk saviour after the defection of Dylan, and Tom Paxton, who had condemned Dylan's flirtation with electric instruments in a *Sing Out!* article as 'folk rot'.

All are possible but did they really wound him deep enough to inspire such a ferocious deluge of spite? Given its immediacy in the wake of Newport, it seems far more likely that the target of contempt in 'Positively 4th Street' is a generic character Dylan used in order to vent his rage at a movement that had so publicly turned against him. Following 'Like A Rolling Stone', the Newport experience had goaded him further into a wired, tumultuous outburst of writing – and this was its apotheosis.

Dylan admitted in a press conference in San Francisco later that year that the song had indeed been designed to 'needle' those who had needled him. In an interview with Scott Cohen two decades later, he said he was still proud of it. 'It's extremely one-dimensional, which I like. I don't usually purge myself by writing anything about any type of "so-called relationships". I don't have the kinds of relationships that are built on any kind of false pretense, not to say that I haven't. I've had just as many as anybody else, but I haven't had them in a long time. Usually everything with me and anybody is up front. My life-is-an-open-book sort of thing. And I choose to be involved with the people I'm involved with. They don't choose me.'

However, perverse as ever, Dylan contradicted himself in his interview for the 1985 *Biograph* box set, strongly denying that 'Positively 4th Street' was a kick back at his detractors. 'I couldn't write a song about something like that,' he said. 'I don't write songs to critics.'

A poisonous song, but a great song, 'Positively 4th Street' saw the assembled throng through the rest of the afternoon, Dylan characteristically stopping and starting as he changed things around, before they got two complete takes down to his satisfaction. With lyrics as vitriolic as 'Do you take me for such a fool / To think I'd make contact / With the one who tries to hide / What he don't know to begin with', and a delivery as snarling as Dylan conjured up, there was little anyone else could do to exaggerate the venom. Al Kooper's grumbling organ was its main instrumental feature, with Bloomfield's guitar supplying a savage undercurrent, Frank Owens playing lively runs on the piano, a bristling Bobby Gregg keeping it rooted on drums and a fraught Russ Savakus contributing a glowering bass line.

Dylan was exuberant and keen for the session to go on and even made attempts to work another new song, 'Desolation Row', into the day. He was convinced his new album was now cooking and ready to take shape and wanted to ride with his own energy. But it was 6 pm, the unionized studio technicians wanted to knock off and the band were tired and irritable. Dylan was content enough. The songs were taking form in exhilarating fashion and while 'Positively 4th Street' was ultimately not included on the finished album (it was released only as a single to follow-up 'Like A Rolling Stone'), the recording had energized and inspired him and in that sense was central to the rest of the sessions for *Highway 61 Revisited*.

Dylan marched out of Studio A that day and went straight home to write some more material.

Chapter 7

I NEED A DUMP TRUCK MAMA TO UNLOAD MY HEAD

'Everybody is making love / Or else expecting rain / And the Good
Samaritan, he's dressing / He's getting ready for the show / He's
going to the carnival tonight / On Desolation Row'
Bob Dylan, 'Desolation Row'

When they reconvened in Studio A the following afternoon, Dylan was raring to go again. He had more songs, more belief, more energy, more attitude. He *knew* they were cooking up a storm.

During the day, however, the cast list changed. Bass player Russ Savakus is listed on the session notes as having spent the whole day at Studio A and he was certainly booked to be there. But he was not happy; he could not get to grips with the way Dylan worked and he was full of foreboding about the forthcoming day's session. Tony Glover, Dylan's old cohort from Minneapolis, who was in Studio A at the time, said that Savakus simply 'freaked out'. He had found the marathon 'Tombstone Blues', with its constant stopping and starting as a result of Dylan's free-form approach to recording 'on the hoof' particularly stressful and wearing.

There was some sympathy among the other musicians for Savakus. He had proven his talent in various jazz sessions, but generally playing stand-up double bass – he had no previous studio experience playing electric bass guitar. When Bob Johnston had booked Savakus for the session, he had neglected to mention the electric requirement. An adept and adaptable musician, Savakus did not imagine he would have a problem with this – and initially he was right – but he became more and more unsettled as he recognized he was overstretching himself. As Dylan worked on his latest ideas, a still stressed Savakus decided he had better things to do with his time and bailed out.

Al Kooper had called his friend Harvey Brooks the night before to put him on standby for the session. Now he called him again. For while Savakus was on the verge of cracking during 'Tombstone Blues', Bob Johnston was already scouring his vast reservoir of contacts for a possible replacement bass player. Ever alert to such opportunities, Kooper spoke to Johnston at the end of the day's session and suggested he knew just the man to fill his shoes. When it became obvious that Savakus was not willing to play on the rest of the album, Johnston gave Kooper the nod to get his man in.

Brooks – also known as Harvey Goldstein – was a fine bass player whom Kooper was confident had the immense reservoirs of patience, tolerance, cool, instinct and adaptability that Dylan was increasingly demanding of those around him. It was handy to be a good musician, but if you were going to be around Dylan for any length of time, strength of character, a thick skin and an easy-going nature were crucial.

Kooper had such an engaging personality and gift of the gab he could probably have persuaded Dylan that Muhammad Ali and Mickey Mouse would be suitable replacements for the troubled Savakus. As it was, Johnston readily accepted Kooper's fulsome recommendation about Brooks and told him to make the call.

'I got to know Russ … he was a very straight shooter and a real good bass player,' Brooks told Dylan biographer Clinton Heylin. 'But I think he did also have some difficulty with the style of music because as I was to learn, this was a case of just "go for it". You were only going to get one or two shots, maybe, at each song.'

Brooks admits that initially on arriving at Studio A he did not have a clue what was going on. He took comfort in the fact that nobody else seemed to have much of a clue either, not even Dylan himself, who was tinkering around on piano and guitar trying different things out, seemingly constructing two or three different songs at the same time. Wandering into the studio anew it seemed a case of organized chaos … except there was nothing organized about it.

It was not long, though, before Brooks realized he was in the company of genius. Unlike the recording sessions for any of his previous albums, Dylan was now in complete control and, in his head at least, was fast arriving at a train of thought where he knew exactly what he wanted to do. The problem came when he tried to unload what was in his head and the others were forced to translate his random instructions into some tangible sense of direction.

'Bob comes into the studio and … it goes quiet and everyone starts listening to him to what he's gonna say and what he wants to do,' said Brooks. 'He ran the whole session. Bob Johnston was there just to keep it going. He was supposed to say if somebody was in tune or out of tune, but that was a useless concept to try and get *anything* in tune.'

As far as Bob Johnston was concerned, whatever Dylan did was fine by him. Dylan himself commented wryly on this in his *Chronicles* autobiography. 'He (Bob Johnston) thinks that everything I'm recording is fantastic. He always does. He's thinking that something is gonna strike pay dirt, that everything is totally together. On the contrary. Nothing was ever together. Not even after a song had been finished and recorded was it ever together.'

They kicked off that day with 'From A Buick 6', or 'Lunatic Princess No 3', as it was originally listed on the recording sheet. The original 'Lunatic Princess' was another song he had been trying to put together during the recording of 'Like A Rolling Stone'. Snapping into action at the signal of a single drumbeat crack, it gallops happily along over a now supremely confident Al Kooper organ fill, reflecting the energy and upbeat mood Dylan was imparting on the proceedings. 'Like A Rolling

Stone' was riding high in the charts and here was pop star Bob, unconcerned by the niceties of the recording process, launching without prevarication into another song that had evolved gradually into something radically different from its origins.

During the recording sessions for *The Freewheelin' Bob Dylan* three years earlier – a time when his songwriting was structured more to rejigging and updating folk and blues rather than destroying the mould – he had played around with 'Milk Cow Blues'. It was a song indelibly associated with a bootlegger from Lovejoy, Georgia, called James 'Kokomo' Arnold. One of life's drifters, Arnold moved around the States doing various jobs before arriving in Chicago in 1929, illegally smuggling alcohol into the country during the prohibition.

As a child, Arnold had learned the rudiments of guitar and he also managed to gain popularity – and a less risky supplementary income – with his lightning, aggressive left-handed slide guitar playing and intense blues singing. He made his first records, 'Rainy Night Blues' and 'Paddlin' Madeline Blues', in Memphis in 1930 under the name Gitfiddle Jim. When prohibition ended in 1933 and finished his bootlegging business, Arnold was forced to concentrate on music to make a living. In 1934 he recorded his two greatest tracks for Decca. One was based on an old Scrapper Blackwell blues inspired by the Kokomo brand of coffee, which Arnold released as 'Old Original Kokomo Blues'. The song proved so popular that he became known as Kokomo Arnold and was a profound influence on, among others, Robert Johnson, who based his 'Sweet Home Chicago' on 'Old Original Kokomo Blues'.

On the other side of Arnold's recording of 'Original Kokomo Blues' was 'Milk Cow Blues'; Johnson re-invented this one too as 'Milk Cow's Calf Blues', which 20 years later was covered by Elvis Presley as one of his seminal Sun recordings at Sam Phillips' studio and re-titled again to 'Milk Cow Blues Boogie'. Kokomo Arnold continued to record for a few years but disappeared off the radar in the 1940s and never resurfaced, despite being sought out by young enthusiasts when the blues were in vogue in the early 1960s. Working in a factory in Chicago, Arnold had little appetite for a potential rebirth of his musical career and rejected the opportunity – gobbled up by so many of his contemporaries – to record again. He died, aged 67, in Chicago after suffering a heart attack.

Although Dylan's original fascination with 'Milk Cow Blues' might have been inspired by the Elvis version, he would also have been aware of the highly individual, very different interpretation of the song by one of his heroes, Sleepy John Estes. The great Tennessee blues man was assumed long dead by the blues revivalists, but he was rediscovered in 1962 – blind and living in abject poverty. Sleepy John's taut, pained version of 'Milk Cow Blues' had been included on Volume 4 of the *Harry Smith Anthology of American Folk Music*, which Dylan had listened to intently and which played a major role in his musical education in his nascent years as a would-be teenage hobo. When Dylan sang 'Milk Cow Blues' in the early part of the *Freewheelin'* sessions in April 1962 he employed the Elvis rock'n'roll snarl, but in one take he instinctively added a verse from another blues classic – Leadbelly's 'Good Morning Blues'.

'My songs,' he told Robert Hilburn of the *LA Times* with, you imagine, some sense of irony in 2005, 'are either based on old Protestant hymns or Carter Family songs or variations of the blues form. What happens is I'll take a song I know and simply start playing it in my head. That's the way I meditate. A lot of people will look at a crack in the wall and meditate or count sheep or angels or money or something and it's a proven fact that it'll help them relax. I don't meditate on any of that stuff. I meditate on a song. I could be driving a car or talking to a person or sitting round or whatever and I'm listening to the song in my head. At a certain point some of the words will change and I'll start writing a song.'

There's a clear thread from 'Milk Cow Blues' to 'From A Buick 6'. The roots of Sleepy John Estes' vigorous interpretation of the song are plainly visible in the rhythmic trundle of 'Buick 6' and a similar lyric structure that rhymes 'kid' with 'hid' in the opening line. Dylan's pauses and jerky vocals perfectly mirror the pronounced Estes vocal style.

'I got this graveyard woman, you know she keeps my kid / But my soulful mama, you know she keeps me hid,' chirped Dylan as the band whipped through the song with a minimum of decorum, getting the day's proceedings underway with one of the slighter, warmer songs on the album. Bo Diddley gets a mention ('She walks like Bo Diddley and she don't need no crutch …') amid the evocative image of being lost on the highway in an iconic car ('Well, when the pipeline gets broken and I'm lost on the river bridge / I'm cracked up on the highway and on the water's edge ...').

Founded in 1903 by a Scots-American David Dunbar Buick, who soon sold out for a minimal fee (and died flat broke in 1929), Buick became the biggest car manufacturer in the US under the control of William C. Durant. In time Durant bought up many of his rivals to create the giant General Motors. Yet Buick retained its identity and status. A Buick was always considered near top of the range – only Cadillacs were more prestigious – and when Dylan was evolving his song, the distinctive Buick design was considered a mark of true style, with a front grill that seemed to ape human features and became known as the 'dollar grin'.

Dylan's almost loving lyrical observations in the song portray a reassuring protector, littered with allusions to travel, highways and time that run through the *Highway 61* songmaking process. The Buick 6 was an early model from 1919 though it was probably the powerful, cast-iron Buick V6 engine (the 'Fireball'), which was introduced in 1962, that captured Dylan's imagination sufficiently to employ it as a symbol of strength, faith and power on this updated take on 'Milk Cow Blues'.

They spent a couple of hours on 'From A Buick 6' in Studio A that day and got four takes down, the fourth the version that wound up on the finished album. Dylan's laissez-fair approach, coupled with Bob Johnston's attitude that whatever Bob did was great, meant that they hurtled through the track without paying too much attention to the finer qualities of recording. Little things such as whether or not they were in tune were conveniently overlooked as the musicians were all caught up in the momentum of the recording and Dylan's own desire to rattle it all off as fast as humanly possible.

It was a policy that tried the patience of the older musicians, but it found favour with the suits at Columbia, many of whom still saw Dylan as a trivial waste of space and an irritating distraction to the core business of show tunes and classic song interpreters like Johnny Mathis. This was before the days of independent productions and in-house Columbia staff handled every aspect of the sessions. The producer, studio engineers and those logging details of the sessions were all Columbia personnel. One of the (uncredited) studio engineers on the session was Roy Halee. He later became associated with everything Simon & Garfunkel committed to vinyl but right now he was, by his own admission, clueless – an excited, nervous passenger trying to get the hang of the strange recording process. He was not to know that this was not how it was usually done.

When he turned up at the 'Like A Rolling Stone' sessions, he felt like he had walked into a circus of madmen. The musical world he knew was classical, where recording techniques were straight down the line; a single mic hung above the conductor's head and that was the way it was done. Working with Dylan was not like that. No one hung a mic over Dylan's head. He liked space, he wanted freedom, he could not keep still in the studio and if that meant it made him difficult to record, then that was someone else's problem. Halee was faintly appalled by Dylan, with his gruff attitude and curt abruptness towards those around him, but he made the best of it and was summoned back to help engineer the rest of the album.

Partly scared by Dylan, partly following everybody else's kowtowing and partly because he simply did not know any better, Halee kept his head down and unquestioningly did Dylan's bidding. When Dylan suddenly announced he wanted to record his vocals on 'From A Buick 6' right next to the drum kit, Halee did not think twice. This was unheard of in studios at the time and in terms of recording quality it really was not a good idea, but Halee was instantly there, setting up the mics without raising an eyebrow. He would worry later about how to prevent the sound bleeds, as Dylan's vocals spilled into the drum microphones and were muffled by the drums.

'Classical music was very schooled and orderly but with this stuff you had to come up with all kinds of sounds and mic techniques,' said Halee. 'You really had to stretch what you knew and it was a big challenge – there was a lot of experimentation. And not everything worked out every time, of course, but the attitude was good and I think it helped me in later years.'

If Halee was baffled by the random working practices Dylan had employed while recording 'From A Buick 6', he was struck dumb as Dylan unleashed a more demonic, vicious and troublesome creature entirely: 'Can You Please Crawl Out Your Window?'. Another song of poisonous retribution written in the same caustic spirit as 'Positively 4th Street', it occupied the session for the rest of the day, right through to 10 pm.

The lyrics are vintage Dylan, with many suggestions and mysteries hidden between the lines. Written in the immediate aftermath of Newport, the object of his derision here is even more masked than on 'Positively 4th Street'.

'He sits in your room, his tomb, with a fist full of tacks / Preoccupied with his vengeance / Cursing the dead that can't answer him back / I'm sure he has no intentions / Of looking your way, unless it's to say / That he needs to test his inventions …'

The usual suspects come under scrutiny as the spitting, derisory lyrics are analyzed: are they referring to Warhol, Sara's first husband, Bobby Neuwirth, Al Grossman, Irwin Silber, Pete Seeger? Or, perhaps more pertinently given the style and timing of its creation, a wry bout of self-analysis reflecting on his own perception in the eyes of the audience he was consciously abandoning. 'Why does he look so righteous while your face is so changed / Are you frightened of the box you keep him in …'.

The pursuit of truths in Dylan's lyrics is a thankless, never-ending task: as you chase the threads and end up tying yourself in knots. But the post-Newport Dylan-on-Dylan theory with 'Can You Please Crawl Out Your Window?' does seem to carry more weight the further you investigate the lyrics.

'He looks so truthful, is this how he feels / Trying to peel the moon and expose it / With his businesslike anger and his bloodhounds that kneel / If he needs a third eye he just grows it / He just needs you to talk or hand him his chalk / Or pick it up after he throws it …'.

If this was Dylan teasing and wreaking vengeance on his critics, the song took its own revenge as the early attempts to commit it to tape ended in complete disarray. Dylan's guitar was completely out of tune and his singing was not much better; Mike Bloomfield, Al Kooper, Harvey Brooks and Bobby Gregg struggled to maintain any sense of order in the carnage.

Listed on the recording sheet as 'Look At Barry Run' and colloquially known as 'The Continuing Saga of Baby Blue', the song came to torture all involved in trying to tame it. They had a break at 5.30 pm to clear their heads and have something to eat and then returned to the studio an hour and a half later to put 'Can You Please Crawl Out Your Window?' to bed. But the song refused to go to bed. It was not tired and it had a tantrum.

Through the afternoon and evening they had 17 goes at getting a usable version on tape, but none of them worked and frustration set in. Confusion reigned, with Dylan seemingly unwilling or unable to communicate what he wanted the finished article to sound like, leading the others to presume that he did not actually know. In a process Mike Bloomfield came to describe as 'chucklefucking', they kept charging at the song without the remotest direction from either the author or producer, vaguely hoping that

© Daniel Kramer

Blues guitar maestro Mike Bloomfield.

in the law of averages, they would eventually stumble on a sound that made some sort of sense. Not today it did not.

'There were chord charts for these songs but no one had any idea what the music was supposed to sound like,' Bloomfield told Clinton Heylin. 'It all sort of went round Dylan. I mean, he didn't direct the music, he just sang the songs and played piano and guitar and it just sort of went on around him. But the sound was a matter of pure chance. The producer did not tell people what to play or have a sound in mind … it was a result of chucklefucking … people stepping on each other's dicks until it came out right.'

Bloomfield's palpable frustration was understandable. 'It's a natural,' he said of his empathy with the blues. 'Black people suffer externally in this country, Jewish people suffer internally. The suffering's the mutual fulcrum for the blues.' As such he had a no-messing philosophy when it came to his approach to music – he just wanted to get on and play his guitar. He wasn't one for 'chucklefucking'.

Al Kooper, who had hit it off with Bloomfield from day one, was sympathetic to the guitarist's confusion during the constant takes that day. 'He was years ahead of everyone,' Kooper said admiringly of his friend. 'His melodic sense and feel were incomparable.' That is perhaps why Dylan felt content to give Bloomfield a blank sheet of paper and a licence to play exactly what he wanted as they tried again to make coherent sense out of the tangle of instruments and clashing ideas that conspired to destroy their work that day. Unfortunately, with his irritating silences and apparent inability to formulate a coherent plan of engagement in his own head, let alone anyone else's, Dylan invested the same carte blanche in everyone else, too. The result was a recurring conflict of sounds, styles and philosophies.

As they grew tired and tempers frayed and the evening wore on, Dylan put 'Can You Please Crawl Out Your Window?' to one side. Nobody really knew what was in his mind and whether or not he had finally settled on a version to satisfy his restless soul, or simply decided that discretion was the better part of valour. He did ultimately return to the song on 5 October when, under pressure from Columbia, he went into the studio with the Hawks to record a follow-up single to 'Positively 4th Street'. It was still destined to be problematic. The Hawks had only rehearsed with Dylan for three weeks and experienced the same frustrations the *Highway 61* band had on the day of recording. However, they did manage the take that was released as a single in December (backed with 'Highway 61 Revisited') although it was a commercial flop, failing to make the US Top 50.

He may have been temporarily defeated by 'Can You Please Crawl Out Your Window?', but Dylan was not yet finished, unveiling yet another new song – and another epic – 'Desolation Row'. In his now accustomed manner, he played the song through once for the gathered ranks so they could get the hang of it – and then they were dispatched to their stations to attempt a take. A daunting prospect given the long, drawn-out tussles with 'Can You Please Crawl Out Your Window?', which considering the relative lengths and weights of the songs, was a box of candy compared with the complexities of 'Desolation Row'.

Dylan once claimed he wrote 'Desolation Row' in the back of a cab on the way to the studio, but as the song clocks in at over 11 minutes and contains 659 words, that must have been one hell of a cab ride. The driver might want to check his directions a bit more closely next time he picks up a fare.

Kooper, Bloomfield and the others listened open-mouthed as Dylan sang it to them. Just the opening lines had them spooked:

'They're selling postcards of the hanging / They're painting the passports brown / The beauty parlour is filled with sailors / The circus is in town / Here comes the blind commissioner / They've got him in a trance / One hand is tied to the tightrope walker / The other is in his pants.'

Had there ever been a more vivid, colourful, evocative surreal opening to a song? The Dylanologists searching for inner meaning in the lyrics would be on overtime when they heard those lines. Everyone in the studio was enthralled when they first heard the song. Al Kooper insists 'Desolation Row' is a reference to 8th Avenue in New York, the ensuing verse descriptions portraying the scenes of human neglect and decimation habitually found there at the time.

But there are many other theories, too, especially concerning the literary allusions that repeatedly crop up in the song. T. S. Eliot gets a namecheck in a later verse ('And Ezra Pound and T. S. Eliot / Fighting on the captain's tower / While calypso singers laugh at them / And fishermen hold flowers') triggering speculation that he song was inspired by Eliot's 1922 poem 'The Waste Land', itself a complex, epic work full of veiled allusions and written out of a personal despair reflecting desperate disillusionment with the world around him.

John Steinbeck's *Cannery Row*, a colourful 1945 novel about a seedy waterside street dominated by a sardine factory in Steinbeck's home town, Monterey, during the Great Depression, also falls under suspicion as a direct inspiration for the song. If Steinbeck's *Grapes Of Wrath* inspired Woody Guthrie and, in particular, the rambling narrative of *Tom Joad*, then why not *Cannery Row* for 'Desolation Row'?

Drawn from the journals he kept while working as a fire look-out on Desolation Peak in the North Cascade Mountains of Washington state, the beat poet Jack Kerouac's autobiographical novel *Desolation Angels* – which was published in March 1965, though written much earlier – is also likely to have sparked Dylan's creative juices on the song. Sandwiched between references to the *Phantom Of The Opera* and *Casanova*, one phrase in the song – 'in the perfect image of a priest' – is a direct quote from *Desolation Angels*.

Not that Dylan is ever likely to offer many clues of his own. 'I'm not good at defining things,' he told Robert Hilburn. 'Even if I could tell you what the song is about I wouldn't. It's up to the listener to figure out what it means to him.' Whether 'Desolation Row', 'Like A Rolling Stone', 'Positively 4th Street' or any other song, Dylan has consistently maintained a guarded silence on the exact nature and inspiration for his muse.

'When I'm writing a song like that, I'm not thinking about what I want to say, I'm just thinking, "is this okay for the metre?". It's like a ghost is writing a song like that. It gives you the song and it goes away, it goes away. You don't know what it means. Except the ghost picked me to write the song.'

In the characteristic absence of any revealing nuggets from the man himself, we might have to concur with the rabid Dylanologists who conclude that those gripping opening lines of 'Desolation Row' refer to an incident at the corner of First Street and Second Avenue East in Duluth, Minnesota, on 15 June 1920.

Irene Tusken, a white, 19-year-old stenographer, claimed she had been raped behind a marquee after visiting a travelling circus. Suspicion immediately fell on a group of black labourers working with the circus. Six of the labourers were quickly arrested and locked up in Duluth jail. But, as word of the alleged crime spread through the town, a lynch mob of more than a thousand townsfolk assembled to dish out their own retribution and marched to the City Jail. The police guards refused to use their guns against their own and offered minimal resistance as the mob overpowered them, forced their way into the cells and dragged out three of the accused. Isaac McGhie, Elias Clayton and Elmer Jackson, all in their early 20s, were hauled through the streets and subjected to a mock trial. They were swiftly declared guilty, beaten … and lynched.

The case shamed Minnesota and shocked most parts of America. Hatred, intolerance and barbarity of this severity might be expected in the South, but not in the North. The subsequent investigations did little to cleanse the air. There were 25 indictments for rioting and 12 for first-degree murder, but when it came to the crunch only eight people were tried. Four were acquitted, one trial resulted in a hung jury and three men spent less than 15 months in prison after being convicted of rioting. No one was convicted of murder.

Two black men, Max Mason and William Miller, were tried for the rape of Tusken. Miller was acquitted but Mason was found guilty and sentenced to between seven and 30 years. He was discharged by the parole board after four years on condition he left the state. What was not widely reported at the time was that in the immediate aftermath of the rape,

Tusken was examined by her family doctor, who found no physical evidence of rape or assault of any kind.

Dylan's father – then 10 – was living in Duluth at the time in an apartment not far from where the drama unfolded, so Bob may well have been privy to a first-hand account of the horrific events of 1920. As the song says, there were postcards of the hanging, serving as a grisly souvenir.

The song is like a movie with a succession of strange characters and disturbing images leaping before your eyes, seemingly making no sense at all, yet somehow imparting wider, darker, deeper, more sinister visions of the world at large and America's role in it.

A mood of taut despair and forlorn resignation emerges from the melange of bizarre, mystifying rhymes ('Praise be to Nero's Neptune / The Titanic sails at dawn /And everybody's shouting / "Which side are you on?"') and the succession of oddball characters populating the involved and evocative verses: Einstein disguised as Robin Hood, Dr Filth, the blind commissioner, Cinderella, Bette Davis, Romeo, Cain and Abel, the hunchback of Notre Dame, Ophelia, the Good Samaritan. The fight, it appears, has been beaten out of us (him?) and the righteous anger of our (his?) previous incarnation destroyed by the realities of a life that eats you up, spits you out and tramples on your ideology. 'Desolation Row' was once shrewdly described as Dylan's alternative State of the Union address and when he was later asked at a press conference what he would do if he was president, Bob smirked and said he would force schoolkids to learn all the words to it rather than 'America The Beautiful'.

Helping to vote it No. 4 in *Mojo* magazine's list of Dylan's 100 Greatest Songs in 2005 ('Like A Rolling Stone' was No. 1), the English singer-songwriter Roy Harper said he felt 'Desolation Row' almost represented a suicide note, a final notice of departure. 'It contained all the elements of where we felt civilisation had been for years but it wasn't delivered with the overt sense of humour of his more accessible earlier songs,' said Harper. 'Times had changed for Dylan. He was no longer the carefree young vibe thief of the freewheelin' age. He was now expected by everyone under 20 to become the next messiah, just as he was becoming more human. There were rumours of hard drugs and self-examination. Like a lot of us he was on the verge of floundering. There were no easy solutions any more.'

Harper even believed he had a strong grasp on the significance of the characters dipping in and out of the narrative. 'We all know the characters the song describes. The Millais painting of the drowned Ophelia lingers in my mind, dead in the head at 22, living vicariously, peeping into Desolation Row for moments of delicious embarrassment, only to resume her role in some Salvation Army equivalent. Robin Hood, Cinderella, Bette Davis, etc, they're all there along with a million inferences about the humdrum of seedy human life, usually set at midnight and beyond, while daytime insurance men check that no one escapes to Desolation Row.'

Then again, the poet Philip Larkin once said he could not decide if the lyrics of 'Desolation Row' were 'mysterious' or simply 'half-baked'.

Even in the frenzied world of Chinese whispers that has perennially accompanied the pursuit of meaning in Dylan's symbolism through the years, the lyrics of 'Desolation Row' have been more stringently examined for clues than most.

Presumably due to its length and the heavy demands it makes on the singer, it is not a song Dylan has performed too often live, and on the occasions he has performed it, he has frequently omitted various verses. In Melbourne, on a tour of Australia in April 1992, he stumbled, apparently distressed, as he sang the lines 'Einstein disguised as Robin Hood / With his memories in a trunk / Passed this way an hour ago / With his friend, a jealous monk …' seemingly too overcome to complete the song. Reasons other than the intensity of his own lyrics would surely be attributed to this lapse were it not for the fact that playing in Sydney two weeks later the exact same thing happened the moment he hit the Einstein/Robin Hood reference, he again became upset and had to stop singing. The hardcore Dylan analysts have launched an urgent quest for the true identities of 'Einstein' and 'Robin Hood' ever since.

Back at Studio A, it was approaching 10 pm as the band dutifully attempted a complete take of 'Desolation Row'. With their eyes constantly turned to Dylan, they ploughed bravely through the song, each attempting to create their own individual wall of sound as an impassive Bob delivered his entrancing commentary on the gutters of life. Cautiously optimistic that they might actually have nailed it in one go, they eagerly gathered round to listen to the playback.

It was awful. Dylan's guitar was totally out of tune and the whole thing sounded a terrible mess. Almost as soon as they had started playing it had been obvious to those listening behind the mixing desk – including Bobby Neuwirth, Tony Glover and Al Grossman – that the only place this track would be heading was the garbage. But Bob Johnston cheerfully kept the tapes running and nobody dared say anything or stop Dylan in full flight, fearing his reaction.

When he heard it, Dylan was appalled. He had just wasted more than 11 minutes and a lot of emotional and physical energy recording a demanding track that a small child could have told him was woefully out of tune. 'Why didn't anyone stop me?' he grumbled. 'Don't worry Bob, you'll get it next time,' said Grossman. Everyone else looked at their shoes.

There was no more to be done in Studio A that day. It was late, it was a Friday night and Dylan's mood was too dark to contemplate any more serious creativity. The weekend loomed ahead and he was off to spend it writing the rest of the album....

Chapter 8

HOWLIN' AT THE MOON

'Now the rovin' gambler he was very bored /
He was tryin' to create a next world war …'
Bob Dylan, 'Highway 61 Revisited'

Dylan worked constantly on his songs during his 'free' weekend in Woodstock. He enjoyed an enduring affiliation with the area, which had a long-standing reputation as an art colony. Driving back to New York with Al Grossman after a gig in Syracuse a couple of years earlier, Dylan told Grossman about the artistic vibe of Woodstock and they had a detour to take a look. Grossman was instantly smitten. He saw a palatial house for sale, decided it was his perfect country retreat and within days had bought it. Grossman's love affair with Woodstock never wavered and it was to be his main home for the rest of his life.

Dylan also took up residence in Woodstock, renting a room above the Tinker St café for a while, where he wrote 'It Ain't Me Babe' and 'My Back Pages'. During his 1965 UK tour he visited John Lennon at his mansion in Berkshire and decided that he would like to buy somewhere similar, so he headed back to Woodstock and rented a cabin there with Sara Lownds, which is where he wrote 'Like A Rolling Stone'. Shortly after recording this track, he bought his own 31-room house in the area, in Byrdcliffe – part of an art colony that had been set up in 1903 and had become a haven for artists of all descriptions. He drew inspiration from the tranquillity of the surroundings with its artistic ambience and it was there he wrote most of the material that appeared on *Highway 61*.

Initially, he was very visible in the local community. John Herald, a member of bluegrass band the Greenbriar Boys, for whom Dylan had opened at Gerdes Folk City in 1961, had moved to Woodstock and recalls Dylan hanging out at the café in the days after recording 'Like A Rolling Stone', eager to play the acetate to anyone who wanted to listen.

In 1965 Woodstock was already attracting a lot of summer visitors but the small town still provided Dylan with the semblance of sanity he required to hone his songs before his return to Studio A. It would not stay that way for long, however. Dylan found that he could not write extensively in the same place twice ('I can't stand the smell of birth,' he explained) and his initially inspirational new home was to stymie his creativity after *Highway 61*.

Worse, the tranquillity that had attracted him to the area in the first place was quickly decimated, in part by his own celebrity. His presence in Woodstock – particularly after his marriage to Sara in November 1965 – indirectly triggered its new reputation as a hotpoint of counterculture, which resulted in an unwanted (especially by Dylan) wave of new visitors. Dylan was even forced to buy a gun and rifle as protection against the swarm of strangers beating a path to his door.

But for this weekend at least, Woodstock remained quiet as Dylan, Al Kooper and Tony Glover installed themselves in his new house, drinking, talking and trying out some of the ideas Dylan wanted to use on the rest of the album. It was a relaxed environment as Dylan wrote out chord charts and fitted the words that seem to be constantly tumbling out of him to existing tunes in his head.

Reinvigorated, Dylan was developing fully sketched ideas, going back to songs already started, committing fleeting thoughts and couplets to paper, polishing up songs he was readying to record, sitting at the piano for hours on end knocking them into shape. He was completely focused and thoroughly inspired. Nothing distracted Dylan in muse mode. He stayed up all night working and, suddenly finding himself in the middle of the richest, most creative strain of his life, he just kept at it until it was time to go back to the studio.

On Monday evening he bounced back into Studio A to greet Bob Johnston, Mike Bloomfield, Al Kooper, Paul Griffin, Bobby Gregg and Harvey Brooks, with the rest of the album in his pocket. And burning a hole in that pocket was Dylan's pride and joy, the song he felt defined the album so much it wound up as the title. 'Highway 61 Revisited' incorporated most of Dylan's favourite ingredients – it spoke of the road, of roots, history, literature, deceit and payback. And it defined – quite literally, given the path of the Highway itself – where he had come from. What it did not seem to know, amid the random vagaries of his characteristically disguised metaphors, was precisely where it was going.

It is impossible to listen to 'Highway 61 Revisited' without imagining Dylan was recalling his own spectacular musical journey and relating it to the Bible, to the blues icons, to the uncertain fate of America, to whatever popped into his head at the time he was painstakingly forming it into a colourful, dizzying, electrifying *tour de force* in the course of the weekend. Both escape route and gateway to hell, the Highway 61 he had known so well growing up represented many conflicting visions, both historic and futuristic, and the song reflected this confused sense of tangled wonder and mangled roots.

If the horrors of the lynching that shamed Duluth had triggered 'Desolation Row', then it is highly possible that his birthplace was still on his mind as he crouched over his guitar that same weekend, piecing together 'Highway 61 Revisited'.

'What I recall mostly about Duluth,' he writes in *Chronicles*, 'are the slate grey skies and the mysterious foghorns, violent storms that always seemed to be coming straight at you and merciless howling winds off the big black mysterious lake with treacherous ten-foot waves. People said that having to go out onto the deep water was like a death sentence. Most of Duluth was on a slant. Nothing is level there. The town is built on the

The house in Duluth, Minnesota, where Dylan spent his earliest years.

side of a steep hill and you're always either hiking up or down.'

But, in Dylan's lucid and vivid account of his childhood in Duluth, he also says: 'Mostly what I did growing up was bide my time. I always knew there was a bigger world out there.'

Part of that bigger world – indeed, in practical terms, the *key* to that bigger world – was Highway 61, with a dangerous stretch north of Duluth that was full of twists and turns, unprotected by any guard rail, and the cause of numerous deaths through the years. It was especially dangerous as it twisted around cliffs overlooking Lake Superior and it was not too unusual for cars to lose control in the ice and snow and plunge over a 100-foot ravine into the freezing waters. To the young Robert Zimmerman, Highway 61 represented his escape route out of Duluth, but it also carried with it a stirring sense of the unknown, full of mystery and hidden dangers.

As a scholar of the blues, Dylan was also well versed in the historical significance of Highway 61. He has said he often uses a form of 'meditation' to provoke new songs, blotting everything else out of his mind and sending an old folk or blues song spinning round his head until something new and original spills out of it. The song infiltrating his head that weekend was surely Mississippi Fred McDowell's '61 Highway'.

Dylan had been at Newport Folk Festival the previous year, when McDowell (who was born in Rossville, Tennessee, and was well into his thirties before he moved to Mississippi) had played the main stage to a rapturous reception. One of the songs he played was 'Milk Cow Blues' – which Dylan, as we have seen, transmogrified into 'From A Buick 6' – and another was '61 Highway' (subsequently included on *The Blues At Newport 1964 Part 1* album, released earlier in 1965).

Steeped in the rural traditions of the Deep South, Fred had thrilled the Newport audience with his intense voice, peerless bottleneck guitar and uncompromising Delta blues, creating a bridge between the modern sound and legends such as Charley Patton, Robert Johnson and Son House. A farm labourer for most of his life, McDowell had originally played his celebrated slide guitar with a pocket knife, though he refined this to a slide made out of a beef rib bone before settling on a glass slide held on his ring finger. Glass, he said, created a far clearer sound than anything else.

McDowell was one of several musicians playing authentic blues introduced to the wider world by Alan Lomax, who recorded him on one of his famous field research trips in Mississippi in 1959. Accompanied by the young English folk singer and banjo player Shirley Collins, Lomax was in Como recording the brothers Lonnie and Ed Young and ended up staying with them. They got on so well that Lonnie invited his neighbour round to play Lomax some of his songs. The neighbour, a 55-year-old man wearing blue dungarees after a hard day in the cotton fields, was Fred McDowell.

Shirley Collins now admits that she was enjoying the music of the Young brothers so much she was initially irked by McDowell's arrival. In her book *America Over The Water*, she wrote: 'I'm ashamed to say at first I resented the intrusion by a younger man into the atmosphere made by the old musicians with their ancient and fascinating sounds. I didn't want that spell broken.'

Those reservations were blown away the instant McDowell began playing. 'Fred started to play bottleneck guitar, a shimmering and metallic sound. His singing was quiet but strong and with a heart-stopping intensity. By the time he'd finished his first blues we knew we were in the presence of a great and extraordinary musician.'

The first song he sang for them was '61 Highway'. 'Lord, the 61 Highway is the only road I know / She runs from New York City right down by my baby's door / Now some folks say the Greyhound buses don't run / Just go to West Memphis, baby / Look down Highway 61 …'.

Alan Lomax wrote one word in his notebook – 'Perfect'.

Lomax and Collins subsequently spent four days staying with the Youngs in Como, recording the tracks that inflamed enough excitement to launch Fred McDowell on the path to a bona fide legendary status among the cognoscenti of the 1960s folk and blues revival. He went on to make many albums, play concerts all over the world and work with some of the young R&B bands he helped inspire, including The Rolling Stones. He died of a heart attack 13 years after his discovery by Alan Lomax and was reputedly buried in a silver lamé suit the Stones had given him.

Highway 61 was, in any case, a popular topic of song for blues artists from the 1920s onwards. 'Up The Country Blues' had been recorded by Sippie Wallace, with pianist Eddie Heyward in Chicago in 1923. Originally from Houston, she first started singing blues as a teenager in tent shows, in which temporary big tops were erected along the dusty back roads of the South to bring vaudeville acts – dancers, singers, acrobats, comedy skits, rhythm bands and animal acts – to poor black audiences. This was how the likes of Ma Rainey and her protégé Bessie Smith helped build their reputations through the early 1900s.

Beulah Thomas – nicknamed Sippie at school because the gaps in her teeth made her sip everything – met and sang with jazz greats including Joe 'King' Oliver, Clarence Williams and Louis Armstrong after moving to New Orleans, where she was billed as 'the Texan Nightingale'. Unusually, she also wrote much of her own material, including 'Up The

Country Blues', one of the first cuts she recorded after moving to Chicago with her brothers George and Hersal and her husband Matt Wallace.

All three men were destined to die young – Hersal from food poisoning, George in a street car accident, Matt from natural causes. For 40 years Sippie confined her singing to the Leland Baptist Church in Detroit but was rediscovered in the 1960s, recording with Victoria Spivey. She later collaborated with Bonnie Raitt on the *Sippie* album, nominated for a Grammy in 1983, by which time she was 85. She died three years later.

Other variants of 'Up The Country Blues' emerged in the wake of Sippie Wallace's version – among them one-armed Dixieland jazz trumpeter/singer Wingy Manone in 1927 – while the Highway 61 theme was taken up in recordings by other blues and jazz artists like the McCoy Brothers, Skip James, Jack Kelly's South Memphis Jug Band featuring blues fiddle player Will Batt, cigar-chomping blues pianist/singer Roosevelt Sykes and Delta blues slide guitarist and singer Big Joe Williams. Each of them romanticized Highway 61 either as a means of escape, the path to find a lost loved one or a route to retribution, finding favour among the blues cognoscenti and reinforcing Highway 61's appealing image as the blues highway.

In 1937 the great harmonica player, singer and leading light of the post-war Chicago blues scene, John Lee 'Sonny Boy' Williamson recorded his own version of 'Up The Country Blues', detailing a search along the length of Highway 61 for an absent lover. With his distinctively slurry voice, caused by a speech impediment, Williamson was essentially the man who turned the harmonica into a lead instrument in blues bands. While Dylan's own early harmonica playing was based more on the style of Sonny Terry, Dylan still had to thank Williamson for giving the harp that exposure in the first place. Indeed, Williamson became a revered icon among folk revivalists (his first record on Bluebird, 'Good Morning Schoolgirl', was subsequently covered by The Yardbirds and The Grateful Dead).

Williamson was killed, aged 34, in 1948, when he became involved in a robbery on Chicago's South Side while walking the couple of blocks home from a gig at the Plantation Club and died with a fractured skull after being hit with an axe.

Bizarrely, his name lived on in Aleck Rice Miller, another brilliant harmonica player, also originally from the Deep South, who claimed to be the original Sonny Boy Williamson, alleging that John Lee had appropriated the name from him. It was one of many doubtful stories told by the alternative Sonny Boy as he nurtured his own legend – he told interviewers he had been good friends with Robert Johnson, who had died in his arms. It worked, though. Rice Miller found great favour in the 1960s blues boom, particularly in Europe, where he worked with the young Eric Clapton and Jimmy Page. He also hosted the popular *King Biscuit Time* radio show and even jammed with Levon Helm & The Hawks, before they became The Band.

Rice Miller died in his sleep three weeks before Dylan recorded 'Like A Rolling Stone' but even then the myths grew around him, with unconfirmed rumours emerging that Dylan had been planning to use him on the *Highway 61 Revisited* sessions and take him on his next tour.

Robert Shelton, whose warm *New York Times* review of Dylan's support set to The Greenbriar Boys at Gerdes Folk City in September 1961 had effectively triggered the whole Dylan bandwagon, was in no doubt about the historical importance of Highway 61 on his music. 'A lot of great basic American culture came right up that highway and up that river and as a teenager Dylan travelled that way on radio,' he said in a BBC documentary. 'If you'd been born in a place like Duluth and if you were raised in a very parochial town like Hibbing, Minnesota, you had to start making your escape plans very early. Highway 61 became, I think, to him a symbol of freedom, a symbol of movement, a symbol of independence and a chance to get away from a life he didn't want in that town.'

Oh God said to Abraham, 'Kill me a son,'

Abe says, 'Man, you must be puttin' me on'

God say, 'No.' Abe say, 'What?'

God say, 'You can do what you want Abe, but

The next time you see me comin' you better run'
Well Abe says, 'Where do you want this killin' done?'
God says, 'Out on Highway 61.'

As baffling as it appeared on the surface, the opening verse of 'Highway 61 Revisited' also had deep resonances in Dylan's personal history: Dylan, whose family were part of a small Jewish community in Hibbing, was rewriting Genesis 22 from the Old Testament. In about 1800 BC, God brought Abraham from the ancient city of Ur to the new world of Canaan to found the Hebrew nation. He told Abraham he would lead a mighty race but, as a test of Abraham's faith, he gave him a task. Abraham had to sacrifice his own son, Isaac, on a mountain top.

> 'And it came to pass after these things that God did tempt Abraham. And he said now take thine only son, Isaac, who thou layest and get thee to the land of Moriah and offer him up there for a burnt offering upon one of the mountains which I will tell thee of.' (Genesis 22)

Abraham duly took Isaac to the top of Mount Moriah and, with imagery mirroring the death of Christ nearly two thousand years later, made him carry the wooden altar on which he intended to burn him as a sacrifice. When they reached the spot God had identified, Abraham bound his son to the altar and prepared to kill him. However, as he raised his knife to plunge it into Isaac, an angel appeared and told him to spare the boy and go home – he had passed the test.

The story's significance to Dylan – who, in his book *Chronicles*, describes a very remote relationship with a father who didn't understand him – becomes even more pronounced and loaded when you remember that Bob's father's name was Abraham Zimmerman.

'Growing up, the cultural and generational differences had been insurmountable,' wrote Dylan. 'Nothing but the sound of voices, colorless unnatural speech … when I left home, I was like Columbus going off into the desolate Atlantic.'

Substituting Moriah for Highway 61 and setting Abraham's test into the context of his own rock'n'roll soul and desire to escape can lead to some deep and perhaps harsh, circumstantial assumptions about Dylan's attitude to the Jewish faith. There was no rabbi in Hibbing and when it was time for his bar mitzvah, in 1954, an old rabbi with a white beard and black hat arrived on a bus from New York to meet Bob in an apartment above a café to prepare for the big day. In 1983 Dylan recorded 'Blind Willie McTell' – a song not released until eight years later on the *Bootleg Series Vol. 1–3* – which seemed to allude to a journey along Highway 61 as a metaphor for America's ills in the South, notably with the line 'This land is condemned all the way from New Orleans to Jerusalem.'

It has been widely assumed that, on leaving Hibbing, his adoption of Woody's mannerisms as a drifter from Oklahoma and a whole new identity as Bob Dylan was a deliberate rejection of Judaism. Greenwich Village contemporaries Barry Kornfield and Mark Spoelstra suggest as much in Bob Spitz's *Dylan: A Biography* and Dylan's own garbled, fantasy explanations of his background in his early days in New York avoid any reference to Judaism. 'I've never felt Jewish,' he told *Sing Out* magazine in 1968.

In a TV interview with Ed Bradley for CBS in 2005, Dylan made a wry observation on all the speculation about his religious motives. 'If the common perception of me out there in the public was that I was either a drunk or a sicko or a Zionist or a Buddhist or a Catholic or a Mormon – all of this was better than "Archbishop of Anarchy!".'

It may be overly simplistic, if tempting, to see 'Highway 61 Revisited' as Dylan's denouncement of his religious upbringing, but perhaps it would be fair to assume that, written in the middle of a radical reassessment of his musical ideology and with it an earth-shaking shift in the route he was taking, the song marks his own personal deal with the Devil at the crossroads. Just as it had been for a lot of the old blues acts who had preceded him taking the road north in search of employment and better days, Highway 61 is a metaphor for Dylan's own migration, real and imagined.

The rest of the song – assembling four different, random, but equally ugly scenarios and pitching them as part of the same journey – seems to mark Highway 61 more as road to hell than an escape to salvation, a metaphor that reflected Dylan's own childhood fears about the dangers of the highway and mirrored the experiences of the old blues guys who had sung about it through the years.

> Well Georgia Sam he had a bloody nose
> Welfare department they wouldn't give him no clothes
> He asked poor Howard where can I go?
> Howard said there's only one place I know
> Sam said tell me quick man I got to run
> Ol' Howard just pointed with his gun
> And said that way down on Highway 61.

Georgia Sam was a name once used as a pseudonym in a recording studio by Blind Willie McTell (his real name was McTier, McTear or McTell, depending on who you ask) and as we were to discover from Dylan's later song named in his honour, McTell was a particular hero to Bob – a blues singer who really told it how it was and exposed the iniquities of the Deep South and its roots in slavery, in addition to having a voice of rare beauty.

Introducing Willie McTell into the song neatly interlinks with other intriguing reference points on the album. McTell had a rough time growing up in Statesboro, Georgia, attending a school for the blind. But he became a master of the 12-string guitar – an instrument popular in Atlanta at the time – which he adopted because he could get more volume out of it when busking in the streets.

Among his first recordings, in 1928, was the song for which he will forever be remembered: 'Statesboro Blues', a part-autobiographical epic born of loss, despair and personal pain.

> My ma died and left me reckless
> My daddy died and left me wild wild wild
> No I'm not good looking, but I'm some sweet woman's
> angel child.

'Statesboro Blues' came to be regarded as one of the ultimate blues classics, later covered – albeit in abridged form – by a number of artists, most famously The Allman Brothers and Taj Mahal. Yet what was not immediately obvious was that Willie McTell himself had adapted 'Statesboro Blues' from Sippie Wallace's 1923 recording of 'Up The Country Blues', which later germinated into '61 Highway', completing the circle that that span round Dylan's head as he pieced together 'Highway 61 Revisited'. Dylan may not have consciously drawn on these reference points but he was a great believer in the importance of the subconscious in songwriting. He subscribed to Pete Seeger's notion that songwriters were merely 'links in the chain', and described his own songs as 'more confessional than professional' in an interview with Paul Zollo in 1991. 'It's nice to be able to put yourself in an environment where you can completely accept all the unconscious stuff that comes to you from your inner workings of your mind and block yourself off to where you can control it all, take it down,' he said.

Dylan's brutal song goes on to finger Highway 61 as the place you can sell anything:

> Mack the Finger said to Louie the King
> I got forty red white and blue shoe strings
> And a thousand telephones that don't ring
> Do you know where I can get rid of these thing
> And Louie the king said let me think for a minute son
> And he said yes I think it can easily be done
> Just take everything down to Highway 61.

It is an almost prophetic verse about the destiny of the consumer society, where everything must go and nothing remains that cannot be sold. Several generations before eBay and car-boot sales, Highway 61 was portrayed as the rubbish dump of the world, masquerading as a people's market populated by chancers and opportunists.

It doesn't tell us who Mack the Finger might be or, indeed, Louie the King. Some assume Mack is a corruption of Mack the Knife, given Dylan's fondness for and influence by the work of Bertolt Brecht and the seedy saga of *The Threepenny Opera,* in which Mack the Knife appears. Dylan confesses in *Chronicles* he had a particular penchant for the lyrical imagery in the song 'Pirate Jenny' from the opera. 'Each phrase comes at you from a 10-foot drop, scuttles across the road and then another one comes like a punch on the chin,' he writes. 'It's a nasty song, sung by an evil fiend and when she's done singing there's not a word to say.'

Yet the Mack the Knife theory makes little sense in the context of the verse and, far from being the kidnapper in *The Jungle Book* movie as some have ventured, the red, white and blue shoe strings suggest 'King Louie' makes more sense as a reference to one of the French kings. As he supported the rebels in the American War of Independence, Louis XVI is the likeliest candidate to have triggered Dylan's imagination – the last king before the French Revolution had a problematic sex life with his queen, Marie Antoinette, and met his bloody end in 1793 at the hands of Madame Guillotine.

There follows the most baffling verse of all, concerning 'the fifth daughter on the twelfth night' who 'told the first father that things weren't quite right.' It continues the riddle with 'Let me tell the second mother this has been done / But the second mother was with the seventh son / And they were both out on Highway 61.'

Some Dylan enthusiasts with rampant imaginations on fan websites have taken this to be a description of a rabidly incestuous family, but while intriguing, the clues are too thin to offer a logical explanation, though plenty have tried.

The final verse foists the last indignity on Highway 61 as gutter of the world.

> Now the rovin' gambler he was very bored
> He was tryin' to create a next world war
> He found a promoter who nearly fell off the floor
> He said I never engaged in this kind of thing before
> But yes I think it can be very easily done
> We'll just put some bleachers out in the sun
> And have it on Highway 61.

This has often been seen as a reference to the Vietnam War, but the bigger picture harps back to the Mack the Finger verse and the idea that everything has profit potential, even human misery. Vietnam was the first rock'n'roll war, where soldiers smoked pot and marched into battle with a rock soundtrack playing in their heads. Public opinion was swayed by the protest music of the young generation of singers such as Country Joe & The Fish, Buffy Sainte-Marie, Joan Baez, Tom Paxton, Phil Ochs, Bob Dylan et al and played a significant role in ending the war.

Battle footage and the music of the day intermingled to such a degree they seemed joined at the hip. Vietnam was in everybody's front rooms as its musical commentary played on the radios and record players and footage of death and destruction filled the TV screens. The bleak realities of an Asian war that few Americans understood were piped into people's homes ... and some of them expected to see John Wayne storming across the screen to save the day just to prove it was all for the cameras.

So Vietnam gave the first indication that future wars would be televised and Dylan's darkly logical conclusion was that if this was the case, then there would be somebody in a sharp suit waiting in the wings to sell tickets and make a buck. The killing would be financial as well as literal. Black humour, indeed.

The amalgamation of the extreme scenarios of doom, despair and degradation combine to paint Highway 61 as a cesspit where greed, immorality, deceit and evil vomit over one another, drowning in each other's rank, disgusting stench. It did not feel like it when Dylan sang the verses in, for him, a relatively jaunty style, but 'Highway 61 Revisited' was one of his most fraught and barren songs, completely devoid of hope or salvation.

This attitude of resigned defeat alienated his old supporters on the political left of the folk movement even more. For the likes of Pete Seeger and Joan Baez, the cause of their dismay was not so much whether Dylan played electric guitars or not as the fact that his old clarion calls to fight the good fight and name and shame the enemy had been replaced by a sign saying 'Abandon hope all ye who enter here'. Dylan himself more or less acknowledged as much in later interviews. 'I've conceded the fact that there is no understanding of anything,' he said, 'it's just winks of the eye and that is all I'm looking for now I guess … philosophy can't give me anything that I don't already have.'

Dylan came back down into New York from Woodstock to resume recording on Sunday 1 August in readiness to resume hostilities in the studio the following day. He was armed with enough material to complete the album and excited enough by it to deliver it in one big session.

More relaxed working at night, when his voice had warmed up, Dylan asked Johnston to call everyone together for an 8 pm start. While fresh, Dylan decided to get things rolling with a tentative try of 'Desolation Row'. Fizzing now, he was keen to unveil 'Highway 61'. The other musicians who'd assembled in the studio were similarly keen … Frank Owens, Al Kooper, Sam Lay, Mike Bloomfield, Bobby Gregg and Harvey Brooks were all there ready for action, while Bob Johnston and the tape engineers, Roy Halee and Larry Keys, set up the equipment for what they knew from Dylan's upbeat attitude would be a key recording session. Dylan grabbed something he saw lying around the studio and stuck it in his harmonica harness. Sam Lay later claimed the toy whistle was part of his artillery for the occasion. After a couple of run-throughs of 'Highway 61', Dylan suddenly blew the whistle as the band flew into the track, giving it a mock police-siren effect to kick things off and establish a powerfully inappropriate cavalier mood of knockabout fun. It was to be the song's bizarre identity card.

Still fine-tuning as he went along, recording the song probably came less easily to Dylan than writing it. In the event, they recorded 10 different takes of 'Highway 61 Revisited' over the next couple of hours before Dylan was content. As usual, Bob Johnston and the others did not know what was going on in Dylan's head through the process and he shared nothing. They did his bidding and looked to him for signs of approval or disgruntlement to discover whether they or he had got it right.

'Bob worked really spontaneously and fast and we didn't spend a lot

Dylan nails another one at Studio A during the Highway 61 sessions.   © Daniel Kramer

of time looking for the perfect notes, it just had to feel right,' said Harvey Brooks. 'The way we'd listen was "Yeah, that's okay, there's a couple things there that might not be right, but they felt good." If the take felt good we went on. There were no microscopes at that session. The only microscope was in Dylan's head, and from his point of view did the song come off? That's all he was concerned about.'

The final version of 'Highway 61' sounded like a devil-may-care party track driven along by a romping rhythm and charging keyboards, while Dylan sounded enthused and joyous. It had all the upbeat elements of a carnival song, a natural to coax his new audience off their seats and on to the dance floor, a feel-good boogie for the happy generation and it is only when you start to analyze it that you realize it is totally the opposite. But while the frivolous mood may have contradicted the complex bleakness of the song, Dylan – blowing on his toy police siren to the end – was clearly having fun with it.

On a roll now, Bob did not want to waste a second of whatever inspirational muse had gripped him and instantly started tinkering away at his next opus.

> When you're lost in the rain in Juarez
>
> And it's Eastertime too …

The next song was subsequently recorded in the studio log as 'Juarez', the border town in Mexico that featured in the typically alluring opening line, but by the end of the session Dylan had rechristened it with its mysterious proper title, 'Just Like Tom Thumb's Blues'. Tom Thumb merits no mention in the song, either as mythical diminutive hero of folklore, the 'General' of Barnum circus fame or as a bizarre metaphorical reference point, and the title appears to be one of Dylan's more deranged private jokes, especially given the slightly bizarre content of the song bearing the name.

> And your gravity fails
>
> And negativity don't pull you through …

It is hard to know if 'Just Like Tom Thumb's Blues' is comedy, burlesque, tragedy or all three. The swirling images emanating from a debauched visit across the border again suggest that a movie, book, drug trip or a lost weekend might have provided the inspiration for this one.

> Don't put on any airs
>
> When you're down on Rue Morgue Avenue ...

Just across the border from El Paso, Texas, Juarez is a large city in the state of Chihuahua, demonized in the American press as the 'city of death' because of its infamous reputation as a centre of drug trafficking, unregulated drinking dens, seedy brothels, suicides, disease, garish fleshpots, political corruption and homicide, with a history of unsolved serial murders for good measure.

> They got some hungry women there
>
> And they really make a mess outa you.

Juarez (or to use its proper name, Ciudad Juarez) features in Jack Kerouac's *On The Road* – a seminal book for Dylan – as the hero, Sal Paradise, crosses Texas en route from New Orleans to San Francisco, in the rain (but sadly not Eastertime).

'Straight ahead,' wrote Kerouac, 'lay the distant lights of El Paso and Juarez, sown in a tremendous valley so big that you could see several railroads puffing at the same time in every direction, as though it was the Valley of the World. We descended into it.'

There is no Rue Morgue Avenue in Juarez but an infamy of sorts surrounds the name on the back of the Edgar Allen Poe story 'The Murders In The Rue Morgue', a double murder mystery set in Paris and made into a film starring Bela Lugosi in 1932. It would not be the first or last time Dylan jumbled up his literary references. He did, however, acknowledge his love of Poe. 'I was into the hardcore poets,' he told Robert Hilburn. 'I read them the way some people read Stephen King. Poe's stuff knocked me out in more ways than I could name.'

> Now if you see Saint Annie
>
> Please tell her thanks a lot
>
> I cannot move
>
> My fingers are all in a knot ...

It is claimed by some that Dylan himself went on a binge in Juarez in 1964, which would obviously bring the inspiration for 'Tom Thumb' closer to home, but neither Dylan himself nor any of the other likely suspects of the time have ever publicly alluded to it and it remains an unsubstantiated assumption. He did go on a road trip from New York to San Francisco via New Orleans, purportedly with a jar of marijuana on the dashboard and the beginnings of 'Mr Tambourine Man' swimming round his head in 1964, retracing at least some of Kerouac's steps, but nobody has said anything about a detour through Juarez.

I don't have the strength

To get up and take another shot ...

The other unconfirmed consequence of this hypothetical visit was rumoured to have been the contraction of a nasty anti-social disease – possibly from a prostitute called (or at least represented by) Saint Annie.

And my best friend, my doctor

Won't even say what it is I've got.

He had used a very similar line at the outset of the *Highway 61* sessions recorded on one of the 'Like A Rolling Stone' warm-up songs, 'Sitting On A Barbed Wire Fence', at Studio A six weeks earlier, with the line 'The Arabian doctor comes in and gives me a shot but he wouldn't tell me what it is I'd got....' Well, a good line is a good line, why not recycle it?

Sweet Melinda

The peasants call her the goddess of gloom…

Dylan once elucidated – in his own typically cryptic, tongue-in-cheek fashion – on the genesis of 'Just Like Tom Thumb's Blues', introducing it at a concert in Melbourne, Australia, in 1966. 'This is about a painter down in Mexico City who travels from North Mexico up to Del Rio, Texas, all the time. His name is Tom Thumb and right now he's about 125 years old but he's still going. Everybody likes him a lot down there, he's got a lot of friends and this is when he was going through his blue period. He's made countless amounts of paintings you couldn't even begin to think of. This is his blue-period painting. I just dedicate this song to him.' Yeah, *right*, Bob.

She speaks good English

And she invites you up into her room …

Another possible influence is the nineteenth-century surrealist poet Rimbaud, whose 'Ma Bohème' includes the line: 'I tore my shirt, I threw away my tie, Dreamy Tom Thumb, I made up my rhymes as I ran.'

And you're so kind

And careful not to go to her too soon …

The innocent in a strange land and an even stranger scenario trying to bite off more than he can chew … before finding it biting him back very much harder.

And she takes your voice

And leaves you howling at the moon.

In 1951, Hank Williams had a hit with 'Howlin' At the Moon'. It was the song of a desperate, deranged man driven to extreme, self-destructive behaviour by the love of a good woman. Or maybe the love of something far more sinister – alcohol and hard drugs. Less than two years after he recorded 'Howlin' At The Moon', the infamously unreliable, irresponsible Williams died in the back of a Cadillac taking him to a New Year's Day gig in Canton, Ohio, a bottle of whiskey still in his hand. Such an iconic image of one of America's most influential music heroes would not have been lost on Bob Dylan.

Up on Housing Project Hill

It's either fortune or fame …

The Jack Kerouac link runs throughout 'Tom Thumb'. Housing Project Hill crops up in Kerouac's *Desolation Angels*, a work that was also an inspiration for 'Desolation Row', from which, as we have seen, the line 'in the perfect image of a priest' is taken.

You must pick up one or the other

Though neither of them are to be what they claim …

The cavalier road adventure suddenly starts to sound bruised and worn. In *On The Road*, Sal and the other protagonists stop whoring as reality sets in, illness strikes and they start to drift apart. Dylan mirrors their disillusion – and perhaps his own – in the comedown.

> If you're lookin' to get silly
>
> You better go back to from where you came …

In the control room listening intently as Dylan took the band through the song again and again were Al Grossman and Bobby Neuwirth, who may have afforded a smirk every time he heard the opening line. He always claimed it was he who coined the phrase 'When you're lost in the rain in Juarez and it's Eastertime too.' When the two musketeers later fell out, the 'Juarez' line and Neuwirth's perception of Dylan's ingratitude for his part in it was cited as one of the reasons.

> Because the cops don't need you
>
> And man they expect the same.

The musicians watched in wonder as the song evolved and took shape. Frank Owens had a starring role, playing delightful honky-tonk piano fills around Bloomfield's dramatic guitar riff, while Dylan told his multicoloured story of misadventure across the Mexican border in a studied, clearly enunciated voice, emphasizing the last words of each line with an exaggerated drawl.

> And picking up Angel who
>
> Just arrived here from the coast
>
> Who looked so fine at first
>
> But left looking just like a ghost.

They got it down in 16 takes, Dylan finishing in a flourish as the pay-off nail was hammered into the Juarez coffin – a long, loving harmonica solo, just like the old days, to see the last verse on its way.

> I started out on burgundy
>
> But soon hit the harder stuff …

The song's adventure, clearly, was taking a grimmer turn with a reference most took to be about drugs, but the finale seemed to goad the main man on to drag out the forlorn resignation of it all with some relish.

> When the game got rough
>
> But the joke was on me
>
> There was nobody even there to call my bluff …

The whores, the beer joints, the crooked cops, the used and abused, the comrades in arms ... all now abandoned to their fates and the book closes.

I'm going back to New York City

I do believe I've had enough.

It was 11 pm. They all needed a break.

Chapter 9

SOMETHING'S HAPPENING HERE

'There ought to be a law / Against you comin' around /
You should be made / To wear earphones …'
Bob Dylan, 'Ballad Of A Thin Man'

'It seemed I'd always been chasing after something, anything that moved – a car, a bird, a blowing leaf – anything that might lead me into some more lit place, some unknown land downriver. I had not even the vaguest notion of the broken world I was living in, what society could do with you.'

In *Chronicles* four decades later, Dylan confirmed he was an artist in constant need of the thrill of the chase. Mostly, he had no idea what he was chasing and he has protested until he is blue in the face that we should not draw too many inferences and conclusions from these songs of his. They were just words that happened to fit at the time and the important thing was the groove … the rhythms, melodies and moods that stuck them all together. Don't you dare call him spokesman for a generation or conscience of the disaffected youth. They were just songs and he was just a bloke who built them and sang them.

But since recording 'Like A Rolling Stone' his artistic imagination seemed to know no limits. Dylan had barely put his pen down or been separated from his typewriter in those heady weeks since dancing in delight around Al Grossman's apartment as he played the 'Like A Rolling Stone' acetate. The uproar at Newport had fanned the flames and, while the preceding years had seen him produce an extraordinary volume of quality material, the six months since 13 January – when he had started recording *Bringing It All Back Home* – had been the most productive and creative phase of his life.

It was midnight in New York and Dylan did not want to go home. By nature a night owl, he had decided his best work was done after dark and lost patience with the routine daylight-hours working that was the norm in Columbia studios. On a high after 'Just Like Tom Thumb's Blues', he was ready to roll with two more songs that he figured would complete the album. He was impatient to get on with it.

With Bob Johnston bowing to his every whim and his star at Columbia rising with every new chart placing notched up by 'Like A Rolling Stone', Dylan was now calling all the shots. His confidence in the studio had grown immeasurably even in the months since *Bringing It All Back Home*. Dylan now had an unshakeable faith in his new material and a steely belief in the new direction his music was taking. He did not know where it was taking him, but that was kind of the point.

The other musicians knew they had to hang around until Dylan was ready to go and then they had better be *really* ready. They realized from the first couple of *Highway 61* sessions that if somebody had a problem or was dissatisfied with his tone or something he had played and called a halt, then there was a good chance that Dylan would abandon the song completely and try something else. If he started something then he wanted it finished, and quickly. If not, move on. It was one of the trials of working with Dylan that Russ Savakus found so hard to suffer.

Yet there could be immense satisfaction, too, for the musicians who found that, despite his lack of communication, Dylan was always open to different ideas. Al Kooper discovered this when he risked Tom Wilson's wrath to play keyboards uninvited on 'Like A Rolling Stone', only to find that Dylan loved what he did and demanded it was turned up in the mix. On the other hand, Dylan later insisted Kooper's rumbling organ through 'Ballad Of A Thin Man' was buried low in the mix.

Mike Bloomfield's instinctively explosive guitar additions also found favour with Dylan, who was particularly enthused by his searing lead on 'Tombstone Blues'; it gave the track an almost demonic edge that Dylan had not originally envisioned. Dylan's songs were inspirational to those around him but he also enjoyed being inspired by the musicians that he worked with, and he took a lot of energy from Bloomfield's unpredictable volleys. He told Robert Shelton in an interview for the *New York Times* a month later that he saw 'Tombstone Blues' as a 'breakthrough' and that nothing like it had been done before. He certainly couldn't have done it without Mike Bloomfield.

Tonight, though, Dylan was so focused they all knew they had to stick with him come what may. They could hear how good these songs were, and even if he couldn't communicate his ideas and relied totally on their own judgement, they were by now getting the general drift of what he was after. The early evening session had been hard but satisfying and they were all on a high. Nobody grumbled about going back into Studio A at midnight and finishing the album – however long it took.

Enter Queen Jane.

Perhaps the warmest, most engaging and least prickly song on the album, 'Queen Jane Approximately' could be good cop to the bad cop of 'Like A Rolling Stone' and has inspired its own cult of speculation regarding who or what the song is actually about. In 'Like A Rolling Stone', the spoiled and fallen princess apparently deserves all she gets ... a barrage of triumphant sneers from Dylan's poison pen. In 'Queen Jane Approximately', she has not had that fall yet and Dylan is seemingly offering a safety blanket to give her a soft landing.

When – and it is decisively *when* and not *if* – it all goes horribly wrong, our hero will be there with the hand of friendship and no recriminations. You never quite trust Dylan to say exactly what he means – or indeed mean what he says – but, superficially at least, it seems a tender, sympathetic song that scarcely fits in with the tempestuousness of the lyrical assaults that dominate most of the album.

'When your mother sends back all your invitations ...' A family rift? A wedding cancellation? A personal calamity? 'And your father to your sister he explains / That you're tired of yourself and all of your creations ...'. It is someone clearly in torment, whatever the circumstances. 'Won't you come see me, Queen Jane?'

As the verses unfold, the message remains on track, the offer reaffirmed over and over without malice aforethought. Flower ladies whose roses lose their bouquet appear in a second verse that suddenly takes on a more desperate slant with the revelation that Queen Jane – whoever she may be – has children who resent her.

Then there are clowns who 'have died in battle or in vain' and, even more disturbingly, '... advisers heave their plastic / At your feet to convince you of your pain.' Are we talking shrinks? Clinical madness? Paranoid conspiracy theorists? And then 'Trying to prove that your conclusions should be more drastic ...'.

At this point, you really fear for Queen Jane and bitterly resent whoever it is doing whatever it is that they are doing to destroy her. And if we pursue the shrink/mental-illness line, it starts to sound like we should all seek her out and get her out of that environment right away. 'Trying to prove that your conclusions should be more drastic ...'. What does he mean? How drastic? Are there demons trying to convince Queen Jane that suicide is painless?

'Now when all the bandits that you turned your other cheek to...'. She sounds nice, Queen Jane. But naive. 'All lay down their bandanas and complain...'. Who are these bandits with bandanas? Are they opportunists? Exploiters? Hangers-on? 'And you want somebody you don't have to speak to ...'. The interesting word here is 'have'. To whom is Queen Jane forced to speak that is playing with her mind and driving her to the brink of suicide? Managers? The press? The business heads? The money men?

Won't you come see me, Queen Jane?
Go see him, Queen Jane. Go see Uncle Bob, he'll sort you out.

It's usually assumed Queen Jane is a metaphor (almost inevitably given the verse about her turning the other cheek to bandits) with Joan Baez in the frame as the most likely candidate. The similarity in the names is sufficient to be deemed conclusive proof by many people who love to unravel the puzzles Dylan poses. To them, Queen Jane and Saint Joan are one and the same. It somehow seems unlikely: Dylan is never usually this compassionate in his songs about Baez.

'Queen Jane is a man,' said Dylan, cryptically, when quizzed about it once, triggering a new trail of red herrings, most of them leading back to the conclusion that again he is addressing himself.

The real Queen Jane? The regal Joan Baez.

Rarely for a Dylan song, it has a literal meaning that holds up. Queen Jane was a real Queen of England, albeit a tragic one who survived only nine days on the throne (or 13, depending on whether her reign is dated from the day on which she was crowned or from the death of the previous king) and is now a cause célèbre in history.

The great-granddaughter of Henry VII, Lady Jane Grey was born in Leicestershire in the English Midlands in 1537, the eldest daughter of the Marquess of Dorset and Lady Frances Brandon. A devout Protestant, she grew up learning Latin, Greek and Hebrew, among other subjects, played harp, lute and cittern and was regarded as one of the most intelligent and best-educated people in the country.

She was fifth in line to be monarch and thus grew up with little expectation of ascending to the throne. But these were times of great religious tension as the English Protestants fought bitterly to keep Scottish Catholic hands off the monarchy. The mess left by Henry VIII's six marriages made succession anything but clear cut, with half the contenders deemed too sympathetic to Catholicism.

Henry VIII's son Edward VI (by his third wife Jane Seymour) came to the throne at the age of nine in 1547 with John Dudley, the Duke of Northumberland, heading the council that ruled and advised on behalf of the sickly child. As Edward's health deteriorated and he became terminally ill with tuberculosis, crisis loomed for the monarchy. In the event that his son Edward died childless, Henry VIII's nominated successor was Mary Tudor, his daughter with his first wife Catherine of Aragon.

Desperate to prevent Catholic-sympathizer Mary becoming queen, Northumberland secretly connived to convince Edward and the rest of the council to nominate Edward's cousin Jane to succeed him to the throne rather than his half-sister Mary. And, in a neat aside to strengthen his own hand, Northumberland also arranged for Jane to marry his own son, Guildford Dudley.

So, at the age of 16 – to her own surprise and dismay – Lady Jane Grey was not only pressured into marrying a man she barely knew and didn't like, she was declared Queen of England. In fear of her own life in this new set of circumstances Northumberland had orchestrated, Mary Tudor mobilized her own forces and, in an unexpected surge of public support, the country rallied behind her. It did not take long for Northumberland's masterplan to unravel in disastrous fashion for both Jane and Northumberland himself. Nine days after she had been reluctantly crowned, Queen Jane was marched to prison and Mary I was declared queen.

Fearful that the deposed teenage queen still posed a threat as long as she was imprisoned and could rally sympathizers to incite a rebellion, Mary decided Jane would have to go. The order came for both Lady Jane Grey and her new husband to be executed.

Most accounts say that when the fateful day came, Jane was perfectly calm. She read the 51st Psalm to the huge crowd that had gathered at Tower Hill and, believing she would be able to see her own dead body if she didn't cover her eyes, she then tied a handkerchief over her eyes and lay her head on the block. Before beheading her, the executioner knelt down beside her to ask forgiveness for what he was about to do.

Of course, Dylan's song might be about another Jane altogether and, in truth, it is more likely to refer to Jane Seymour, the mother of Edward VI. Seymour, Henry VIII's third wife, died 12 days after giving birth to Edward in 1537, a tragedy that caught the imagination of the nation to such an extent that dramatic and romanticized stories of the death-bed scene arose. These in turn inspired the folk song 'The Death Of Queen Jane' – annotated in the late nineteenth century by Francis Child as Child Ballad No. 170, though there are records of the ballad dating back to 1612 and it is thought to have evolved from 'The Lamentation Of Queen Jane'.

According to the ballad, the dying Jane Seymour pleads with the king to assent to an early version of a Caesarean section so that at least the baby may live. 'Oh royal King Henry do one thing for me / Rip open my two sides and save my baby.' Henry eventually agrees and Edward is saved while Jane perishes.

Historians are adamant that this is not what happened. Childbirth was a common form of death for women at the time and the fact that royal births were usually viewed by several members of the court to ensure the new baby was indeed of royal stock meant there were plenty around who refuted the rumour that Jane had died under the knife. But facts have never stood in the way of a good ballad and the song – and myth – gained common currency.

Dylan would have heard the song when hanging out on the London folk scene, and when he later hooked up with Joan Baez, one of the big ballads she sang was 'The Death Of Queen Jane', her voice squeezing every ounce of drama and heartbreak from the song, which she recorded in 1964. The persistent theory that Baez was Dylan's intended target is perhaps supported by this connection with the old ballad.

It is easy to see how the imagery of the folk song would have appealed to Dylan. The saintly Jane Seymour had already had to suffer the indignity and cruelty of being married to a bloated, ill-mannered king with antisocial habits; then had to sacrifice herself giving birth to his only son. Equally, if he had studied his English history, Lady Jane Grey was another victim whose downfall was caused by others using and abusing her, and her inability to overcome their greed and thirst for power.

Whoever the subject, Dylan's ploy of updating traditional songs and replanting them in a modern environment – like Guthrie and others before him – had surely been utilized brilliantly again to create 'Queen Jane Approximately'.

As midnight approached, Paul Griffin – who had been away working on another session – arrived to play the graveyard shift, replacing Frank Owens, who had sat at the piano earlier that evening. Griffin immediately made his mark with the jaunty piano intro that sets the laid-back mood of 'Queen Jane'. Al Kooper, emboldened by the praise being heaped on his accidental work on 'Like A Rolling Stone', added his by-now-familiar, and reassuring, organ runs behind Mike Bloomfield's unerringly insistent guitar and Bobby Gregg's light, sympathetic drumming (Sam Lay, like Owens, having departed earlier in the evening). They set an easy, rolling pace, allowing Dylan's out-of-tune strumming, leisurely harmonica and unthreatening vocals to stamp their own marks on a track of bruised, imperfect loveliness.

The lyrics were compassionate, the all-consuming mood of the track was mellow and the melody strikingly beautiful and by the time they had finished, the track sounded like a happy stroll in the park. In fact, it was nothing of the sort. 'Queen Jane Approximately' proved to be the most difficult recording of the day, as the musicians stumbled through it with a series of false starts and unforced errors. Dylan, almost impervious to the problems and tunnel-visioned about perfecting it in the quickest time possible, scarcely blinked and ploughed on with take after take as the band struggled. His disciplined energy communicated itself to the others, who remained upbeat and continued to take their cue from the main man.

Dylan was not concerned with the niceties and decided that seven takes was quite enough for any song about an English queen. He wanted to move briskly on, still determined to put the album to bed before they were through at Studio A that night. He duly unveiled another new song he had been fitfully working on over the past couple of weeks. The cult of 'Ballad Of A Thin Man' began almost from the moment Dylan played it in those early hours at Studio A.

In instant contrast to the upbeat, almost frivolous mood generated throughout the repeated attempts on 'Queen Jane Approximately', Dylan was suddenly icily forbidding as he produced 'Ballad Of A Thin Man', a song of cold, snarling hate, full of sinister undertones and unnerving imagery revolving around the mysterious, clearly loathed Mr Jones. The first time Dylan delivers the line 'Because something is happening here / But you don't know what it is …' you know something has really needled him. 'Do you, Mr Jones….' That silent-assassin sneer cuts you down with scorn and you know that whatever it is Mr Jones has done and whoever Mr Jones is, this time it's personal.

Countless listeners have tried to fathom out the true meaning of the song and the identity of Mr Jones, but Dylan surely lays his cards on the table in the opening line:

You walk into the room with your pencil in your hand …

Bob was not a fan of the press and famously terrorized interviewers, offering surreal, nonsensical answers to their banal questions. Indeed, exposing the stupidity of the press became a bit of a sport for Dylan at the time, throwing their inconsequential nonsense and earnest attempts to garner true meaning and relevance from his work right back in their faces with vicious wit and at times sheer cruelty.

'He just wanted to record a press reception so we could all hear how ridiculous and infantile all reporters are,' a Dylan acolyte told journalist Keith Altham when he enquired why Bob even bothered going through the whole charade.

Captured on film by D. A. Pennebaker for *Don't Look Back*, the unfortunate Laurie Henshaw attempted to interview Dylan for British pop mag *Disc Weekly* in London on 12 May 1965, with hilarious results (though Laurie may not have thought so at the time).

Henshaw: Let's talk about you. Your clothes, for instance. Are your tastes in clothes changing at all?

Bob: I like clothes. I don't have any particular interests at all. I like to wear drapes. Umbrellas, hats…

Henshaw: You're not going to tell me you carry an umbrella?

Bob: I most certainly do carry an umbrella. Where I come from everybody carries an umbrella. Have you ever been to South Dakota? Well, I come from South Dakota and in South Dakota people carry umbrellas.

Henshaw: What has been the greatest influence on your life?

Bob: You! Your paper happens to influence me a lot. I'm going to go out and write a song after I've seen you … I don't want to be interviewed by your paper, I don't need it and you don't need it either. You can build up your own star.

Henshaw: Why should we bother to interview you if we didn't think you were worth interviewing?

Bob: Because I'm news. That's why I don't blame you. You have a job to do. I know that. There's nothing personal here, but don't try to pick up too much, you know?'

Laurie: 'When did you start making records?

Bob: I started making records in 1947 – that was my first recording. A race record. I made it down South. Actually, the first record I made was in 1935. John Hammond came and recorded me. He discovered me sitting on a farm.

Laurie: What kind of people do you take an instant dislike to?

Bob: I take an instant dislike to people that shake a lot. An instant dislike – wham! Most of the time I throw them against a wall....

The legend of Dylan's sulking monosyllabic press conferences is one of his defining characteristics at the time: straight-faced he countered dumbness with numbness.

Q: How many people who major in the same musical vineyard in which you toil, how many are protest singers? That is, people who use their music and use the songs to protest the, uh, social state in which we live today, the matter of war, the matter of crime, or whatever it might be?

Bob: Um, how many?

Q: Yes, how many?

Bob: Erm, I think there's about, uh, 136.

Q: You say about 136? Or do you mean exactly 136?

Bob: It's either 136 or 142.

'Being expected to answer questions,' Bob confided later, 'it's enough to make anybody sick really.'

And, in an interview with Jenny De Yong in Sheffield in April 1965: 'Newspaper reporters, man, they're just hung-up writers, frustrated novelists. They don't hurt me none by putting fancy labels on me. They got all those preconceived ideas about me, so I just play up to them.'

'Ballad Of A Thin Man' seems undoubtedly to have been inspired by the idiocy of journalists and those bizarre press conferences that plagued him at the time. The second verse, in particular, is a brilliant puzzle of mind games that surely sums up his own feeling of being a ringmaster of fools.

> You raise up your head
> And you ask, 'Is this where it is?'
> And somebody points to you and says
> 'It's his'
> And you say, 'What's mine?'
> And somebody else says, 'Where what is?'
> And you say, 'Oh my God
> Am I here all alone?'

It is a funny exchange, summing up the zany pointlessness of an encounter with the massed ranks of the press. It sounds like harmless fun, until he hits that confrontational pay-off line again with steel in his voice, hatred in his heart and a knife in his hand.

> Because something is happening here
> But you don't know what it is
> Do you, Mister Jones?

In the early 1960s, before all the madness started in earnest, Dylan established contact with the veteran British journalist Max Jones, who wrote about jazz and blues for the British music weekly *Melody Maker*. Jones had interviewed Louis Armstrong, Billie Holiday, Count Basie, Duke Ellington, Peggy Lee and Ella Fitzgerald and was on friendly terms with many jazz legends. With his trademark black beret, slightly eccentric mannerisms and endless anecdotes, Jones was something of a legend when Dylan started corresponding with him, inquisitive about certain records and artists.

A 21-year-old Dylan visited Britain for the first time in November 1962, braving one of the worst winters in history to fight his way through snowdrifts to appear in a BBC television drama *The Madhouse On Castle Street*. The maverick director Philip Saville had spotted him playing in Greenwich Village and decided he would be perfect for the role of Lennie, the troubled, rebellious young singer who is the focal point of the play. The BBC flew Dylan to London, paid him £500 and put him up at the Mayfair Hotel.

But when he met the trained actors he was due to be working with, it became obvious that it was not going to work. Dylan just was not equipped to take on a play of this stature and a role of such magnitude, and even the bold Saville recognized that Dylan's acting would be disastrous for the production.

But instead of dumping Dylan completely, Saville – perhaps mindful of the already considerable financial outlay – enterprisingly split the role. The young British actor David Warner played the speaking parts, while Dylan slouched on a staircase and sang as and when the plot demanded. It worked too, sort of.

With time on his hands, it also proved to be Dylan's crucial entrée to the thriving British folk circuit, and he spent time hanging out with the likes of Martin Carthy and learnt a lot of traditional English songs. Once, in Carthy's apartment, it was so cold they chopped up an old piano for firewood.

Dylan also paid a visit to the *Melody Maker* building in Fleet Street to meet Max Jones. Arriving in the evening when most of the staff had gone home, he ambled into the building and bounded up the stairs towards the magazine's offices. A security guard spotted him, took one look at his wild, rampaging hair, beatnik clothes and vacant expression and took him to be a vagrant off the street. As the security guard grabbed him, an indignant Bob protested he was there to see his friend Max Jones, but he was catapulted out the front door before he could finish his explanation.

Some time later Max Jones and Bob Dylan did meet and Bob always seemed to have a soft spot for Jones. Playing at London's Earls Court in 1978, the only thing Dylan said during the whole concert was 'Is Max Jones here tonight?'

As it happened, Jones *was* there that night. Still the jazz correspondent for *Melody Maker*, he had been sent – under protest – by editor Ray Coleman to use his old influence and get an interview with His Bobness. It was the last thing Max wanted to do; he had no interest in Dylan's music. He had entertained a perfunctory interest in Dylan's early work due to his interest in the folk-blues tradition and the connection with Woody Guthrie, and maintained correspondence with Dylan during Bob's early years, but Jones was a jazz man at heart and cared little for Dylan's cryptic lyrics and his post-*Bringing It All Back Home* folk-rock direction.

Indeed, Max did not put Dylan on any pedestals, and if asked by the great man what he thought of his later work he would have no problem telling him *exactly* what he thought of it. It is perfectly possible Max dissed one of his records in a letter or damned it with faint praise and, as Phil Ochs would discover, Bob did not always take kindly to criticism from those he trusted. So there may have been the motive there for Bob to retaliate and Max certainly wasn't keen to renew acquaintances.

But by this time *Melody Maker* was in a circulation war with *NME*, and a Dylan interview was the one they all wanted. The editor had ordered Max to pull out all the stops, go to Earls Court and call in all his old favours to get an audience with Dylan. Fully aware of Bob's fondness for red wine, Max went backstage after the show clutching a bottle of the finest claret, was waved through the various cordons of security and ushered into Bob's presence.

'Max Jones!' said a genuinely delighted Dylan. 'Bob Dylan!' said a not-so-bothered Jones. As they went to shake hands the claret fell out of Max's hand and smashed all over Dylan's leg. He made his excuses and disappeared to clean himself up. Max sheepishly slunk away into the night. They never met again.

Yet aggrieved as he may have been, Dylan surely had too much respect for Jones to use him for target practice in 'Ballad Of A Thin Man' – didn't he? Prior to the notorious press conference shown in the *Don't Look Back* movie, when Bob savaged everyone within spitting distance, he pulled Max Jones aside and told him to stay out of the way of the cameras. The press mauling that followed was clearly premeditated and he did not want Jones caught in the crossfire.

It is *almost* inconceivable that Max was the intended target of the song and if he was, he certainly was not aware of it. Yet, perhaps miffed by Max's lack of enthusiasm for his music after initially being so encouraging and supportive when he was starting out, Dylan may have adopted the name 'Jones' as a generic reference for the press reporters who padded after him like puppy dogs without any real understanding of Dylan, his music or the culture that had spawned him.

If there was a specific Mr Jones that Dylan had in mind when he wrote 'Ballad Of A Thin Man', then it could also have been Jeffrey Jones, a young New York reporter on *Newsweek*, who plagued Dylan for an interview during the 1965 Newport Festival weekend.

In a piece for *Rolling Stone* magazine, Jeffrey Jones later 'outed' himself as the likely Jones in Dylan's sights, saying he did speak briefly to Dylan in his trailer in the aftermath of the Newport storm. He freely admitted that, as a young reporter who was green round the ears, his line of questioning was particularly infantile and that he probably deserved the ridicule meted out to him in the song and, apparently, on the few other occasions they met in person. Then again, never trust a man who volunteers himself as the victim of someone else's ridicule.

It is unusual for Dylan to be so literal, though, and as the song meanders on, weaving its unsmiling web of accusation and surreal scenarios, its point becomes less clear. Another verse involves a one-eyed midget shouting the word 'NOW', unleashing another surreal train of thought.

> And you say, 'For what reason?'
> And he says, 'How?'
> And you say, 'What does this mean?'
> And he screams back, 'You're a cow
> Give me some milk
> Or else go home ...'

Another verse concerns a kneeling sword swallower wearing high heels, who enquires how it feels and then says: 'Here is your throat back / Thanks for the loan'. This still inspires excited messages in Dylan chat rooms from gays insisting that Bobby was writing about a homosexual blow job. And in the context of a straight (in every sense) being completely out of kilter in a changing culture, he may well have done.

> And says, 'How does it feel
> To be such a freak?'
> And you say 'Impossible'
> as he hands you a bone ...'

This verse about geeks and freaks is perhaps the cleverest of all, twisting the accepted norm on its head so the 'straight' man (in whichever sense of the word you choose to interpret it) finds himself in alien territory where his whole sense of convention is overturned and he finds himself disorientated. He could be the office worker in a suit and tie at a party full of transvestites, or the respectable disapproving stockbroker in the midst of a gaggle of long-haired bikers. Or he could be the hapless journo trying to make sense of the new music with its strange characters, bewildering lyrics and loud backings.

The writer Robert Shelton described Mr Jones as one of Dylan's greatest archetypes. 'He's a Philistine, an observer who does not see, a person who does not reach for the right questions. He piously pays his social dues through self-serving tax deductions, pays to watch freak shows but doesn't like the entertainment, is superficially educated and well bred, but not very smart about the things that count.'

A teasing Dylan would also insist that Mr Jones was a real person, but without throwing too much light on his real identity. 'He's a pinboy. He also wears suspenders. He's a real person. You know him, but not by that name. I saw him come into the room one night and he looked like a camel. He proceeded to put his eyes in his pocket. I asked this guy who he was and he said, "That's Mr. Jones." Then I asked this cat, "Doesn't he do anything but put his eyes in his pocket?" And he told me, "He puts his nose on the ground." It's all there, it's a true story.'

On stage in 1986, he gave a more cogent account of the song. 'I wrote it in response to people who ask questions all the time ... I figure a person's life speaks for itself, right? So every once in a while you gotta do this kinda thing ... put somebody in their place. This is my response to something that happened over in England in '63 or '64.'

Sounds more Max Jones than Jeff Jones then....

The musicians in Studio A rattled through 'Ballad Of A Thin Man' with a haste that pleased Dylan and Bob Johnston no end. Dylan played rhythm piano in a melancholic grumpy fashion as Al Kooper hit the top keys on his organ, eerie howling notes soaring into the night. It is like a slow-motion blues, shuffling along with a satanic air simmering beneath the surface of the scenarios painted by Dylan's lyrics ... and it feels ready to explode at any moment.

There is a hint of a stumble as Dylan starts to play the first verse and he laughs as he sings 'You try so hard but you don't understand' – and its effect is spine-chilling. It is one of those supreme accidental moments that would instantly cause most artists to stop and start again. Most artists would not dream of compounding the error by leaving it on the finished album.

But Dylan is not most artists. He swaggered on and the suppressed tension in his voice and the measured restraint of the band has a cold and deadly conviction. It somehow makes 'Thin Man' so much more personal and the effect is spellbinding. Compared with most of the rest of the album, it is a sparse arrangement, as if the others are holding back, in awe, perhaps, of the suppressed rage lurking behind Dylan's words. And while months of board meetings and focus groups designed to sort out the best arrangement for the song would not have predicted it in a million years, it worked like a charm.

It was 2 am, but they recorded 'Ballad Of A Thin Man' in three takes, with a fourth added for good measure to provid 'drop-in' inserts at the editing stage. A bright-eyed Dylan could see the end of the album in sight. With his tail up, he wanted another crack at 'Desolation Row'. He had been sparring with it before and had attempted a couple of takes both on his own and with the band, but still had not worked out the best way of tackling it. It seemed like months ago now, but the first thing they had tried when they hit the studio earlier that day was 'Desolation Row'. Dylan was still clueless about the best way of approaching it, but he knew it was a special song and, despite the late hour, he was on a high. His philosophy was to wind up the band, let the tapes roll and trust that something brilliant would happen. He mobilized the band for a grandstand finish.

In typical Dylan fashion, there was no direction, no guidance, no indication whatsoever of what was in his mind. But, unlike most of the other new songs he had dropped on them, at least they had heard this one and had some idea of the best way to do it – or at least the best way to get through it without screwing up completely. So they let rip through one of the biggest songs Dylan had written.

© Daniel Kramer

Dylan in 1965 at his second home – Studio A.

Al Kooper played ghostly organ, Bloomfield tore it up on guitar, Bobby Gregg beat out the rhythm and Paul Griffin pounded the piano keys, while Harvey Brooks did his level best to hold it all together on bass. Dylan, at the peak of his creative strength, adrenalin surging through him, wailed away on the harmonica and sang his socks off.

After about an hour of solid playing in various permutations, they had five takes in the bag and felt they had tamed the monster memorably described by biographer Clinton Heylin as 'an 11-minute voyage through a Kafkaesque world of gypsies, hobos, thieves of fire and historical characters beyond their rightful time'.

It was gone 3 am now and Dylan allowed himself a small moment of satisfaction. This had possibly been the single most creative, productive, energized and inspired day in the whole of a career already bursting at the seams with brilliance and ingenuity. In seven intense hours, an almost superhumanly motivated Bob Dylan had driven Bob Johnston and the musicians to ever more resilient heights to get the job done. 'He can't help what he's doing,' said Bob Johnston. 'I mean, he's got the Holy Spirit about him – you can look at him and tell that.'

The band were never entirely sure of their expected roles in the project, or what fulfilling Dylan's artistic dream for the album would entail. But they fed off Dylan's own energy and drive, which was so concentrated and fierce that they would have played all night, if necessary, in order to deliver the required result. In three long, complex, arduous yet exhilarating sessions on 29–30 July and 2 August they had delivered 10 tracks. Add the barrier-crushing 'Like A Rolling Stone', recorded six weeks earlier, and that was ample material for a new album. Job done.

Johnston had an acetate made of rough mixes of the tracks – including 'Positively 4th Street' and the electric, full-band version of 'Desolation Row' – to give to Dylan at the end of the session. Including 'Like A Rolling Stone', the running time was almost an hour. Dylan might have won the day after making the big guns at Columbia choke on their lunches when he gave them a six-minutes-plus single to release, but an hour-long LP? Even Al Grossman would have a job bullying them into that one. Something had to give. Johnston presented Dylan with the acetate so he could decide which tracks to leave off.

There was still the small matter of a title and cover artwork, plus mixing and the other paraphernalia surrounding the last stages before the release of a new album, but to all intents and purposes, Dylan had completed his artistic end of the bargain. Diving off the shocking, thrilling, pulsating, liberating springboard of 'Like A Rolling Stone', he had produced strange, challenging, fulfilling new songs he knew would transport him irrevocably to somewhere very different.

This was new territory and he had no idea what the long-term ramifications would be, but that really was not the point. The dramatic three days at Studio A had been the rocket ship that took him a million miles from The Other Place that had put him in a strait-jacket, drained him of energy, creativity and self-respect and where the natives were getting distinctly unfriendly. At these recording sessions he called all the shots, broke all the rules, didn't give a damn about protocol or anything else and did exactly as he wished. And they represented the most frenzied, exhausting, thrilling artistic peaks of his life since he formed his first band, the Golden Chords, in Hibbing, Minnesota in 1955.

He knew it too. He had struck such a rich torrent of ideas and artistry that he did not quite know how to handle it or what he should do with it. He was desperate not to waste it. The only thing he worried about was failing to justify his own genius. But as he reflected on the work they had done over the last week with 'Highway 61 Revisited', 'It Takes A Lot To Laugh, It Takes A Train To Cry', 'Queen Jane Approximately', 'Tombstone Blues' et al, he felt good.

He was quietly relieved. He was not bothered about critics, about anybody at Columbia, about those who had booed at Newport, about Bobby Neuwirth or Al Grossman, or even about the reaction of his fans. Right then, the only person he wanted to satisfy with his new work was himself. And he thought he had done it.

Except, when he got that damn acetate home and listened to it, he realized that he hadn't....

Chapter 10

GETTING READY FOR THE FEAST

*'At midnight all the agents / And the superhuman crew / Come out
and round up everyone / That knows more than they do ...'*
Bob Dylan, 'Desolation Row'

L istening to the fruits of his labours over the next day left Dylan feeling
excited yet frustrated. He couldn't quite put his finger on it but the
album didn't feel quite finished.

'Desolation Row' had been a bone of contention for him since it first
began to take shape. They had had several cracks at it over the last few
days but somehow it still did not sound right. It was such a huge song, a
true epic even by Dylan's standards, that he instinctively felt it needed a
big sound to carry it. He had the band, he had the words, he had the desire
... yet quietly listening to it away from the madness of the studio, he was
dissatisfied by it.

Half the instruments were hopelessly out of tune, of course, but that
did not bother him – they were out of tune on most of the rest of the
album, too, and the songs still sounded fine. In fact, he was convinced that
any attempt to polish the sound and imbue it with technical perfection
would kill stone-dead the atmosphere he wanted to create. He liked the
roughness, the erratic, bar-band mood that resulted from his insistence
that the band played on instinct alone without rehearsals.

It went totally against the grain of most session musicians and the general working practices of Columbia Records or indeed the record industry at large. Virtually all aspects of the recording process at the time were controlled by the record companies, and they would select the producers, studio engineers, tape operators and session musicians – often quite randomly, wilfully ignoring likely suitability or sympathy with the artist.

But Dylan had a staunch ally in the man at the desk, Bob Johnston, and a formidable figure in his own corner, Al Grossman. Ostensibly Columbia's eyes, ears and mouth to ensure everything stayed on message and within the accepted financial, union, time and quality restrictions, Johnston was no company man. His first loyalty lay with the artist. He loathed the fact that recordings at Columbia and elsewhere were still largely in the hands of people with no feel, understanding or empathy with the individuality of the performer. Johnston allowed the artists he worked with the scope to achieve their full potential. Some might say he gave them enough rope to hang themselves, but Johnston did not see it this way.

If they had realized how indulgent he was allowing Dylan to be in Studio A at the time, Johnston's bosses at Columbia might very well have taken a different view and stepped in either to pull the plug or to install someone else. But the buccaneering sense of freedom and exploration encouraged by Johnston's acquiescence is an essential part of what ultimately made *Highway 61 Revisited* such a groundbreaking album. Johnston is sometimes ridiculed for his lack of creative involvement – Al Kooper described him as 'the kinda guy that just pats you on the back and says you're fantastic' – and there were those who scorned him as Dylan's willing lapdog, obediently concurring with whatever mad notion Dylan came up with next.

Dylan and Grossman had a fractious relationship with Columbia. Grossman had serious issues with John Hammond and the two had barely spoken since Grossman had tried to extricate Dylan from his contract, although Dylan maintained personal affection for Hammond and was forever grateful for his support in the early days.

And then there was Tom Wilson, mysteriously ejected from the project after 'Like A Rolling Stone', a producer who favoured a more hands-on approach. His ideas and eagerness to help Dylan explore the possibilities of setting his songs in a rock context certainly lit the fuse of the whole process, yet freed Dylan's own rampant imagination to such a degree that the singer came to resent such outside interference. And when all was said and done, Wilson was still Columbia's man. So was Johnston, supposedly, but you wouldn't know it. Dylan wanted to do it his own way. Johnston's key contribution was cheerfully allowing him to do just that.

The conventional recording practices of the day decreed that the producer would present the tapes to the record company, who would then make all the serious decisions about titles, artwork, mixing problems, running order, pre-release singles and the like. But in this case the acetate went direct to Dylan, who listened intently and felt strangely uncomfortable with some parts of it, particularly 'Desolation Row'. It is odd that on an album where the electric band was such a vital ingredient of the album and a symbol of all it stood for, Dylan did not think it worked on this particular track … and not just because they were playing out of tune.

Less than 36 hours later Dylan was back in the studio with Johnston. They had planned a day of mixing the album, but listening to the acetate had persuaded Dylan to take another crack at 'Desolation Row'. This was one occasion, he told Johnston the day before, on which he thought the blazing electric backing was detrimental to the song and he wanted to try it acoustic, maybe with just a double bass.

Johnston called Russ Savakus. The bass player had recovered from the trauma of the 'Tombstone Blues' experience, accepting that he just wasn't cut out to play electric bass guitar, at least not on something as wildly unpredictable and unstructured as Dylan sessions tended to be. Upright double bass, however, was an entirely different matter – he was adept on this instrument and had recently been playing it with popular married Canadian duo Ian & Sylvia – who had played at the 1963 Newport Folk Festival and had a big hit in Canada with 'Four Strong Winds' – and the great North Carolina folk and bluegrass singer/guitarist Doc Watson.

Whatever the problems with 'Tombstone Blues', Johnston knew Savakus's sensitive touch would make him the right man to play upright bass on an acoustic 'Desolation Row'. Savakus had been booked to play another session that day, but the persuasive producer explained that he just needed him to play a quick part that he could do in his sleep, and that would only take a few minutes.

Already wary of Dylan, Savakus agreed. However, when he arrived he was fretful, watching the time, worrying about being late for his next gig, keen to do whatever it was he had to do and get on his way. But Dylan was not in a hurry. And nobody told Savakus the track they wanted him to play was over 11 minutes long.

So, after Newport, after alienating the folkies, after firmly nailing his colours to the rock mast, after committing himself to a band sound, Dylan made a sudden U-turn and decided that his biggest song and the one earmarked to close the album would sound best acoustic. He had not suddenly lost his nerve and did not see this as a retro step or admission of defeat, but simply believed that the band sound muddied the song and that it would benefit from a stripped-down treatment. If nothing else, it would act as a balance to the rest of the album.

And then occurred one of those strange, happy coincidences on which tracks – and, indeed, albums – stand and fall.

Charlie McCoy was a friend of Bob Johnston's who happened to be visiting New York from Nashville. That was where Johnston had originally met him during Bob's days as a songwriter working up material for Elvis Presley movies. Johnston went to Nashville to record some demos and needed someone to put a band together to create a progressive country feel for the session. He was directed to Charlie McCoy, who he was already aware of as the harmonica player on the scores for some of Presley's films.

McCoy was already a familiar figure in Nashville, a popular musician in the two main studios in the town and his diary was full. If anyone needed a harmonica on their record, McCoy was the man they would call, though they also knew he was pretty special on the guitar and could turn his hand to bass.

Born in Oak Hill, West Virginia, in 1941, McCoy grew up in Miami where he learned to play harmonica and very quickly decided he wanted to spend the rest of his life playing music. In 1959, he moved to music city, Nashville, Tennessee, determined to make it happen.

It was not all plain sailing. The then 18-year-old McCoy found work for a harmonica player hard to come by in the capital of country music, where the local musicians were well entrenched and sessions were something of a closed shop to outsiders. Resilient, talented and committed, he met knock-back after knock-back, but refused to give up.

He did everything he could think of to keep his dream alive. He had singing lessons, he constantly practised the guitar, he enrolled in courses on musical theory, he played for free in bars, he knocked on the door of every music-industry person he could think of in his quest to carve out a niche that would justify staying in Nashville.

After two years of doors being slammed in his face and worrying where the next meal was coming from, Monument Records offered him $49 to play harmonica on a new Roy Orbison record, 'Candy Man'. Three hours later he emerged from the studio $49 richer, his first hit record under his belt and his career as a Nashville session man well and truly launched. His harp riff that opened the track was such a key element to one of the Big O's early hits that Nashville looked anew at the guy who had been bugging them so persistently. There were just two significant recording studios in Nashville – Owen Bradley and RCA – with a regular pool of musicians used to play on most of the records. But after 'Candy Man', McCoy suddenly found himself in big demand and the work flowed in.

Johnston and McCoy hit it off immediately when they got together in Nashville in 1964. In fact, Johnston and Nashville hit it off immediately. When McCoy put the band together to play on Johnston's Presley session demos, Johnston was struck by how much trouble they took for him – a stranger in town and as far as the musicians were concerned, a complete unknown. McCoy and the others paid great attention to detail and showed they really cared about the music, something that in Johnston's experience rarely happened in New York or LA, where the attitude was to get in, do the job, get your money and get out again as quickly as possible. Johnston's scorn for the New York industry underlined his support for Dylan's independent spirit. This in turn led him to keep the record company at arm's length ... and naturally endeared him to the Dylan camp.

Johnston was in Dylan's ear throughout the *Highway 61* sessions. He urged him to escape New York and fly with him to Nashville to record some tracks. Far from the narrow-minded, clichéd, traditional country conclave, he said, Nashville was a hotbed of imaginative, enthusiastic and committed young musicians who really cared about music, and would bring something different to the party and give Bob a new perspective. It would make a refreshing change from the cynicism of New York and would energize and inspire him. Dylan's Nashville experience lay further up the road, with *Blonde On Blonde*, but in the meantime a little bit of Nashville came to Dylan.

By chance, McCoy had arrived in New York to visit the World's Fair and called Johnston, who sorted him out with tickets for a Broadway show. When Dylan decided to go and do some more recording on 4 August, Johnston suggested McCoy should come to Studio A and collect the tickets there. An upbeat and friendly Dylan was delighted to meet McCoy and hear of his adventures in Nashville when he duly turned up at Studio A. It might have been preconceived and it was very likely Johnston's plan all along, but Dylan suddenly said to McCoy: 'Hey, why don't you play on this song?'

McCoy, who had no instruments with him – was momentarily nonplussed. 'What do you want me to play?' he asked. 'Oh just grab a guitar ...' said Dylan, waving at an acoustic in the corner as he started to pick out 'Desolation Row'. 'He never told me what to play, nothing like that,' says McCoy. 'But playing on a song I don't know is what I do every day. There were no suggestions about playing harmonica or anything else and apart from the bass player there wasn't anyone else around.'

He did not think too much about it at the time, and did not feel that there was anything especially unusual about the way Dylan was working. 'I've worked with many like him. I didn't think there was anything weird about it at all.'

He immediately liked the song, though. 'It was fine. An easy melody with great lyrics – the stuff country music is made of.' he says. He had already learned that humility was a vital requisite when you stepped into somebody else's session, and while he had never come across Dylan before, he genuinely liked him. 'When you're a session musician, the artist and the song is always the number one item,' he explains. 'You check your ego at the door and go in there and do what you can to make this record the best it can be.'

McCoy had been given no hint of what would await him when he turned up at Studio A, but, hey, if this charismatic guy with the shaggy hair, black jacket, shades and cigarette hanging out of his mouth wanted to hear him play, then play he would. They were similarly informal in Nashville. He was unfazed by Dylan's nonchalance and quietly listened to the studied lyrics, the rolling melody and the long, flowing structure and wondered how Grady Martin would play it.

Grady Martin was one of Charlie McCoy's all-time heroes. A supremely gifted guitar picker from Tennessee, Martin was one of the great legends of the Nashville session scene. 'He was like an interior decorator who could walk in, look at a bare room and visualize the result,' said McCoy.

The first big hit he played on was Johnny Horton's 'Honky Tonk Man' in 1956, and his most fêted moment came later that year, with the evocative Spanish guitar runs (played in one take on a borrowed guitar) that had a key role in turning Marty Robbins' 'El Paso' into a massive crossover success.

Martin's most innovative contribution – albeit accidental – came when he played on another Marty Robbins record, 'Don't Worry', in 1960. A technical malfunction as he was playing his guitar solo created a distorted fuzz effect, which was not only kept on the record, but achieved a landmark status in guitar folklore and influenced generations. The only musician to work with both Hank Williams and Elvis Presley, not to mention Patsy Cline and Woody Guthrie, Martin was in 1965 the king of the Nashville session scene.

Charlie McCoy worshipped the man and, unexpectedly finding himself in Columbia Records' Studio A in New York – with Bob Dylan thrusting an acoustic guitar into his hand as he introduced him to a long, involved song about heaven-knows-what – Charlie wondered how Grady Martin would play it.

The gorgeous, fluid flamenco runs that McCoy delicately played around Dylan's rather more primitive strum were pure Grady Martin, and proved perfect for the track. Dylan's voice softened in sympathy as McCoy's graceful guitar danced behind him, adding another dimension entirely to a song he'd previously only seen in aggressive mode. 'It was a poor imitation of Grady Martin,' McCoy modestly reflects decades later, but Dylan and Bob Johnston were grinning from ear to ear at the end of it.

The combination of Savakus on double bass, Dylan playing rhythm and McCoy's Grady Martin impression gave the song a relaxed and natural feel; the music seemed to warm up the further they went into the oblique scenarios of the song, almost imperceptibly gathering pace and intensity until Dylan delivered his pay-off lines: 'Right now I can't read too good, don't send me no more letters, no / Not unless you mail them from Desolation Row.' Dylan laughed at the end of it. His instincts about an acoustic version had surely been proved right. Johnston suggested they play it through again, McCoy varying the guitar frills around Dylan's ragged rhythm as he again unveiled the bizarre world of 'Desolation Row'.

McCoy looked quizzically at Dylan as they finished. 'Was that okay?' 'Yeah, great …' said Dylan offhandedly, going to listen to a playback. Charlie had assumed he was being auditioned for another track and did not know that Johnston had been recording it. But Russ Savakus departed immediately after they had finished the take and McCoy realized the 'audition' had been the real thing. Both Dylan and Johnston announced themselves happy with what they had on tape and indicated that Charlie's duties at the session were complete. He collected his tickets from Bob Johnston, shook hands and went off to see his Broadway show, barely giving another thought to what had just happened.

Dylan and Johnston stayed in the studio listening to the two takes, debating the pros and cons of each. In the end they decided on elements of both, splicing the two takes into one which they felt preserved the soulful melancholia of the song, while lacing it with steely menace.

Dylan also had issues with 'Tombstone Blues'. And in a moment he considered divine inspiration, he decided to hire The Chambers Brothers to sing back-up vocals to dub on to the track. As spaced out as he was after being up all night with Mike Bloomfield, Al Kooper and the others trying to knock songs into shape for their own set at Newport, Dylan had watched in awe on the Sunday morning as The Chambers Brothers raised the roof at the festival's gospel concert. Their soaring vocals, passionate harmonies, bluesy sensibility and intense conviction had thrilled the Newport audience, Dylan included.

The Chambers Brothers at Newport heading for the 'Tombstone Blues'.

Part of a poor sharecropping family from Lee County, Mississippi, George, Willie, Lester and Joe Chambers had developed a polished vocal harmony style borne of their childhood days singing in the Baptist church choir. They had disbanded as a singing group when George was drafted into the army in 1952, but re-emerged with a modernized approach in LA a couple of years later. George had learned to play bass, while Willie and Joe played guitars. Lester opted for the harmonica, persuading Sonny Terry to give him a lesson in return for cooking him a traditional Southern meal. Gradually they began to make their mark on the folk scene, playing smaller clubs in southern California.

Yet they were still unrecorded and relatively unknown when they arrived at Newport in 1965 and became one of the unexpected hits of the festival. Combining authenticity with real stage awareness, and a set that gained momentum as it went along, wielding real spiritual depth, they connected with everyone who saw them that weekend. They ended up with two tracks, 'I Got It' and 'Bottle Music', included on the Newport Folk *Festival 1965* album subsequently released by Vanguard.

As enraptured as everyone else, Dylan thought that their rich, charged-up harmonies would give a lift to any track they sang on. He talked to them at Newport and they said they would be happy to come along and sing on his new record. Listening to 'Tombstone Blues' now, he decided this was the track that needed them.

So they cheerily came along to Studio A, still flush with excitement from the reaction at Newport, happy that their careers seemed to be regenerating, delighted to be in the company of new friends, thrilled by the opportunity. Dylan played them the track and outlined what he wanted them to do. They sang their part quickly, without fuss … there was a natural empathy between them and they did not spend time prevaricating or working out harmonies. They just went in and did it – it was a philosophy that Dylan understood and respected.

And that was it. It did not take long and The Chambers Brothers went on their way to their own three-record deal with Paramount, a well-received debut LP, a strong live following and a move into R&B territory. They even added a white drummer, Brian Keenan, who gave them a rockier feel.

It brought them a hit single, 'Time Has Come Today', but they ultimately disappeared in a welter of writs and accusations of being ripped off by record companies. However, they always thought kindly of Dylan and the day that they sang on 'Tombstone Blues'. Lester Chambers later even named one of his sons Dylan.

But when *Highway 61* was released The Chambers Brothers were not on it. Dylan listened intently to the playbacks of 'Tombstone Blues' with The Chambers Brothers' vocals added to the track and still was not happy. He listened to Bloomfield's sinister guitar attacks, the scatter-gun drumming, the dirty, rumbling, dishevelled rhythms and his own belligerent vocals, and decided that The Chambers Brothers clouded the issue. Mike Bloomfield had become such an integral part of the sessions and his demonic playing on 'Tombstone Blues' was surely his finest moment on the album. Neither Dylan nor Johnston wanted to sacrifice it and The Chambers Brothers' version was reluctantly shelved.

The final mixing did not take long. At the time, stereo recordings were something of a novelty and of minority value, so the stereo and mono mixes were done separately by different (and uncredited) members of Columbia's studio staff; this created differences between the two formats in both length and sound quality.

Most stereo recordings were equalized at the mix-down stage of the production process for the purpose of cutting vinyl, but *Highway 61* was different. Unusually, the stereo version of the LP was cut from its own mix tapes, giving it a much fuller-bodied sound than was normal, and giving the songs more impact as a result. Quality had to paid for, however, and newspapers advertised the mono version of *Highway 61 Revisited* for retail at $3.78, with the stereo version at $4.66 (though some newspaper deals offered discounts and the *Syracuse Herald Journal* was offering the mono version for as little as $1.88).

Dylan and Johnston rehashed the running order from the rough acetate made for Dylan a few days earlier. Johnston's acetate started with 'Can You Please Crawl Out Your Window', followed by 'Sitting On A Barbed Wire Fence', 'Like A Rolling Stone', 'Ballad Of A Thin Man', 'Just Like Tom Thumb's Blues', 'Highway 61 Revisited', 'Positively 4th St', 'It Takes A Lot To Laugh, It Takes A Train To Cry', 'Tombstone Blues', 'Desolation Row', 'Queen Jane Approximately' and 'From A Buick 6'. (Johnston's original acetate was later bootlegged as *I Never Talked To Bruce Springsteen* on vinyl and later still on CD as *Highway 61 Revisited Again*).

Both Johnston and Dylan instinctively felt that 'Like A Rolling Stone' – the launchpad of the whole direction of the album – should be the opening track. 'Can You Please Crawl Out Your Window' was in any case quickly discounted. Dylan was dissatisfied with the track and resolved to go back to it at a later date. He later re-recorded it with Robbie Robertson and The Hawks when under pressure from Columbia to produce some fresh material to release as a follow-up to 'Positively 4th Street'; it came out as a single four months later. A rogue copy of the *Highway 61* recording did briefly slip out on a single, before being swiftly withdrawn and replaced by the later version.

Originally recorded for the *Bringing It All Back Home* album, 'Sitting On A Barbed Wire Fence' – which had helped start the ball rolling as the second track attempted at the 'Like A Rolling Stone' session – was also jettisoned on the grounds that it did not fit into the general context of the album and had been surpassed by the subsequent material they had recorded.

Dylan felt that 'Tombstone Blues' was key, especially as he listened again to Bloomfield's savage guitar blasts and decided it was the logical track to follow 'Like A Rolling Stone' on the album before easing into the more mellow 'It Takes A Lot To Laugh'. It was then a question of putting the rest of the tracks into a sequence that made sense in terms of musical balance. The frenetic 'From A Buick 6' was nominated to follow 'It Takes A Lot To Laugh' with Dylan and Johnston electing the controlled fury of 'Ballad Of A Thin Man' as a suitably dramatic climax to side one.

They decided to open the second side of the LP with the beguiling

'Queen Jane Approximately', breaking the listeners gently back into the album before hitting them with the full velocity of the disturbing 'Highway 61 Revisited'. Dylan was very keen that the album should end on the acoustic version of 'Desolation Row'. As the LP was opening with the brutal explosion of 'Like A Rolling Stone', he felt an acoustic conclusion, built around McCoy's quietly dancing guitar, gave the album perfect symmetry, notwithstanding the disturbing nature of some of the scenarios painted in the lyrics of the concluding track.

Not everyone agreed. Al Kooper thought an acoustic closing track jarred with the rest of the album, although his view may have been coloured by the fact that, deep into the early hours of the marathon session on 2 August when he and bass player Harvey Brooks were the only musicians left in the studio, he finally got to play electric guitar on yet another take of 'Desolation Row', and harboured hopes that this would make it on the album.

Dylan and Johnston had already decided 'Positively 4th Street' would not be on the LP. Ever since 'Like A Rolling Stone' had charted, Columbia was anxious to get a follow-up hit single ready as soon as possible to keep the bandwagon rolling and as soon as he heard it, John Hammond was convinced that 'Positively 4th Street' was the perfect track. It was cut from the same cloth of tempestuous anger and vitriol with the same rumbustious, cavalier style that had given 'Rolling Stone' so much impact, and Hammond felt that it had the potential to be an even bigger hit.

Dylan himself was ambivalent about singles. It was not something that came into the radar of folk, jazz or any other genre artists and it was a major shock to the mainstream when Dylan hit the UK Top Ten with 'The Times They Are A-Changin'' in April 1965. 'Subterranean Homesick Blues' made it to No. 9 in the UK the following month (it reached No. 39 in the US), but until 'Like A Rolling Stone' Dylan did not take much notice of the market potential of singles.

'I never wanted to make singles,' Dylan said in an interview three decades later. 'Folk singers made albums, they didn't make singles.' But getting 'Like A Rolling Stone' played on national radio had opened enough doors to make him change his mind.

After initially dragging its heels and displaying insulting ambivalence to 'Like A Rolling Stone', Columbia roused itself to get the album out quickly, in order to capitalize on the success of 'Like A Rolling Stone', the enduring controversy over Newport, the Dylan bandwagon that was gaining momentum all the time and the obvious fact that the album delivered to them was something very special indeed.

Dylan believed that 'Highway 61 Revisited' was one of the album's defining tracks and, considering the song's strong sense of personal history, travel and crossing new boundaries, he thought it logical to name the whole album after it. This was a whole lot better than the *Yet Another Side Of Bob Dylan* or *A Whole New Bob* options that Dylan feared Columbia might suggest. In his Dylan biography *No Direction Home*, Bob Shelton attests there were indeed murmurs of dissension from the suits at Columbia who still had to approve such things, because they just did not think the title made any sense. But, perhaps daunted by the prospect of an irate Grossman ranting at them if they went against Dylan's wishes, word eventually came back that Columbia was willing to go with Dylan's chosen title. He had also already chosen his cover shot several weeks earlier.

Brooklyn photographer Daniel Kramer had been a staunch Dylan fan since he first saw him, singing 'The Lonesome Death Of Hattie Carroll' on the Steve Allen TV show in 1964. He pestered Al Grossman for months to allow him a shoot with Dylan; Grossman finally relented and invited him to his house in Woodstock. Kramer and Bob hit it off immediately and it was this session that produced the famous shot of Dylan with Al Grossman's wife, Sally, in the background, which ended up on the front cover of *Bringing It All Back Home*.

Both Grossman and Dylan enjoyed the shoot so much that Kramer was invited into the inner sanctum. He went on tour and became Bob's official photographer, in deed if not in title. With a new album on the horizon, Grossman turned again to Kramer and asked him to come with ideas for a sleeve picture.

Kramer took Dylan to one of his favourite New York haunts – a café in East 18th that Dylan always referred to as O. Henry's; it was once the regular haunt of the writer O. Henry, who was reputed to have written one of his best-known works *The Gift Of The Magi* in one of the booths at the front. It was actually called Healy's Café (it later became Pete's Tavern) and Kramer had already photographed Dylan there several times. He took various shots of Dylan seated outside and they then wandered through the area around Union Square, finding other locations and trying out different ideas.

After a couple of hours, Kramer decided that Dylan's scruffy old clothes just wouldn't cut it on the cover of an album that Dylan insisted would signal a new beginning (even though he was then still to record it). So they went to a men's store around the corner and bought some new clothes.

Intending to take the clothes back once they had finished with them, they shot several more rolls of film in the multi-coloured shirt and smart trousers that still had the tags on. Exhausted after wandering around the city, but finally satisfied that they had got a suitable shot for the cover, they retreated to nearby Gramercy Park, where Dylan was staying in Grossman's apartment.

When they got there, Dylan produced his pride and joy, a new motorcycle T-shirt, and asked Kramer if he would take a shot of him wearing it. Kramer was not keen – they were all tired after a long day of shooting and as, far as he was concerned, the cover was done and dusted. But few people said no to Dylan when he had a bee in his bonnet, so he agreed.

Dylan sat on the steps and Kramer looked at him through the camera. The shot seemed bare, so he asked Bobby Neuwirth to stand behind him in his stripey shirt. It still seemed sterile, so Kramer dug into his bag and pulled out the Nikon SP that he had been using at the café, and gave it to Neuwirth to hold. He shot two frames, put the camera away and then went home to develop the pictures.

Kramer felt that he had at least half a dozen shots from the session that would make a good cover. They included one of the afterthought

© Daniel Kramer

Bob in his favourite T-shirt: the shot after Daniel Kramer's Highway 61 Revisited cover shot.

photographs of Dylan on Al Grossman's steps. There was something hypnotic about Dylan's slightly quizzical, slightly menacing stare at the camera that somehow symbolized the challenging mystery of the man's music. When Kramer showed Dylan his own personal shortlist, Bob instantly picked out the motorcycle T-shirt shot. From that point there was to be no further discussion about the cover image.

There now remained just one more task for Dylan to complete before signing off the new LP package to Columbia – writing the sleeve notes. Most artists of the day had a tame journalist, producer, record executive or fellow musician contribute some fluff about the album, but this was not

Dylan's way. He wrote his own sleeve notes in his own inimitable style.

Dylan had been plagued for months by *Tarantula*, a book that he had been commissioned to write and that had seemed like a good idea at the time, although he now regarded it as a recurring sore. It felt like a dark cloud hanging over him and a distraction from what he really wanted to be doing. He scribbled constantly, filling page after page with random inner thoughts and obscure observations, and these scattered thoughts had become a *de rigueur* element of his albums, reinforcing the image of songwriter as poet.

John Lennon's surreally comic *In His Own Write* had been published the year before, followed by the equally oddball *Spaniard In The Works*, and Dylan's own zany thoughts were eagerly awaited. But it was one thing to jot stuff down as it came into your head and quite another to concentrate it into a coherent book. For all his literary aspirations, Dylan was finding the book impossibly tough to write.

But, in his own mind at least, it was a style that fitted the sleeve notes for the new album:

> On the slow train time does not interfere & at the Arabian
> crossing waits White Heap, the man from the newspaper &
> behind him the hundred inevitables made of solid rock &
> stone – the Cream Judge & the Clown – the doll house
> where Savage Rose & Fixable live simply in their wild
> animal luxury ...

It continued in similar vein across the back of the album sleeve, introducing Vivaldi (and his green jacket), John Cohen, Quasimodo and Mozart into a story that made no sense at all, however deeply you analyzed it. There were, however, crumbs of clues as Dylan wrote: 'The songs on this specific record are not so much songs but rather exercises in tonal breath control ... the subject matter, tho meaningless as it is – has something to do with beautiful strangers ...'.

With the sleeve notes complete, all that remained was for Bob Johnston to wage and win an argument with Columbia over getting Tom

Wilson a sleeve credit for 'Like A Rolling Stone' and the album would be ready for lift-off.

On 30 August 1965, less than four weeks after Charlie McCoy found himself imitating Grady Martin on 'Desolation Row' and Russ Savakus had been worrying about making it to his other session, *Highway 61 Revisited* was released.

For those involved – and many who heard it – nothing would ever be quite the same again.

Chapter 11

I SHALL BE RELEASED

'And the only sound that's left / After the ambulances go /
Is Cinderella sweeping up / On Desolation Row ...'
Bob Dylan, 'Desolation Row'

On the day *Highway 61 Revisited* was released, 'Like A Rolling Stone' was still riding high in the US singles charts. But, initially kept off the top spot by The Beatles' 'Help!', it was now No. 3, behind Barry McGuire's 'Eve Of Destruction' and We Five's 'You Were On My Mind' (written by Sylvia Tyson of Canadian folk duo Ian & Sylvia; a subsequent cover version was a hit for Crispian St Peters in Britain).

As Dylan embraced rock music, the charts seemed to be turning folk. It must have rankled that, having been eased away from the No. 1 spot by such fans as The Beatles, his path to the top was now blocked by 'Eve Of Destruction', a bombastic anthem for the apocalypse written by a teenage P. F. Sloan in a contrived, almost cynical attempt to tap into the mood of the times and out-Dylan Dylan. Sloan wrote 'Eve Of Destruction' with The Byrds in mind, crafting it as a less obtuse statement than 'Mr Tambourine Man'. The Byrds turned it down, but producer, songwriter and music publisher Lou Adler passed it on instead to Barry McGuire, a friend of The Byrds, who had recently launched a solo career after leaving The New Christy Minstrels.

While Dylan was in the early stages of recording *Highway 61*, Barry

McGuire recorded his charged-up version of 'Eve Of Destruction' in one take at the end of a long recording session, his voice rough and raspy as he read the words from a crumpled piece of paper on a music stand. At one point McGuire bellowed 'Aaaaahhhh!', which everyone assumed reflected the gradual intensifying, as the lyrics got to him, of his angry frustration at the state of the world. In fact, the only thing it reflected was his frustration at losing his place.

McGuire planned to go back into the studio the following week to re-record his vocals properly, but by then record promoter Ernie Farrell had already taken the demo from Lou Adler's desk and arranged for it to be played on leading LA radio station KFWB. A single was rapidly mixed, pressed and shipped out, and before long was beating Dylan to the No. 1 spot and selling six million copies around the world, to a surreal backdrop of teenagers dancing wildly to its prophecies of impending doom and carnage. The promotion pictures had a grim-faced McGuire emerging from a fall-out shelter; these were indeed bizarre times when a song predicting the end of the world succeeded in becoming a joyous pop hit.

'Like A Rolling Stone' hit the top spot in the *Cashbox* chart, but only made No. 2 in *Billboard* and *Record World*. Not that this unduly bothered anyone in the Dylan camp. They knew what had been going down in Studio A and they knew there were plenty more powerful songs where 'Like A Rolling Stone' had come from. Al Grossman, Bob Johnston, Mike Bloomfield, Al Kooper and the rest were thrilled with the *Highway 61* sessions and, for once, Columbia, too, was excited by what it was hearing, sensing that it would soon be riding high on top of a remorseless wave that would turn Bob Dylan into an international superstar.

This assessment was not too wide of the mark, although things did not pan out exactly as Columbia might have anticipated. Columbia executives saw the commercial potential but not the lasting impact of the music on the album. In fact, Dylan's singles career went into rapid decline after 'Like A Rolling Stone'. 'Positively 4th Street' (backed with 'From A Buick 6') made the Top 10 in both the US (No. 7) and UK (No. 8) without achieving levels of radio play or mainstream attention remotely comparable to 'Like A Rolling Stone'. And the re-recorded 'Can You Please Crawl Out Your Window?' – released in America just before Christmas 1965 – stalled at No. 58 (No. 55 in *Record World*). 'Rainy Day Women #12 and 35' reached No. 2 on both sides of the Atlantic the following summer, but it was over three years before Dylan troubled the charts again with 'Lay Lady Lay', still his last Top 10 hit to date.

Immediately after recording 'Like A Rolling Stone', Dylan was telling anyone who would listen that it was the best thing he had ever done. It was a view he reiterated in his *Playboy* interview with Nat Hentoff the following February. '"Like A Rolling Stone" changed it all,' he said. 'I didn't care any more after that about writing books, poems or whatever. I mean, it was something that I myself could dig. It's very tiring having other people tell you how much they dig you if you yourself don't dig you. It's also very deadly entertainment-wise. Contrary to what some scary people think, I don't play with a band now for any kind of propaganda-type or commercial-type reasons. It's just that my songs are pictures and the band make the sound of the pictures.'

Similarly, at a press conference in San Francisco in December 1965 he made his pronouncement that *Highway 61 Revisited* was the best album he had ever made, or was ever likely to make. 'I'm never gonna make a record better than that one,' he said, 'it's just too good. There's a lot of stuff on there I would listen to ...'

It was an album created on a flood of adrenaline issuing from the absurd levels of inspiration and energy that enveloped Dylan as he wrote classic song after classic song within a matter of weeks. Apart from Mike Bloomfield, there was nothing considered about the choice of musicians on the album – some, like Al Kooper and Harvey Brooks, were relatively raw and new to the session scene; others, such as Paul Griffin and Bobby Gregg, were tried and trusted session players. But through the happy accident of convenience, opportunity and luck, this seemingly random selection of musicians combined to inspire Dylan and encourage the stretching of his vision and imagination, enabling *Highway 61 Revisited* to reach a whole new level of outrageous artistic genius.

Dylan knew how good the album was and how much it stimulated him and, with the arch-opportunist Grossman constantly in the background, he was still seduced by the long-enduring fantasy of fame beyond his wildest dreams – even if he had already had enough to know he loathed all that came with it. He might not have anticipated the phenomenal impact the album would have or see it as the innovative, crusading masterpiece it was, but he clearly recognized it as *his* masterpiece.

It was much later that he offered a more measured response to *Highway 61*. 'In retrospect it really wasn't any breakthrough,' he said in 2005's *No Direction Home*. 'Everything I had done up to that point had led up to writing a song like that ['Rolling Stone'] just effortlessly.'

Not that Bob hung around to admire his handiwork. In his quieter moments he might have rued the short Newport set as ill-advised and ill-prepared, but with a completed album under his belt and the whole concept rather more refined, he could not wait to play it on stage. Nor could Al Grossman, who was in the process of setting up a lucrative, but crippling, US tour to take Dylan through the rest of 1965 and, as it transpired, much of 1966, when he would also take on Europe and Australia. It would guarantee the destruction of a sizable number of brain cells and set Bob on the inexorable path to burnout.

Immediately after finishing the album, Dylan went into the Bob Carroll rehearsal studio in New York, one of his favourite haunts, to prepare for the first full live performance of his new sound. He was desperate to get the message across that there was a new Bob on the block, convinced that once the folk fans saw and heard him play this stuff properly with a hard, tight band, opposition would crumble and there would be no need to explain himself. There was no thought of retirement now.

Newport might have been a whim, a fantasy impulsively acted on that merely confused and angered people, but writing and recording the album had convinced Dylan that he was on to something that was startling even himself, and he didn't want to blow it. He invited the key musicians on the album to join him on stage to confront the masses properly.

Al Kooper was keen, of course, and Harvey Brooks instantly agreed to join the party on bass. Paul Griffin was booked out on a session, but Frank Owens, who had also played piano on *Highway 61* was available and readily agreed to join the band. However, the one contributor that Dylan really wanted with him to interpret *Highway 61* on stage made his excuses and declined the invitation.

Mike Bloomfield had his differences with Paul Butterfield but, partly on the back of their own appearances at Newport, the Butterfield band had the chance of making a high-profile album of their own on a major label, with Albert Grossman stepping in to smooth their path. Big things appeared to be happening for the Butterfield band and Bloomfield did not want to miss out. They had their own dates to play and their own albums to make and, still essentially hooked on playing blues, Bloomfield told Dylan that he was sorry he couldn't make the live dates but he was staying with Paul Butterfield.

First choice drummer Bobby Gregg's diary was already groaning under the weight of sessions that had him booked up for the rest of the year and he, too, regretfully told Bob he could not make the dates. So Bob began the search for replacements.

Dylan's friend John Hammond Jr had seen guitarist Robbie Robertson, drummer Levon Helm and keyboard player Garth Hudson in Canada backing Ronnie Hawkins. They were, said Hammond, 'an insanely good live band'. He invited them – and Mike Bloomfield – to play on his own foray into electric music, the 1965 album *So Many Roads*, stoking up classics by the likes of Muddy Waters, Willie Dixon and Bo Diddley. Bloomfield, humbled by Robertson's phenomenal lead-guitar playing, generally played piano at the sessions. Dylan had caught one of their rehearsals with Hammond earlier in the year and been impressed. The memory stuck with him and, looking for another guitarist to drive his sound in the absence of Mike Bloomfield, Dylan sought out Robertson. Al Grossman's secretary,

Mary Martin knew Robertson and put them in touch.

Robertson was born in Toronto. His mother was a Mohawk and Robbie was partly raised at the Six Nations 40 Indian Reservation in Ontario, learning guitar from relatives visiting the reservation when he was in his early teens. By the time he was 15 in 1958 he was playing in various bar bands around Toronto. He was writing songs, too, and came to the attention of Ronnie Hawkins, a rockabilly singer from Arkansas who had relocated to Canada and was big on the Ontario club circuit. Hawkins recorded a couple of Robertson's songs, 'Hey Boba Lu' and 'Someone Like You', on his *Mr Dynamo* LP in 1960 and invited Robbie to join his band, The Hawks, initially as bass player and then on lead guitar. Robertson and the other Hawks (Levon Helm, Rick Danko, Richard Manuel and Garth Hudson) stayed with Hawkins until 1964, regularly touring Canada and the US and joining package tours with the likes of Chuck Berry, Jackie Wilson and Carl Perkins.

With Robertson's fluid guitar style steadily evolving, The Hawks decided to cut loose from Ronnie Hawkins and decamped to New York, where they built a reputation as a band guaranteed to get any joint jumping. However, that was all most people saw in them and the three singles they released, one as The Canadian Squires and two as Levon & The Hawks, all flopped.

The Hawks seemed to be going nowhere fast when Dylan called Robertson to ask if he wanted to try out for the backing band he was putting together. Robertson readily agreed to join Dylan for a run-through at Bob Carroll's New York rehearsal room. Not that he knew too much about Dylan when he met him for the first rehearsal.

'I didn't know a lot about folk music,' Robertson told *Rolling Stone*. 'I wasn't up to speed with the difference he was making as a songwriter. I remember somebody playing "Oxford Town" from *The Freewheelin' Bob Dylan* album and thinking "There's something going on here." His voice seemed interesting. But it wasn't until we started playing together that I really understood it.

'There was a hardness, a toughness, in the way he approached his songs and the characters in them. That was a rebellion in a certain way against the purity of folk music. He wasn't pussyfooting around on "Like A Rolling Stone" or "Ballad Of A Thin Man". This was the rebel rebelling against the rebellion.'

Robertson was excited by Dylan's songs and the emotion and energy that he put into them, describing him as 'a great musical actor'. After years of playing in pokey clubs and bars, the idea of appearing in large concert halls was also appealing – it was not lost on him that he could play a couple of weeks' solid gigging with the Hawks and still not reach as many people as he would during one show with Dylan. Robertson immediately hit it off with Dylan and the initial rehearsals with Al Kooper, Harvey Brooks and Frank Owens went smoothly. Robbie was, however, deeply unimpressed by the drummer Dylan was auditioning for Bobby Gregg's spot and persuaded Dylan that he knew someone far better suited for the job. He called Levon Helm.

The son of a cotton farmer from Elaine, Arkansas, Levon Helm was raised on country music and listening to the Grand Ole Opry on the radio. He would tell interviewers later that seeing his first gig – Bill Monroe & his Bluegrass Boys – when he was six years old had 'tattooed' his brain. He was given his first guitar at the age of nine and hung out at the KFFF studios in Helena, watching Sonny Boy Williamson broadcast his radio show *King Biscuit Time*. In 1954 the 14-year-old Helm went to see Johnny Cash and Carl Perkins in concert in Helena and further down the bill was a young Elvis Presley playing rockabilly with Scotty Moore on guitar and Bill Black on stand-up bass. He saw Elvis again when he returned to Helena the following year, this time with a drummer, DJ Fontana, and Levon was hooked. Fontana and Jerry Lee Lewis's drummer Jimmy Van Eaton inspired him to turn to take up the drums and before long, still at high school, he was playing in his own rock band. In 1957 he was recruited by Ronnie Hawkins to join his backing band, The Hawks, on a tour of Canada.

He was still with The Hawks eight years later, when he took the call from Robbie Robertson asking if he wanted to join Bob Dylan's band. At this stage, Helm knew no more than Robertson about Dylan. 'I was into B. B. King and Muddy Waters and I still felt Ray Charles had the best band,' he said. But at their first meeting he was immediately impressed. 'I couldn't believe how many words this guy had in his music,' said an amazed Helm. 'It sounded a little like country music to me. I thought the songs were a little bit long, but that was alright with me.' And when Helm turned up at the rehearsal room and immediately slotted into the band seamlessly behind Dylan, Robertson, Kooper, Owens and Brooks, there was no more discussion about who should play drums with them.

On 28 August 1965, just a couple of days before the official release of *Highway 61 Revisited*, Dylan played a sold-out show at the open air Forest Hills Tennis Stadium in Queens, New York, for 15,000 people.

According to Helm the band were 'ragged' at rehearsals, although two weeks of rehearsals seemed an indulgence after the shambolic single night of preparation that had preceded the Newport show. There was nervous anticipation among the band as the gig approached – 'walking on the edge', as Helm put it. The shadow of Newport loomed large and, with *Highway 61* still to be released, the audience did not know quite what to expect at Forest Hills or even whether Dylan was planning to continue or abandon his electric experiment.

Ever the tease, Dylan kept people guessing. Talking to Robert Shelton in the *New York Times*, he said: 'I have no idea what I'll be doing. I'll have some electricity and a new song or couple or three or four new songs. Time goes by very fast up there on stage. I think of what not to do rather than what to do.' Posed with the question about a possible hostile reaction when he turned on the electricity, Dylan went off on one of his surreal diatribes: 'If they can't understand green clocks, wet chairs, purple lamps or hostile statues, they're missing something …'.

The local press did their bit to stir up interest in the gig, warning of the imminent influx into Forest Hills of 'the purists, the socially conscious, the thousands of young boys who grow their hair long and wear rag-tag clothes as a tribute to their spokesman.'

Well prepared for the flak this time, Dylan had decided to hold the band back and play a 45-minute solo acoustic set for the first half of the concert. This was partly as a sop to the old guard that he knew would be gunning for him and partly due to the lack of time there had been to organize a full set with the band. Bob wanted the musicians prepared enough to deliver sufficient songs to avoid the fiasco of the three tracks they had rustled together at Newport; they had worked hard getting it right, but there was still not enough material for a whole show.

It was cold and wet when they arrived at Forest Hills and Dylan was nervous and jumpy, complaining about the incessant demands on his time as he watched Al Grossman prowling around the back of the stage,

© Daniel Kramer

Bob and Al Kooper finalize the set list before blowing Forest Hills away in 1965.

barking orders as they prepared to soundcheck. The stage had been erected at one end of the tennis court facing the huge stadium and anybody still in doubt as to Dylan's intentions would have seen what was coming as soon as they saw the huge banks of speakers being set up. It was an intimidating scenario and Dylan's mood scarcely improved as the swirling wind played havoc, intensifying the problems of mixing the band's sound into any kind of coherent state. They spent a long time on the soundcheck – Dylan desperately wanted to get it right this time.

The rain had relented by the time the crowd arrived and a local DJ, Gary Stevens, came on stage to introduce the extrovert pop DJ and self-styled prince of hipspeak Murray the K to – disconcertingly – a volley of boos. It might have been pantomime but there was real tension in the air.

Dressed in a striped shirt and Cuban-heeled black boots, a solo Dylan eventually appeared, launching the show with 'She Belongs To Me' and dominating the stage. The crowd rose to him and cheered in a reaction that was a mixture of ecstasy and relief – it seemed to them as if the prodigal son was returning to the fold. Sounding in good shape, Dylan gave them no reason to doubt him. He played mostly material from *Bringing It All Back Home*, as well as 'To Ramona' from *Another Side Of Bob Dylan* and 'Desolation Row' from the new album – all played immaculately on acoustic guitar and harmonica, and all rapturously received. Just as at Newport, he ended with two songs from the acoustic side of *Bringing It All Back Home*, 'It's All Over Now, Baby Blue' and 'Mr Tambourine Man'.

During the interval, Dylan rather uncharacteristically addressed the band and warned them of the hostility that may greet them from some sections of the audience and the need to ignore them and get on with the show. They were here, he reminded them, to have fun and to hell with the consequences. 'There's gonna be some kind of circus out there – just ignore whatever happens and play the show,' he told Kooper. For his part Kooper – who had, after all, been on stage at Newport and knew exactly what Bob was getting at – offered a few choice phrases about those gearing up to boo the minute they turned on the electric instruments. Their fears were not misguided. 'There's a new swinging movement in the country and Bobby Baby is definitely what's happening, baby!' shrieked Murray the K in his trademark hysterical fashion and as soon as Dylan walked back on stage, accompanied by Al Kooper, Robbie Robertson, Levon Helm, Harvey Brooks and Frank Owens, the jeers started and the circus began.

As instructed, the musicians ignored the booing and blasted straight into 'Tombstone Blues', instantly hitting a groove that suggested those two weeks of rehearsals had not been wasted. But, determined to be outraged, the 'lemmings' (as Al Kooper described them) slipped easily into their divine roles as unforgiving protectorate of the acoustic strum and booed heartily. As the band came out of 'Tombstone Blues', parts of the crowd maintained a barrage of chanting: 'We Want Dylan, We Want Dylan!' and 'We want Ringo!'.

The band ploughed on into 'I Don't Believe You (She Acts Like We Never Have Met)' and 'From A Buick 6', but the protests did not subside, the rumble of dissatisfaction gathering in pace and resounding across the stadium at any break in the play. If Dylan was fazed he did not show it, leading from the front and barely uttering a word to the band or audience. Standing at the piano playing the opening bars to 'Ballad Of A Thin Man', he stared defiantly out at the audience. According to Al Kooper, Dylan repeated the opening chords over and over for five minutes, giving rise to an urban myth that is not supported by bootlegs of the concert. There is, though, an unmistakeable savagery in Dylan's delivery of the definitive line 'Something's happening here / But you don't know what it is / Do you, Mr Jones?'. There were signs he was winning them over and bootlegs evidence suggests the crowd sang along with the chorus of 'It Ain't Me, Babe' but it was a fierce night and a stern test of Dylan's resolve.

The critic Paul Nelson was there. An old friend of Dylan's from his short spell at the University of Minnesota, Nelson was such a staunch supporter of Bob's new rock persona that he quit his job as managing editor of *Sing Out!* following the fury that contributors to the magazine directed at Dylan after his defection from protest songs. At Forest Hills he made it his business to counter the negative reactions by cheering and clapping as loudly as he could. 'It *was* scary,' he said. 'People would come up to me and say, "Joan Baez would never sell out like that" and I'd say, "what does *she* have to sell out?". When Phil Ochs did the same thing at Carnegie Hall a decade later, people reacted the same way.'

The celebrated *Village Voice* columnist Jack Newfield was also there and reported that the mood grew increasingly ugly as the concert wore on, and the 'mods' v 'rockers' cultural rivalry, which had seen running battles in seaside towns in the UK over the previous year, spilled into America. In their trademark leather biker gear, the rockers identified with the macho image of Marlon Brando in *The Wild One* and rock'n'rollers such as Gene Vincent and Eddie Cochran, and they aligned themselves fully to the new rock Dylan. The mods, who prided themselves on their sharp clothes and sophistication, and chose scooters as their vehicle of choice over motorcycles, forcefully voiced their disapproval of Dylan's move away from folk music. There were scuffles between the rival factions and as Dylan played, fruit was hurled around the audience, some of it landing at the feet of the band. A few members of the audience attempted a stage invasion and one even made it on stage and took a swing at Al Kooper. The organist barely blinked. He brushed himself off, watched the guy being wrestled away by security and got his head down again to pick out the tune as the band played remorselessly on.

They ended – ebulliently – with 'Like A Rolling Stone' and marched off. There was still a torrent of booing but it was mixed with some roars of approval and calls for more. The band had worked up 'Baby Let Me Follow You Down' and 'Highway 61 Revisited' in readiness for an encore but Dylan was not quite bullish enough to attempt one. Instead he jumped into a car with photographer Daniel Kramer and sped straight back to Gramercy Park.

Yet, despite it all, Dylan was jubilant about the Forest Hills gig. He felt that the band had gelled well, while the new songs worked and the crowd's reaction merely gave him a huge adrenaline rush and cemented his belief that he had chosen the right path. Back at Al Grossman's apartment afterwards, he hugged Al Kooper in delight, happily describing the show as 'a real carnival'.

Not everyone else was similarly convinced. After years of playing bars in Canada, Arkansas and New York and being well used to charged situations and hostile audiences, Robbie Robertson and Levon Helm had thought that they had seen it all, but were alarmed and shell-shocked when they came offstage at Forest Hills, not quite comprehending why the show had caused such mayhem. 'Some of those folk purist crowds in the electrical portion of the show …' winced Levon Helm as the dust settled afterwards, '… we got all the booing and hissing and stuff.' He wondered what he had walked into – this sort of thing never happened to The Hawks. 'We'd never been booed in our lives before! After a while it wasn't a whole lot of fun. I figured maybe we should practise or something.'

They were confused, too, by the fact that Dylan seemed so delighted by it, but he was now playing the long game and told anyone who asked that he loved the booing. It inspired him. It convinced him he was getting it right. He wanted them to boo more, not less, he said. There was only scattered booing six days later when the same band flew to LA to do their next gig at the Hollywood Bowl, playing exactly the same set. Yet the circus had come to town in a startling fashion and Dylan was already feeling the strain. After the LA concert there wasn't room to swing a cat in his suite at the Hollywood Sunset Hotel, but he was besieged by a constant flux of well-wishers and hangers-on wanting a piece of him, or just to be close to him. Al Kooper recalled that Bob became so frustrated by the incessant demands suddenly being made of him he stuffed an egg sandwich into the mouthpiece of a phone to try and get rid of one unwanted caller. And when that did not work, he poured a glass of milk into the mouthpiece.

And then they hit the rest of America, promoting an album that was now starting to stop people in their tracks as its full majesty became apparent.

Initially, there was a surprisingly low-key press reaction to the release of *Highway 61 Revisited*; no trumpet fanfares or breast-beating announcements rang out of an LP destined to change the shape of music. The earth did not move, nor the world shudder on its axis. Reviews were sparse and not overly enthusiastic. Newspapers and magazines rarely reviewed left-field LPs in any sort of depth in any case (although California's *San Mateo Times* did describe the new work as 'Dylan at his brilliant best'). But in general terms, the new albums by Peter, Paul & Mary (*See What Tomorrow Brings*) and Joan Baez (*Farewell Angelina*) generated more interest and anticipation than *Highway 61 Revisited*.

The kid with the nasal whine, the funny cap and the unintelligible lyrics was howling a lot louder with some louder instruments behind him, that was all. As is the case with so many pioneering, perception-changing landmarks, *Highway 61 Revisited* was scarcely hailed as such at the time. Yes, the hardcore Newport folk crowd were still fuming and those in Dylan's immediate circle were thrilled and elevated, but few acclaimed the album as a classic, partly because so many of the songs seemed so impenetrable. But, as both Dylan and Al Grossman shrewdly recognized, boos were good for business, sparking a controversy that was generating headlines and indomitably turning Bob into the superstar that he had always craved to be. Except that now he viewed his celebrity with abject horror. The full appalling reality of his new status dawned on Dylan during the rugby scrum that followed back in his hotel suite after the Hollywood Bowl concert, but there was no stopping the monster now it had been unleashed. Grossman's schedule made sure of that. Everywhere Dylan went there was someone in his face either demanding to know what the hell he thought he was doing dumping on folk music, pleading to know the identity of Mr Jones or simply wanting to know him. Sometimes he did his best to answer seriously, mostly he mercilessly sent them up in a manner that had become familiar to his own elite circle of friends, talking in riddles and contradictions. He dutifully fulfilled the promotional round of interviews and press conferences set up for him, refusing to take any of them seriously.

'Nobody destroyed folk music,' he told the *LA Free Press*, 'Folk music is still here, it's always going to be here if you want to dig it. It's not that it's going in or out.' Again and again, he strenuously resisted all attempts to account for his influence and responsibility as a spokesman for a generation: 'All I can do is be me – whoever that is – for those people that I do play to and not come on with them, tell them something I'm not. I'm not going to tell them I'm a great cause fighter or the great lover or the great boy genius or whatever. Because I'm not, man. Why mislead them?'

In a rare outbreak of patient explanation, he seemed to take a shine to Margaret Steen of the *Toronto Star Weekly* as he attempted to put *Highway 61* into context during an interview in his suite at the swanky Inn On The Park. She wanted to know why he was not writing songs like 'With God On Our Side' anymore. Instead of the usual torrent of acidic irrelevance, he treated the question seriously.

> *It's a good song, I'm not putting it down; but this thing I wanted to say, I had to jam it into a very timed, rigid stylized pattern. But now ... well, for one thing the music, the rhyming and rhythm, what I call the* mathematics *of a song are more second-nature to me. I used to have to go after a song, seek it out. But now, instead of going to it I stay where I am and let everything disappear and the song rushes to me. Not just the music, but the words too.*
>
> *Those old songs I used to write, everyone is imitating them now. What I'm doing* now *you can't learn by studying, you can't copy it, someone else can't say he's writing a song "like that".*

She asked if he had been disillusioned by folk music and the ideals of protest song.

> *No, I'm not disillusioned. I'm just not illusioned, either. The civil rights and protest songs I wrote when nobody else was writing them. Now everyone is. But I've found out some things. The groups promoting these things, the* movement, *would try to get me involved with them, be their singing spokesman – and*

inside these groups, with all their president vice-president secretary stuff, it's politics, all politics. Inside their own pettiness they're as bad as the hate groups. I won't even have a fan club because it'd have to have a president, it'd be a group.

They think the more people you have behind something the more influence it has. Maybe so, but the more it gets watered down, too. I'm not a believer in doing things by numbers. I believe that the best things get done by individuals. Back when I used to play in the rock and roll bands I used to get in these hang-ups on the group, *the lowest common denominator. I knew I couldn't make it that way. So I discovered folk, and sang by myself.*

A measure of his confidence in the spurt of inspiration that had animated him throughout the recording of *Highway 61* is indicated by his aside to Steen that he had already had so many life experiences he could now spend the rest of his life writing songs in his room at the Inn On The Park and never dry up. The way things turned out he might not have been joking.

Having divested himself of the hated spokesman-for-a-generation tag, he now found another unwanted label being stuck on him – inventor of folk-rock. It was a phrase bandied around since The Byrds topped the charts with 'Mr Tambourine Man', and *Highway 61* was very quickly seen to define the term. From day one, Dylan loathed the description.

'It doesn't matter what kind of nasty names people invent for the music,' he said in a famous March 1966 *Playboy* interview with Nat Hentoff in which, it later transpired, Dylan had not only answered the questions, he had written most of them too.

It could be called arsenic music, or perhaps Phaedra music. I don't think such a word as folk-rock has anything to do with it. And folk music is a word I can't use. Folk music is a bunch of fat people. I have to think of all this as traditional music. Traditional music is based on hexagrams. It comes about from legends, Bibles, plagues, and it revolves around vegetables and death. There's nobody that's gonna kill traditional music. All these songs about roses growing out of people's brains and lovers who are really geese and swans that turn into angels – they're not going to die. It's all those paranoid people who think someone's going to come and take away their toilet paper – they're *going to die! Songs like 'Which Side Are You On?' And 'I Love You' 'Porgy' – they're not folk-music songs; they're political songs. They're already dead.*

I listen to the old ballads; but I wouldn't go to a party *and listen to the old ballads. I could give you descriptive detail of what they do to me, but some people would probably think my imagination had gone mad. It strikes me funny that people actually have the gall to think that I have some kind of fantastic imagination. It gets very lonesome. But anyway, traditional music is too unreal to die. It doesn't need to be protected. Nobody's going to hurt it. In that music is the only true, valid death you can feel today off a record player. But like anything else in great demand, people try to own it. It has to do with a purity thing. I think its meaninglessness is holy. Everybody knows that I'm not a folk singer.*

He was philosophical about the negative reactions to going on stage with an electric band and, while admitting for the first time that he had been 'stunned' by the reaction at Newport, said he had no regrets.

Either people understand or they pretend *to understand – or else they really* don't *understand. What you're speaking of here is doing wrong things for selfish reasons. I don't know the word for that, unless it's suicide. In any case it has nothing to do with my music.*

So why had he decided to go down the rock'n'roll route?

'Carelessness. I lost my one true love. I started drinking.… The first thing I know I'm in a card game, I wake up in a pool hall …'. There follows one of those bizarre, endless, entertaining yet nonsensical streams of consciousness anecdotes Bob had become an expert in reciting. Further pinned down on the folk-rock question by Joseph Haas in the *Chicago Daily News*, Dylan reared again against the term. 'It's not folk-rock, it's just instruments.... I call it the mathematical sound, sort of Indian music. I can't really explain it ...'.

Why had he given up on folk?

I've been on too many other streets to just do that. I couldn't go back and just do that. The real folk have never seen 42nd St, they've never ridden an airplane.

Many people, Haas told him, felt betrayed by him. 'That's their fault. It would be silly of me to say I'm sorry because I haven't really done anything. It's not really all that serious. I have a hunch the people who feel I betrayed them picked up on me a few years ago and weren't really back there with me at the beginning. Because I still see the people who were with me from the beginning once in a while and they know what I'm doing.'

You could almost hear Dylan shudder when anyone brought up 'protest song' in his presence. The word 'protest', I think was made up for people undergoing surgery,' he said in *Playboy*.

It's an amusement-park word. A normal person in his righteous mind would have to have the hiccups to pronounce honestly. The word 'message' strikes me as having a hernia-like sound. It's just like the word 'delicious'. Also the word 'marvellous'.... Message songs, as everybody knows, are a drag. It's only college newspaper editors and single girls under 14 that could possibly have time for them.

Anybody that's got a message is going to learn from experience that they can't put it in a song. I mean, it's just not going to come out the same message. After one or two of these unsuccessful attempts, one realizes the resultant message, which is not even the same message he thought up and began with, he's now got to stick by it, because, after all, a song leaves your mouth just as soon as it leaves your hands.

No, he said, he hadn't sold out. He wasn't betraying anyone, least of all himself.

> *I never did it for money. It happened, and I let it happen. There*
> *was no reason not to let it happen. I couldn't have written*
> *before what I write now, anyway…. My older songs, to say the*
> *least, were about nothing. The newer ones are about the same*
> *nothing – only as seen inside a bigger thing, perhaps called the*
> *nowhere. But this is all very constipated. I do know what my*
> *songs are about.*

So he had no guilt trip about Joan Baez going on peace marches and
getting draftees to burn their draft cards while he was cleaning up playing
rock'n'roll? Apparently not.

> *Burning draft cards isn't going to end any war. It's not even*
> *going to save any lives. If someone can feel more honest with*
> *himself by burning his draft card, then that's great; but if he's*
> *just going to feel more important because he does it, then that's*
> *a drag…. The only thing I can tell you about Joan Baez is that*
> *she's not Belle Starr.*

Dylan seemed to be bending over backwards trying not to be rude about
Baez, but he could not quite do it, invoking the name of Belle Starr, the
pernicious nineteenth-century bandit queen of the American frontier
(who had a cameo role in 'Tombstone Blues') in order to tease Baez's
'Saint Joan' image.

If Dylan's critics were trying to make him feel guilty, they clearly failed
and his exasperation was understandable. He was on his own journey,
nobody else's; the turn he had taken seemed completely natural to him and
he was genuinely at a loss to understand why others should feel so upset
about it. He was also exceptionally proud of *Highway 61 Revisited*. He
wanted people to understand it and appreciate it. That was why he had
undertaken two weeks' solid rehearsals with the band, trying to put together
a professional show that would show off the new music to its best advantage.
That rehearsal time may have been grossly inadequate by the standards of
many other artists, but for Dylan it represented serious commitment.

After this exciting creative journey, Dylan viewed questions about his abandoning folk music and deserting the protest cause as totally irrelevant. He had, after all, started out as a rock singer but had been diverted by folk. Nobody asked him then what the hell he was doing or challenged him to explain himself for making such a move – and he did not understand why they felt they could now.

Phil Ochs, for one, recognized what Dylan had achieved. One of Bob's staunchest admirers and supporters, even as the denizens of Greenwich Village tried to present them as topical songwriters who were deadly rivals, Ochs had long considered Dylan a genius, comparing him to William Shakespeare.

'Every album up to *Highway 61*, I had an increasing lot of secret fear, "Oh my God, what can he do next?"' he told Dylan biographer Anthony Scaduto. 'And then I put on *Highway 61* and I laughed and said it's so ridiculous. It's impossibly good. It just can't be that good. And I walked away and I didn't listen to it again right away because I thought this was too much. How can a human mind do this? The writing was so rich, I just couldn't believe it.' In an interview with *Broadside* magazine shortly after its release, Ochs described *Highway 61 Revisited* as the most important and revolutionary album ever made, comparing it to a painting. 'He's in his own world now,' said Ochs.

Not that his praise and friendship ultimately held much sway for Ochs. He had voiced none of the reservations or protestations of betrayal of the old folkies – on the contrary he believed Dylan had it in his armoury to become as big as Elvis and was keen for him to follow that route. It was, after all, exactly what Dylan himself had dreamed about all those years ago back home in Hibbing. And even as he deviated into folk music from his original rock roots he still kept half an eye on superstardom.

Subsequently, Ochs was appalled when Columbia decided to release 'Can You Please Crawl Out Your Window?' as a single. He did not like the song but, more importantly, he thought that it was too similar in nature to 'Like A Rolling Stone' and 'Positively 4th Street', and not commercial enough to take Dylan to where he thought he should be. His big mistake was telling Dylan as much. Ochs reacted in lukewarm fashion when Dylan played him the song for the first time, telling him it wouldn't be a hit, igniting an argument that continued as they got into a limo to take them to a club. There were a few more terse exchanges between them and, a few blocks later, an enraged Dylan ordered the car to stop and threw Ochs out, uttering the immortal phrase: 'You're not a folk singer, you're just a journalist.' They barely ever saw one another again.

Al Kooper and Harvey Brooks quit Dylan's band in September. Robbie Robertson and Levon Helm were keen to get the rest of The Hawks on board for the full tour and Kooper said he and Harvey Brooks simply jumped before they were pushed. 'I was gonna get kicked out anyway,' Kooper said in an interview with Peter Stone Brown in 1994. 'Levon and Robbie wanted to bring the rest of the guys in. Me and Harvey Brooks didn't have other guys to bring in. We were just partners.'

In the 2005 documentary *No Direction Home*, however, Kooper came up with a much more entertaining explanation for the decision to bale out. It was just two years since the assassination of Jack Kennedy and, mindful of the anger already inspired by Dylan on the three shows he had played with him so far, Al said he wanted out as soon as he saw Dallas was on the tour itinerary. 'If they didn't like the president,' laughed Kooper, 'what would they think of this guy?'.

Robertson and Helm duly got their way and persuaded Dylan to hire the rest of The Hawks – Richard Manuel on piano, Rick Danko on bass and Garth Hudson on organ – to replace Kooper and Brooks on the tour.

A month after coming out in the States, *Highway 61* was released in the UK to a generally enthusiastic response. 'Where the hell is *that*?' asked Norman Jopling in *Record Mirror* when discussing the location of *Highway 61*, later describing 'It Takes A Lot To Laugh' as 'plodding but hypnotic' and 'Tombstone Blues 'as 'mainly cynical, sometimes blasphemous' and musing on 'Queen Jane Approximately' as 'another interesting Dylan dolly'. Warning Dylan's old folk fans to steer well clear, Jopling concludes: 'It sounds pseudo to say this album is surrealist, but it is.'

Melody Maker writer Bob Dawbarn wrote an article condemning Dylan's new direction with a merciless assault on 'Like A Rolling Stone', savaging the 'horrific backing dominated by syrupy strings, amplified guitar and organ'. He also criticized Dylan's 'expressionless intoning' and a 'monotonous melody'. Dawbarn concluded his piece by urging fans to avoid Dylan's new work at all costs. 'He no doubt enjoys confounding the critics and upsetting the folk fans, who first bought his records, by going over to the electronic enemy. That is his privilege but it is also the record buyer's privilege to reject sub-standard Dylan.' A couple of weeks later, however, the same paper was full of praise for the album. 'Incomprehensible but an absolute knock-out!' enthused its anonymous reviewer. 'As usual a great LP and it caters for fans who like their Dylan quiet and for those who like him swinging.'

The one brave attempt to analyze any of the new material came from Allen Evans in *Music Echo*, who described *Highway 61* itself as 'a rocker about a man on the run', 'Ballad Of A Thin Man' as about 'the rudeness of men towards others' and, most interestingly, 'Desolation Row' as 'a descriptive piece about reincarnation'. Despite opening his review with 'Another set of message and story songs sung in that monotonous, tuneless way,' Evans concluded that it was: 'The type of LP you can play over and over – or not at all.'

The wrath of the old folkies had extended across the Atlantic, though, where – true to type – Ewan MacColl picked up the baton of indignation and pontificated loudly about Dylan's shortcomings. 'The folk boom has been artificially created and won't be over until big money has been made by the people who created it,' he predicted shrewdly to *Melody Maker*'s Karl Dallas. 'We're going to get lots and lots of copies of Dylan – people who have one foot in folk and one foot in pop. I think the folk boom will continue for at least another year.'

MacColl rejected the idea that Dylan, Tom Paxton, Malvina Reynolds or the other American songwriters who had emerged from Greenwich Village had done folk music any favours in the first place. 'What the pop-folk boom does is give people a false idea of what folk music is so that when they hear real folk music, they can't recognize it. They say 'where's the beat?'

'Dylan is for me the perfect symbol of the anti-artist in our society. He is against everything – the last resort of someone who doesn't really want to change the world. He doesn't say anything President Johnson could disagree with. He deals in generalizations – that's always safe. His poetry is punk. It's derivative and terribly old hat.'

But the beast was clearly up and running. Dylan's shift from spokesman of a generation to rock intelligentsia may – in his eyes at least – have been a slow train coming, but its effects were profound. Dylan's acceptance by the mainstream was aided by the artists who covered his songs, such as The Byrds, The Turtles, Sonny & Cher, while his path from prophet/poet to uncompromising, bestselling international superstar was eased by the likes of Manfred Mann – at one of his press conferences, Dylan cited the British band as his favoured cover artist after hearing their versions of 'With God On Our Side' and 'If You Gotta Go, Go Now'. The controversy helped, of course, along with Dylan's natural quirks of style, language and attitude – all contributing to his image of restless rebellion that helped sustain *Highway 61 Revisited* as a pioneering, landmark work. He already had the patronage of The Beatles, whose own work indisputably now took a turn for the more worldly as a direct result of his influence – and others tumbled over themselves to sing his praises and attempt a short-cut to the charts on the back of his songs.

Circumstances and timing contrived to establish *Highway 61* as the conduit of a challenging new era for Dylan personally, and rock music generally, but it wasn't merely happy coincidence – *Highway 61 Revisited* was and is a brilliant album. In the context of the time it was staggering. The album broke many templates and it put Dylan on an artistic high that enabled him to believe in what he was doing, no matter how many people booed. Everyone else involved was swept along by the emotional intensity and artistic urgency of Dylan's muse – experienced and novice musicians alike contributed their own sometimes panic-stricken wrath to the urgent swathes of sound and edgy human foibles that seemed to fly at the listener from the grooves of the LP.

Bob Johnston's laid-back, laissez-faire approach was a crucial factor as Dylan trampled through all the established rules of the jungle. No artists – at Columbia or elsewhere – had been allocated the artistic freedom to spend the company's money doing whatever instinct and whim dictated and Dylan was indulged like no other. The inordinate length of many of the songs, the unconventional mode of recording, the minimal rehearsals, the free-form, improvisational approach, the sessions creeping long into the night, the songs being written and rewritten in the studio, the lack of instructions to the studio musicians… all of these things went against the grain of how records were made at the time.

Nobody stopped to have a quiet word and tell Dylan this was not the way they did things – and *Highway 61* would certainly have been a lesser album if he had allowed himself to be diverted or had diluted the music in any way. This was one man's expression of freedom, borne of cutting loose his old musical chains and discovering himself through a brand new way of storytelling and personal exploration. Nobody in mainstream pop music had ever before committed to vinyl a song with lyrics as viciously hateful and disdainful as 'Like A Rolling Stone'. Nobody had ever constructed a scenario as colourfully rapacious and garishly repellent as 'Desolation Row'. Nobody had snarled and sneered and given anyone the finger with such potent contempt as in 'Ballad Of A Thin Man'. Nobody had ever stuck a movie script into a song in the way of 'Just Like Tom Thumb's Blues'. Nobody had ever introduced such a rich and bizarre mix of characters as those that haunted 'Tombstone Blues'. Nobody had written a modern blues that mixed musical metaphors in the way of 'It Takes A Lot To Laugh, It Takes A Train To Cry'. Nobody had created a compassionate cushion of organ, harmonica and guitar like 'Queen Jane Approximately'. Nobody had constructed a howling tangle like 'From A Buick 6'. Nobody had set a biblical quote into complex vignettes of life in the way of *Highway 61 Revisited*.

The LP broke the mould in so many different ways. The manner of Dylan's approach to the record and the reliance he put on musicians, who in some cases he barely knew, helped to create the irrepressible mood of freshness, spontaneity and urgency that gave the music such force. In this sense it was an album made on a wing and a prayer – but by the force of his own belief and unspoken will, Dylan swept the others along with him and they wholeheartedly partook of the dream without asking too many questions or thinking too deeply about it.

There were key roles and match-winning performances, obviously. Mike Bloomfield was Dylan's masterstroke, an inspirational guitarist steeped in the kind of music Bob himself had revered, but who was hot for the ride and who knew enough to cut loose when Dylan told him at that first run-though of 'Like A Rolling Stone', 'don't play none of that B. B. King shit.' Al Kooper's amateur-hour organ, which popped up randomly throughout the LP, sometimes forbidding, usually compassionate, softened the sound and gave the whole thing the sort of third dimension you would never ordinarily hear on rock records. Charlie McCoy's beautiful, evocative Spanish guitar offered a totally unexpected acoustic levity, enabling 'Desolation Row' to bring home *Highway 61 Revisited* in a radically more mellow fashion than the unmitigated aggression with which it had opened.

As such, listening to the album feels like a journey. Weird and wonderful characters populate the trip as bizarre scenes, colourful cameos, figures from literature, ghosts of the past, spectres of the future and thrilling, scary, seedy locations flash past the window. There are moments of familiarity and recognition and you know that somewhere deep down in its soul lies the blues. But it flickers and disappears as a new visage, with even more outlandish characters, confrontations and cinéma vérité, looms large in front of you, posing more questions without any of the answers. Only clues. Always clues.

Dylan created a whole new songwriting technique on *Highway 61*, one beyond the imagination of anyone involved within the milieu of popular music. Sure, his previous two albums had opened the path and, yes, there are strong roots in blues, country, folk, rock, poetry, literature and his own personal history. But the conflicting emotions in his life at that time combined to inspire an unparalleled burst of creativity. The songs on *Highway 61 Revisited* had gushed out of him in rapid succession just at a point when he had felt at his most battered and bruised. They came from a radical personal reassessment, stemming from boredom with his work up until that point – and disdain for those who passionately clung to his every word. His arrogance and barbed put-downs had become a regular sideshow among his inner circle, but his behaviour was laced with paranoia and resentment about the demands on his time. He was also exhausted from the touring, he was partying hard and he was taking a lot of drugs.

He had first used marijuana during his brief spell at college in Minneapolis and it had escalated since his arrival in Greenwich Village. Producer Paul Rothchild told Dylan biographer Bob Spitz that he introduced Dylan to LSD after a concert at the University of Massachusetts in Amherst in the spring of 1964; interviewed by Nat Hentoff the following year, Dylan acknowledged that drugs were playing a part in his songwriting. While he clearly stated: 'I wouldn't advise anybody to use drugs,' he nevertheless talked freely of their influence.

> *Drugs are medicine, but opium and hash and pot – those things aren't drugs, they just bend your mind a little. I think everybody's mind should be bent once in a while. Not by LSD, though. LSD is medicine – a different kind of medicine. It makes you aware of the universe, so to speak; you realize how foolish objects are. But LSD is not for groovy people; it's for mad, hateful people who want revenge.*

Dylan said on one of the few occasions he attempted to explain 'Like A Rolling Stone' that it was above all else a song about revenge.

But amid the whirl of drugs and clashing emotions – tiredness, boredom, irritation, anger and excess – something exploded inside of him; the great rock poet's words flared into our consciousness in a manner nobody had ever previously conceived in popular song. And it knocked our socks off. From The Beatles down, few who heard it were not impressed or influenced by it. It changed music and it changed the way of making music.

Folk music was never the same force again. For, as much as they recoiled in shock and horror at the irreverence and audacity of it all, most of those in the front line followed Dylan's lead. Peter, Paul & Mary, Phil Ochs and even Joan Baez went on to make electric albums, though it was never part of Dylan's agenda for others to follow suit. He told the Northumbrian singer Louis Killen – a one-time member of The Clancy Brothers – that he had never wanted to cause a musical revolution and his argument was not with those who had condemned his adoption of electric instruments, but with those who thought he was shining a light and copied him.

Dylan copyists sprang up everywhere. He had raised the bar to such a height that suddenly it was no longer enough to rhyme 'moon' with 'June' and rely on romance to populate your lyrics. Music suddenly had to have a purpose beyond mere entertainment and be played with conviction and intent. If Dylan's own intentions were shrouded in obtuse themes and acidic couplets that left his ultimate meanings vague and confused, then that was all part of his enigmatic attraction. The more baffling the sentiment and the more Dylan argued he had no message, the more people assumed he *did* have a message and that it was very profound indeed. It made him the most controversial, talked about and influential musician on the planet, and as much as he might have wanted it to, it wouldn't go away. *Highway 61 Revisited* rocketed Dylan into a whole new arena. Myths and legends grew around him at a frantic rate as his tour careered on, the music got louder and the audiences more hostile, driving him remorselessly to the infamous night at Manchester Free Trade Hall in 1966, during which an audience member called him 'Judas'.

There were too many drugs, too much adrenaline, too much adulation, too much hostility, too much of everything, with burnout and a motorcycle crash waiting around the next corner to bring it screeching to an ugly halt.

But, for now, it was the most incredible, thrilling, challenging, productive period in Bob Dylan's life and its ramifications were deep and enduring. It threw naivety and idealism out of the window, ushering in a more knowing, harsher new age where artistic control switched from the hands of record companies and producers to the artists who felt free to experiment and believed everything was fair game as they plundered fresh horizons. *Highway 61 Revisited* signalled the end of something and the beginning of something else – something that seemed far more important, realistic, honest and exciting. That was how it felt to Dylan – and to most people who heard the LP.

The album did not sell in shedloads. Four decades on, American sales were still under two million and the record's highest chart positions were No. 4 in the US and No. 3 in the UK. But the full might and importance of the album came to be acknowledged as LPs became CDs, groups became bands and magazines began to view rock as an enduring art form with its own history. In 1995, *Mojo* magazine named *Highway 61 Revisited* the fifth greatest album ever made. In 2003, *Rolling Stone* named it the fourth greatest of all time. 'Like A Rolling Stone' is regularly named the best single ever recorded. The album's legend spirals with almost every year that passes.

Caught up by the effects of the LP's dizzying whirlwind, Dylan never contemplated these sorts of consequences. Indeed, he would have been horrified if he had done. He just wanted to make a great album. Once that was accomplished, he took it on the road and the great magical mystery tour transformed into a runaway train, trundling on through a set of recurring images. A new town every night with the same nonsensical scenarios of inane questions from uncomprehending journalists, boos from the folk police when he got on stage and endless partying afterwards. Yet Dylan retained his own counsel and followed his heart, adhering to the principles he knew had been essential in creating an album that still thrilled him every time he thought about it.

He neglected to tell even close allies, but somewhere in the middle of it all he found time to marry Sara Lownds on 22 November 1965, and he kept writing. He could not stop writing. And before the year was over he was back in Columbia Studios to do some more recording and set the wheels in motion to take off to Nashville with Bob Johnston to record his next album, *Blonde On Blonde*.

But that's another story....

WHAT HAPPENED NEXT

Dylan went back into the studio in October 1965 with The Hawks, attempting to fulfil Columbia's request for fresh material for a follow-up single to 'Positively 4th Street'. Bob assumed that he would be able to recreate the magic conjured up during the six days recording *Highway 61 Revisited*, but with only fragments of new material prepared in advance the sessions were something of a damp squib. After two days in the studio (on 5 and 20 October), all they had to show for their efforts was the rehashed version of 'Can You Please Crawl Out Your Window?', which was subsequently released as a (not very successful) single.

The former spokesman for a generation poses for the cover of Blonde On Blonde.

Yet Dylan's purple patch continued after *Highway 61 Revisited*. He toured and wrote constantly and he was keen to record a new album as soon as possible. After a couple of sessions at Studio A in January 1966, Bob Johnston persuaded Dylan to travel to Nashville to record at least part of his next album, *Blonde On Blonde*. The double album – released in May 1966 – included classic songs such as 'Rainy Day Women #12 & 35', 'I Want You', 'Just Like A Woman', 'Sad Eyed Lady Of The Lowlands', 'Visions Of Johanna' and 'Leopard-Skin Pill-Box Hat'.

The tour that occupied Dylan and The Hawks for the end of 1965 and much of 1966 was fractious and momentous. An unhappy Levon Helm could not handle the constant audience abuse that the band endured on stage with Dylan and quit at the end of November 1965, to be replaced by Bobby Gregg. Gregg baled out after a few dates, too, and was replaced by Sandy Konikoff; in April 1966 Konikoff also left the tour, and Mickey Jones took over the drum stool.

The anger stoked up when Dylan swapped his acoustic guitar for an electric continued unabated as he toured Europe in 1966, climaxing with the famous concert at Manchester Free Trade Hall on 17 May 1966, when – amid a volley of slow handclaps and catcalls – a disgruntled fan in the audience watched as Dylan adjusted his harmonica after getting up from the piano at which he had sung 'Ballad Of A Thin Man' and loudly shouted 'Judas'. Dylan's cutting replies: 'I don't believe you' and 'You're a liar', followed by his commanding the band to launch into the loudest, angriest version of 'Like A Rolling Stone' they could muster, remains a classic keynote moment in rock history. The exchange can be heard on the 1998 release *Live 1966*, Vol. 4 in the 'official' *Bootleg Series*.

The identity of the mysterious heckler remained a mystery for over 30 years until a guy called Keith Butler, a second year student at Keele University in 1966 who subsequently emigrated to Canada, read an article about Dylan and confessed he was the 'Judas' man. Others subsequently also 'confessed' to the same thing, disputing Butler's claim – such is the web of intrigue surrounding Dylan mythology.

This crazy, frenetic, charged period of Dylan's life spiralled into excess as the tour thundered on through a sea of hostility, aggression and drugs. But the circus came to an abrupt halt on 29 July 1966, when Dylan broke some bones in his neck falling off his motorcycle. 'I survived,' said Dylan in a *Playboy* interview in 1978, 'but what I survived after that was even harder to survive than the motorcycle crash. That was just a physical crash, but sometimes in life there are things you cannot see that are harder to survive than something you can pin down.'

Many at the time predicted that this signalled the end of Dylan's career, and he has since said that he also did not expect to find the same level of success again. When he eventually did come back it was a very different Dylan, but his iconic status remained – and has done so ever since, through never-ending tours, dozens of albums and even some high-profile awards, something never accorded to *Highway 61 Revisited* during the early years of its existence. He has repeatedly reinvented himself, most recently by adopting a rhythmic, chordal style learned in the 1960s from the blues/jazz artist Lonnie Johnson, effectively restructuring his old favourites to appeal to a younger audience. Dylan continues to tour constantly and lives up to his own celebrity as a mercurial icon and one of the few true geniuses thrown up by rock music.

AL GROSSMAN

The pudgy Chicago motormouth who was Dylan's loud, aggressive and widely unliked manager adopted a ponytail and remained at the helm of Dylan's career until their relationship deteriorated. 'He was a Colonel Tom Parker figure,' commented Dylan in *No Direction Home* (2005), 'you could smell him coming.' His contract with Dylan was not renewed in 1970 and they went their separate ways. Grossman went on to found Bearsville Records, signing Todd Rundgren, Foghat, Paul Butterfield and Jesse Winchester, among others, and also owned a theatre, studios and a restaurant. He died on a Concorde flight from New York to London on 25 January 1986. He is buried behind the Bearsville Theatre in Woodstock, New York.

BOB JOHNSTON

The fabled producer remained on good terms with Dylan after the release of *Highway 61*, persuading him to break with tradition and move to the heartland of country music to record his next album, *Blonde On Blonde* (1966), in Nashville, Tennessee, an event that re-energized the Nashville recording scene. He subsequently became head of Columbia in Nashville and continued to work with Dylan on four more albums: *John Wesley Harding* (1968), *Nashville Skyline* (1969), *Self Portrait* and *New Morning* (both 1970), and built upon his *Highway 61 Revisited* success, producing three seminal albums for Simon & Garfunkel: *Sounds Of Silence* (1966), *Parsley, Sage, Rosemary & Thyme* (1966) and *Bookends* (1968).

Johnston went on to work with a number of other high-profile artists, producing hit albums for Johnny Cash (*At Folsom Prison* [1968], *At San Quentin* [1969], *Hello I'm Johnny Cash* [1970]) and Leonard Cohen (*Songs From A Room* [1969], *Songs Of Love And Hate* [1971] and *Live Songs* [1973]). He left Columbia to work independently and produced Lindisfarne's 1971 album *Fog On The Tyne*. Johnston then moved to Austin and took a back seat for a while, but returned in the 1990s to produce albums by Willie Nelson and Carl Perkins. He remains a revered figure throughout the music industry, especially in Nashville.

TOM WILSON

The Texan producer raised on jazz didn't look back after his sudden, unexplained ejection from Team Dylan after producing 'Like A Rolling Stone'. Using some of the techniques and ideas inspired by Dylan, he turned his attention to Simon & Garfunkel, overdubbing the electric arrangement that transformed 'The Sound Of Silence' from an overlooked album cut into a No. 1 single all over the world. In 1966 he switched from Columbia to Verve, signed the Mothers Of Invention and produced their debut album, *Freak Out!*, following this coup with a string of further triumphs, including The Velvet Underground, The Blues Project (which included Al Kooper) and Soft Machine. Open-minded and innovative, Wilson is acknowledged as one of the most influential producers of the 1960s. He died of a heart attack in Los Angeles in 1978 at the age of 47.

AL KOOPER

Although he quit Dylan's tour band in September 1965, the 'accidental' organist of 'Like A Rolling Stone', who became a key figure on *Highway 61 Revisited,* worked with Dylan again on *Blonde On Blonde* (1966), *Self Portrait* (1970) and *New Morning* (1970) (on which he also co-produced a couple of tracks), and later resumed the partnership on *Empire Burlesque* (1985), *Knocked Out Loaded* (1986) and *Under The Red Sky* (1990). He also joined Dylan on stage at the Prince's Trust Concert at London's Hyde Park in 1996.

After leaving Dylan's band in 1965 Kooper joined The Blues Project (with Steve Katz, Danny Kalb, Andy Kulberg, Roy Blumenfeld and Tommy Flanders), recording a live album with them at the end of that year. He left 18 months later and co-founded Blood, Sweat & Tears, recording just one album with them before leaving to work as an A&R man at Columbia. He teamed up again with Mike Bloomfield – their *Super Session* (1968) with Stephen Stills made the Top 10 – and during the late 1960s worked with The Who, Jimi Hendrix and The Rolling Stones, as well as touring and recording with B. B. King.

In 1973 Kooper discovered Lynyrd Skynyrd and produced their first three albums, which he released on his own label Sounds of the South, and in 1977 he wrote the autobiographical *Backstage Passes*. He has recorded a string of solo albums, including *I Stand Alone* (1968), *Naked Songs* (1973) and *Black Coffee* (2005). Since the late 1990s Koooper has taught songwriting and production at Berklee College of Music in Boston and has continued his musical career with ReKooperators and The Funky Faculty, a band of Berklee professors.

However, Kooper's Hammond organ playing on *Highway 61 Revisited* will probably always remain his greatest claim to fame.

MIKE BLOOMFIELD

The ace blues man resumed his role as lead guitarist with The Paul Butterfield Blues Band after recording *Highway 61 Revisited,* but tensions between him and Butterfield rose. He quit to form the band Electric Flag with Nick Gravenites in 1967 – they debuted at the Monterey Pop Festival – but Bloomfield left before the release of their first album and reunited with Kooper on *Super Session* (1968), jamming with the organ player and Stephen Stills. He spent most of the 1970s working with an informal band, Mike Bloomfield & Friends, and even joined the reunited original line-up of The Paul Butterfield Blues Band, but he struggled with ill-health and drug dependency and his genius had faded. He was found dead in a parked car in San Francisco in 1981, aged 37, after overdosing on heroin.

PAUL GRIFFIN

One of New York's most celebrated session pianists, Griffin worked again with Dylan, on *Blonde On Blonde* (1966). He cemented his reputation working on albums by John Lennon, Dionne Warwick, Solomon Burke, Aretha Franklin, Wilson Pickett, Steely Dan, Neil Diamond, Bonnie Raitt, Peter, Paul & Mary, Van Morrison, Judy Collins, John Denver, Carly Simon and Don McLean (he played on McLean's 1972 No. 1 hit 'American Pie'). He also played on many top-rated jazz albums by the likes of Quincy Jones, Nina Simone, Stephen Bishop and Blues Traveler; and among the leading producers and composers he worked with were Burt Bacharach, Phil Spector, Jerry Leiber & Mike Stoller, Jerry Wexler and Phil Ramone.

Griffin was again called on by Dylan to play on the sessions for *Blood On The Tracks* in 1974. After struggling with poor health, he died of a heart attack at home in New York in 2000, aged 62.

RUSS SAVAKUS

Despite his reservations about Dylan's working practices and his apparent discomfort and unhappiness during the recording of, in particular, 'Tombstone Blues', Savakus remained one of New York's most respected session players, particularly due to his versatility (in addition to upright string bass, he played electric bass guitar again and later also turned his hand to fiddle). He never worked with Dylan again, although his reputation was enhanced by association with the project, notably his stand-up bass work behind Charlie McCoy's guitar on 'Desolation Row'.

After *Highway 61 Revisited*, his next major project was playing on Richard & Mimi Fariña's *Reflections In A Crystal Wind*, released in December 1965. As others followed Dylan's lead, Savakus found himself to be the bass player of choice on many modern folk records and he also worked frequently with Bruce Langhorne. Other memorable sessions included those with Doc & Merle Watson, Joan Baez and Don McLean. He died in 1984, aged 59.

BOBBY GREGG

Already recognized as one of America's top sticksmen before he ever met Dylan, Bobby Gregg was one of the few drummers to have made a solo album, *Let's Stomp And Wild Weekend* (1963). Trusted by the Dylan camp after his sturdy performances on the electric tracks on *Bringing It All Back Home*, Gregg was a natural choice to follow him into the studio on *Highway 61 Revisited*, even though availability meant shared duties with Sam Lay, the Butterfield Blues Band man who had sat in with Dylan at Newport. Gregg was considered a safe pair of hands, able to keep a disciplined beat. He subsequently toured with Dylan for a month or so as a member of The Hawks after Levon Helm baled out in November 1965, but he withdrew a month later when offers of session work piled up.

Gregg went on to drum on a number of Simon & Garfunkel tracks, including the Tom Wilson-produced electric arrangement of 'The Sound Of Silence', and also worked with Peter, Paul & Mary before answering Dylan's call to work on *Blonde On Blonde* (1966). He continued to work as a busy session drummer for several years and his CV included contributions to new albums by Janis Ian, Tom Rush, Eric Anderson, McKendree Spring and The Cyrkle. He extended his style, playing percussion for a challenging 1971 collaboration between The Velvet Underground's John Cale and minimalist composer and pianist Terry Riley on *Church of Anthrax* (1971), a mix of free jazz and experimental rock. He further stretched himself playing bossa-nova rhythms behind the Brazilian star Astrud Gilberto.

HARVEY BROOKS

The New Yorker Al Kooper called to replace Russ Savakus went on to become one of the most famous bass players of all time. Brooks was playing at various clubs at the time of the *Highway 61 Revisited* sessions, and he slotted easily into the mix.

He joined the Dylan band for the initial round of live dates and became a folk-rock hero, playing every night at a different club in Greenwich Village and by day on sessions with everyone from Gordon Lightfoot to Peter, Paul & Mary, Richie Havens, Eric Anderson and Phil Ochs. He said of the experience: 'I was making money but I never imagined what a difference it would make when you became involved with a phenomenon or in that case musical history. One minute you're playing a gig in a club and the next you're in a limo.'

Brooks went on to form Electric Flag with Mike Bloomfield and played live with Jimi Hendrix, The Doors and Miles Davis, working with Davis on the classic *Bitches Brew* (1970). Others he has played with include Mama Cass, John Martyn, John Sebastian, John Cale, Donald Fagen and Loudon Wainwright III. In the early 1990s he relocated to Arizona, where he has continued to gig and play sessions.

CHARLIE McCOY

The man who just happened to call in at Studio A to collect some theatre tickets from Bob Johnston and hung around to play the fluid Spanish guitar that salvaged 'Desolation Row' went on to play a key role in Dylan's subsequent Nashville experience. He played various instruments on *Blonde On Blonde* and was much praised for his guitar part on 'Sad Eyed Lady Of The Lowlands'; Al Kooper has also commented on the remarkable way in which McCoy played trumpet and bass simultaneously on 'Most Likely You Go Your Way And I'll Go Mine'. McCoy went on to contribute bass to *John Wesley Harding* (1968) and *Nashville Skyline* (1969) and remained one of country music's most celebrated musicians on harmonica, guitar or bass into the twenty-first century.

McCoy's session credits include Elvis Presley, Johnny Cash, Joan Baez, Jerry Lee Lewis, Carl Perkins, Leonard Cohen and Paul Simon. He went on to become musical director of the TV show *Hee Haw* for 19 years, regularly won Instrumentalist of the Year at the Academy of Country Music and the CMA Awards and was elected to the Country Music Hall of Fame in 2000. A bona fide Nashville legend, he recorded in his own name and won a Grammy for his 1969 album *The Real McCoy*. He continued to be close friends with Bob Johnston, reuniting with him in 2006 to record a new album by Harper Simon – Paul Simon's son – in what he reported to be his busiest year for a decade. That year, he toured Europe and Japan with his own band and recorded his 32nd solo album.

THE HAWKS

Almost as soon as they had been recruited to play on stage with Dylan, Levon Helm and Robbie Robertson were keen to get the remaining three members of The Hawks involved. When Al Kooper and Harvey Brooks opted out of the upcoming US tour in September 1965, Dylan bowed to their wishes and hired Richard Manuel, Rick Danko and Garth Hudson. Their first date performing together at New York's Carnegie Hall on 1 October went well enough, but subsequent audience hostility on other dates proved too much for Helm, who temporarily retired from music altogether to work on an oil rig. Bobby Gregg was drafted in as a stopgap replacement before Sandy Konikoff, at that point filling Helm's old shoes behind the drum kit with Ronnie Hawkins, took over. He did not settle either and by April 1966, when the tour went overseas to Australia, Dylan had replaced him with Mickey Jones, a Texan who Dylan had originally seen working with Trini Lopez.

Following Dylan's motorcycle crash in July 1966, all except Mickey

Jones (who went on to become an actor) moved to Woodstock. Danko, Manuel and Hudson rented a house called Big Pink and gathered in the basement with Robertson and a recuperating Dylan to play informally, just for the fun of it, although in a relaxed manner they gradually began to work up fresh material. This new material ultimately saw the light of day on Dylan's celebrated 1967 double-LP bootleg entitled *Great White Wonder*, which finally got an official release in 1975 as *The Basement Tapes*.

By this time, the name 'The Hawks' had perished and been replaced by The Band, a joking reference to the dismissive reviewers who had refused to acknowledge them as an entity in their own right on the Dylan tour in 1966, referring to them only as 'the band' (or, possibly, the name could have been a sneer at the 'far out', psychedelic band names that were beginning to dominate the rock scene at the time). Al Grossman signed The Band to Capitol Records, they lured Levon Helm back as drummer and their debut album, *Music From Big Pink,* was released in 1968 to great acclaim.

Robertson developed into a brilliant songwriter and, over the next seven years, The Band achieved their own iconic status as trailblazing rock pioneers of Americana. They worked with Dylan again on his 1974 album *Planet Waves* and his subsequent tour. All keen to pursue individual projects, they staged a grand farewell with the star-studded *The Last Waltz* concert at Winterland, San Francisco on Thanksgiving Day 1976, documented by a triple album and a Martin Scorsese movie of the event.

There were various attempts at reunions, notably in 1983 when Manuel, Danko, Helm and Hudson re-formed with Earl Cate playing guitar, but Robertson always refused to participate. Long troubled by drink and drug problems and suffering from depression, Richard Manuel – whose beautiful vocals haunted so many of The Band's most evocative songs – hanged himself in a Florida motel room. The remaining members pursued solo projects (and, in Helm's case, a movie career) to varying critical receptions. In December 1999 Danko's hard-living lifestyle also caught up with him and he died in his sleep, hours after celebrating his 56th birthday.

THE COVER VERSIONS

There are nearly 600 cover versions of the tracks on *Highway 61 Revisited*, recorded by a motley crew of artists through the years and available on vinyl, CD and download. From The Turtles' and The Four Seasons' interpretations of 'Like A Rolling Stone', released soon after Dylan's original came out, through to Bryan Ferry's slinky 2007 version of 'Just Like Tom Thumb's Blues', as well as numerous unrecorded live treatments, the *Highway 61* material has held an enduring fascination for artists from a range of genres. With over 150 covers, 'Like A Rolling Stone' is the most popular track, but 'It Takes A Lot To Laugh, It Takes A Train To Cry' and 'Just Like Tom Thumb's Blues' have also clocked up around a hundred covers each. Only 'Queen Jane Approximately' remains relatively untouched, barely making double figures. Here is a selective list of some of the more notable covers.

'Like A Rolling Stone'

Glen Campbell (1965), The Four Seasons (1965), The Surfaris (1965), The Turtles (1965), Cher (1966), The Wailers (1966), The Young Rascals (1966), Jimi Hendrix (1967), Flatt & Scruggs (1969), Buddy Greco (1969), James Last (1970), Hugo Montenegro (1970), Paper Lace (1972), Spirit (1975), Johnny Thunders (1980), Johnny Winter (1980), Mitch Ryder (1985), Ana Christensen (1991), The Replacements (1991), John Mellencamp (1992), Judy Collins (1993), World Party (1993), The Rolling Stones (1995), Robyn Hitchcock (1996), Nancy Sinatra (1998), Black 47 (1999), Michael Bolton (1999), Bon Jovi (bootleg, 1999), Reggae Cowboys (2000), Barb Jungr (2003), Patti Smith (2005, live and unreleased), Sandra Bernhard (2006), Steve Forbert (2006), The Waybacks (2006)

'Tombstone Blues'

Tim O'Brien (1996), Sheryl Crow (1999), The Black-Eyed Snakes (2000), The Walkabouts (2001), Marc Carroll (2005), Yonder Mountain String Band (2006)

'It Takes A Lot To Laugh, It Takes A Train To Cry'

Michael Bloomfield, Al Kooper & Stephen Stills (1968), Blue Cheer (1969), Marianne Faithfull (1970), Iain Matthews (1970), Leon Russell (1971), Tir Na Nog (1972), The Grateful Dead (1973), The Earl Scruggs Review (1973), Tracy Nelson (1974), The LA Jets (1976), Frankie Miller (1977), Bad News Reunion (1983), Happy & Artie Traum (1994), Steve Earle (1996), Phoebe Snow (1998), Taj Mahal (1999), Jools Holland (2000), Bruce Hornsby (2000), Fairport Convention (2002), Toto (2002), Beaucoup Blue (2003), Joe Ely (2005), Black Crowes (2006), David Bromberg (2007)

'From A Buick 6'

Alex Taylor (1972), Johnny Winter (1973), Gary US Bonds (1981), Treat Her Right (1991), Wilko Johnson (2003), Mitch Ryder (2004), Richmond Fontaine (2005), Chuck Prophet (2006)

'Ballad Of A Thin Man'

The Grateful Dead (1988), Golden Earring (1995), Dawn of the Replicants (1998), Kula Shaker (1999), Joe Valenti (2000), Willard Grant Conspiracy (2005)

'Queen Jane Approximately'

The Four Seasons (1965), The Grateful Dead (1988), Mojave 3 (1996), American Music Club (2005)

'Highway 61 Revisited'

Terry Reid (1969), Johnny Winter (1969), Wilko Johnson's Solid Senders (1979), Long Ryders (1985), Dr Feelgood (1987), Rita Chiarelli (1993),

P. J. Harvey (1993), World Party (1993), Bruce Springsteen (bootleg, 1995), Billy Joel (1999), John Wesley Harding (2003), Pat Travers (2003), John Waite (2006)

'Just Like Tom Thumb's Blues'

Shawn Elliot (1966), Barry McGuire (1966), Judy Collins (1967), Gordon Lightfoot (1969), Nina Simone (1969), Jennifer Warnes (1969), Medicine Head (1971), Frankie Miller (1977), Rab Noakes (1981), Sir Douglas Quintet (1983), Maggie Holland (1983), The Grateful Dead (1989), Jimmy LaFave (1991), Neil Young (1992), The Bluebirds (1992), Linda Ronstadt (1998), Julie Felix (2002), Tom Russell (2002), Long Ryders (2004), Bryan Ferry (2007)

'Desolation Row'

Marc Ellington (1969), The Grateful Dead (1990), Robyn Hitchcock (2001), The Juggernaut Jug Band (2002), Chris Smither & Bonnie Raitt (2003), Songdog (2005)

FURTHER READING

Baggelaar, Kristin & Milton, Donald. *The Folk Music Encyclopaedia*, Omnibus Press, 1977

Boyd, Joe, *White Bicycles: Making Music in the 1960s*, Serpent's Tail, 2006

Collins, Shirley, *America Across The Water: A Musical Journey with Alan Lomax*, SAF Publishing, 2004

Cott, Jonathan, *Bob Dylan: The Essential Interviews*, Wenner Books, 2007

Crowe, Cameron, *Biograph boxed set notes*, Special Rider Music/CBS, 1985

Dunaway, David King, *How Can I Keep From Singing: Pete Seeger*, Harrap, 1985

Dylan, Bob, *Chronicles Volume One*, Simon & Schuster, 2004

Gray, Michael, *The Bob Dylan Encyclopaedia*, Continuum, 2006

Gray, Michael, *Song & Dance Man 111: The Art of Bob Dylan*, Continuum, 2000

Gross, Michael, *Bob Dylan: An Illustrated History*, Book Club Associates by an arrangement with Elm Tree Books, 1979

Helm, Levon & Davis, Stephen, *This Wheel's On Fire: Levon Helm and The Story of The Band*, Chicago Review Press, 2000

Heylin, Clinton, *Bob Dylan: Behind the Shades Revisited*, Harper Entertainment, 2001

Heylin, Clinton, *Bob Dylan: Behind Closed Doors: The Recording Sessions 1960-1994*, Penguin, 1996

Hoskyns, Barney, *Across The Great Divide: The Band and America*, Hal Leonard, 2006

Irvin, Jim, *The Mojo Collection: The Ultimate Music Companion*, Mojo Books, 2000

Kooper, Al, *Backstage Passes & Backstabbing Bastards: Memoirs Of A Rock'n'Roll Survivor*, Watson-Guptill, 1998

Krogsgaard, Michael, *Positively Bob Dylan: A 30-Year Discography, Concert and Recording Session Guide*, Popular Culture Ink, 1991

Larkin, Colin, *Virgin All-Time Top 1000 Albums*, Virgin, 1998

Lee, C. P., *Like The Night (Revisited): Bob Dylan and the road to the Manchester Free Trade Hall*, Helter Skelter, 2004

McAleer, Dave, *British and American Hit Singles 1960—1990*, Omnibus Press, 1990

Marcus, Greil, *Like A Rolling Stone: Bob Dylan at the Crossroads*, Faber & Faber, 2005

Marqusee, Mike, *Wicked Messenger: Bob Dylan and the 1960s*, Seven Stories Press, 2003

Mojo, *Dylan: Visions, Portraits and Back Pages*, Dorling Kindersley, 2005

Pennebaker, D. A., *Bob Dylan: Don't Look Back*, Ballantine, 1968

Santelli, Robert, *The Bob Dylan Scrapbook 1956-1966*, Simon & Schuster, 2005

Scaduto, Anthony, *Bob Dylan*, Abacus, 1972

Seeger, Pete, *The Incompleat Folksinger*, Fireside, 1972

Shelton, Robert, *No Direction Home: The Life and Music of Bob Dylan*, William Morrow, 1986

Sounes, Howard, *Down The Highway: The Life of Bob Dylan*, Grove Press, 2002

Spitz, Bob, *Dylan: A Biography: The Recording Sessions 1960-1994*, Norton, 1991

Vassal, Jacques, *Electric Children: Roots and Branches of Modern Folkrock*, Taplinger Publishing, 1976

Wein, George, *Myself Among Others: A Memoir*, Da Capo Press, 2003

Williams, Paul, *Bob Dylan: Performing Artist 1960-1973 The Early Years*, Omnibus Press, 1990

Williamson, Nigel, *The Rough Guide to Bob Dylan*, Rough Guides, 2004

DVDs

Bob Dylan: Don't Look Back: 1965 Tour Deluxe Edition, 2007

Festival! – The Newport Folk Festival, 2005

Dylan Speaks: The Legendary 1965 Press Conference in San Francisco, 2006

Bob Dylan World Tour 1966: The Home Movies, through the camera of Mickey Jones, 2006

No Direction Home: Bob Dylan: A Martin Scorsese Picture, 2005

Websites

All Music Guide: www.allmusic.com/

Bob Dylan Official Site: www.bobdylan.com

The Blacklisted Journalist (Al Aronowitz): www.bigmagic.com/pages/blackj

Bringing It All Back Home: www.punkhart.com/dylan

Dylan Pool: http://pool.dylantree.com/

Expecting Rain: www.expectingrain.com

The Farina Files: Newport Folk Festival 1965: www.members.tripod.com/farinafiles1/Newport.htm

Interviews with Bob Dylan: www.interferenza.com/bcs/interv.htm

It Ain't Me Babe: http://www.bjorner.com/Covers.htm

Mix: http://mixonline.com

Wikipedia: http://en.wikipedia.org/wiki/Main_Page

Author: Colin Irwin

London-based music journalist Colin Irwin has been writing about folk music for 25 years. Beginning his career as a sport reporter on a local newspaper, he joined *Melody Maker* in the mid-1970s, eventually becoming assistant editor. He was editor of the weekly pop magazine *Number One* before turning to freelance writing and has presented several BBC series on folk music, both on radio and television. He's also a regular contributor to UK magazines *Mojo* and *fROOTS*, has written for *The Times*, *The Guardian* and *The Independent* and also wrote the book *The Name Of The Game*, a biography of Abba. His book about Irish music, *In Search Of The Craic*, was published to critical acclaim in 2003.

Editor: David Hutcheon

David Hutcheon discovered Bob Dylan when his English teacher lent him *Another Side of Bob Dylan* in 1981, and the essays he wrote for his exams that year were an amalgam of 'My Back Pages' and 'It Ain't Me, Babe'. He is now is a freelance writer and critic for *The Times*, *The Sunday Times* and *Mojo*, and hopes one day to recapture the thin, wild mercury sound of his Higher Grade English work.

INDEX

Index